Searching for Common Ground

Seeking Justice and Understanding in Police and Community Relations

Searching for Common Ground

Seeking Justice and Understanding in Police and Community Relations

First Edition

Phillip J. Mann, J.D.

Old Dominion University

cognella®
SAN DIEGO

Bassim Hamadeh, CEO and Publisher
Alisa Munoz, Project Editor
Susana Christie, Developmental Editor
Celeste Paed, Associate Production Editor
Emely Villavicencio, Senior Graphic Designer
Greg Isales, Licensing Coordinator
Natalie Piccotti, Director of Marketing
Kassie Graves, Senior Vice President of Editorial
Jamie Giganti, Director of Academic Publishing

Cover image: Copyright © 2020 iStockphoto LP/wildpixel.

Printed in the United States of America.

cognella® | CUSTOM
3970 Sorrento Valley Blvd., Ste. 500, San Diego, CA 92121

Contents

Preface

Too often in public discourse, we are a nation of loud voices full of certainty on matters of public import. Doubt, open-mindedness, and curiosity are deemed signs of weakness, or they are otherwise ignored. Those seeking understanding or even compromise are viewed with contempt. In this world, there are the winners and losers or the righteous and unrighteous. The casualties of this approach may be a loss of trust, productive exchange of ideas, and meaningful solutions to pressing societal problems. In short, the common good suffers. The relationship between the community and police is one matter of public import. The deepest, most profound schisms most commonly involve communities of color, but such schisms exist elsewhere. Loud voices alone—although there is a place for loud voices—will not bridge divides between community and police. When community and police hold differing perceptions and beliefs, it helps to clearly identify what they disagree about, but also what they do agree about. This book tries to do both.

In my goal to promote understanding—and the common good—between police and citizens, I have drawn from many sources, including history, laws, regulations, court opinions, sociology, philosophy, psychology, religion, published research, news stories, and personal experience. I am not a recognized historian, sociologist, philosopher, or psychologist, although I am a lawyer and was long a Federal Bureau of Investigation (FBI) agent. Fortunately, I am now a member of the faculty in the Department of Sociology and Criminal Justice at Old Dominion University, where I have gained insight and feedback from my colleagues.

Let us begin by managing expectations. This is not a cookbook, not a one-size-fits-all recipe for establishing healthy and sustained police-citizen relations or, more important, strong communities or nations. It is naïve to think that the complex weave of police-citizen relations can be understood, let alone transformed, by reading any how-to book or manual. My more modest goal is to provide a platform for police and community to reflect upon and choose principles, promote values, and take actions, more often small than great, that just might make some lasting difference over time, much like forming healthy, life-changing habits—and in doing so finding some common ground to serve the common good. This requires education, commitment and engagement.

In my relation to you, the reader, I welcome constructive disagreement with my points and perspectives. If nothing else, I hope this book promotes purposeful, civil, yet robust discourse about police-citizen relations, a discourse that encourages curiosity and inquiry and one that aims for understanding and action. I do not want to reduce public discourse to false or misleading, right-versus-left, or conservative-versus-progressive narratives. When people are predisposed to speak or listen only to like-minded people, much is lost, and little is gained. Rather, when participants are willing to think clearly, exchange ideas and opinions, and even reconsider their own when presented with opposing argument and evidence, they may find answers. This process does "justice" to the intellectual freedom envisioned in the First Amendment of the U.S. Constitution.

But why such intense focus on police? Police officers are perhaps the most common face of government to citizens and communities—our most frequent first responders to crime, tragedy, and countless other difficulties. When they perform their role well, police promote trust and confidence in government institutions and the ability of government to "promote the general welfare." With such special attention directed at police and policing, it is important to examine the relationship between police and citizens in an objective and unbiased manner and explore how law enforcement agencies—together with communities—strengthen their relations in a manner that enhances legitimate core police functions yet supports the community's common good. Greater understanding and transparency on all sides of the relationship—police, citizens, and their communities—are central to the success of any such effort.

Within their broad mission to "protect and serve," police lawfully exercise government's coercive power. Officers stop, frisk, seize, search, arrest, and even use deadly force, all subject to laws, policies, and public expectations. Yet police also respond to varied, and sometimes contrasting, public demands; one moment an officer may detain someone suspected of committing a crime, in the next respond to cries for help from someone trapped in a car after a horrific accident, and in the very next intervene in a domestic dispute. Police also enforce unpopular laws. Do drivers thank an officer who stops their car for speeding 6 miles per hour over the limit? Probably not. In other words, police, cloaked in power and authority, carry out varied, complex tasks requiring not only a practical understanding of human nature, but also an understanding of constitutional and legal limits imposed on them. Much of their work, moreover, is performed in the public spotlight. The stakes are high, and gaining trust and respect in these circumstances is no easy task, but it is an essential one.

This book is not a screed against policing and police officers. However, I do not want readers to presume that I am an apologist for all law enforcement actions. Law enforcement agencies and their officers and agents will make mistakes and do the wrong thing. They are made up of citizens—human beings like you and me—some of whom are quite flawed. Some may, in moments reflecting frustration, bias, or inadequate training, make poor, even grievous decisions where lives are at stake. That said, their actions should be scrutinized by citizens, press, watchdog groups, internal and external auditors, courts, and federal and state legislators alike. Such scrutiny, when performed fairly and objectively, represents a healthy exercise of checks and balances and a process by which police better serve the community. When police effectively serve and protect, they contribute to a community's well-being, and community trust grows. If police violate the public trust, especially when police violate the law or the rule of law, a community cannot and should not be silent, as silence may amount to consent. We must remain a nation of laws; this is not a matter of politics but of basic citizenship. All of government—including law enforcement officers—and the people must promote the rule of law, and the rights, protections, freedoms, and values revealed in the Constitution and its Bill of Rights. Look no further than what happened on January 6, 2021, to remind us of the horror when the rule of law and the U.S. Constitution are flouted.

On a personal note, my decades of experience as an FBI agent and attorney included extensive interaction with other federal, state, and local law enforcement officers. What I witnessed—my personal experience—were public servants faithfully performing their duties. However, despite all the good, selfless, and heroic actions by police, there are real concerns and systemic problems that police and communities must squarely and honestly address. For example, racism, implicit bias, poor training, bad judgment, and certain police practices must be addressed more effectively. Many departments are trying to do just that. But whether your personal experiences and opinions about police are favorable or not, there are approaches that better serve all of "the people" and promote the common good. In this book, I also offer guidance about what officers may or may not lawfully do and what guides and shapes police practices.

There are many myths about state and local police and U.S. government agencies, including some I have heard from well-meaning students. For example, when I teach students about electronic surveillance, they commonly express their belief that the FBI intercepts everyone's phone conversations, implying that 1) the FBI can do whatever it wants to citizens—that the FBI's power is boundless—and 2) the government (which includes the FBI) has little or no concern about personal privacy or Fourth Amendment rights. Generalities such as these offered in the classroom got and get my attention, and with it some frustration, although I also see it as an opportunity.

In response to the first belief, I tell them that FBI investigations are limited in scope—that is, the FBI is largely limited to seeking information, intelligence, and evidence of crime or matters pertaining to national security. This sounds bland, but it is true. I explain that FBI activities and operations are circumscribed by the *Attorney General's Guidelines for Domestic FBI Operations* (hereafter *AG guidelines*). I became acutely aware of the AG guidelines' importance in my assignment to the FBI's Office of General Counsel and later as an FBI chief division counsel in Norfolk, VA. In fact, the AG guidelines were established in response to findings of the Church Committee (also known as the *U.S. Senate Select Committee to Study Governmental Operations with Respect to Intelligence Activities*), a committee that in 1975 investigated abuses by the Central Intelligence Agency (CIA), the National Security Agency (NSA), the FBI, and other agencies. There were many such abuses.

What do these guidelines look like? Refer to the October 3, 2008, press release by the U.S. Department of Justice's Office of Public Affairs announcing and attaching the 2008 AG guidelines signed by then Attorney General Michael Mukasey (U.S. Department of Justice, 2008). The AG guidelines are another level of oversight superimposed over existing federal laws and regulations and, most important, the U.S. Constitution. While not riveting reading for most readers, the AG guidelines lay out what FBI agents and professional support can and cannot do without running afoul of Department of Justice and congressional oversight. The AG guidelines serve as checks and balances on the FBI; they represent an attempt to promote the safety and security of the American people while protecting their civil liberties. In this effort, as noted in the press release, "these guidelines reflect consultation with Congress as well as privacy and civil liberties groups" (U.S. Department of Justice, 2008). To be clear, the FBI's authority to open investigations against groups and individuals is quite bounded, and that is a good thing—as the AG guidelines minimize the exercise of arbitrary power by an important institution of government. It was and remains my conviction that the AG guidelines, founded on and coupled with constitutional and other legal principles, have been effective.

If I still have students' attention, I respond to their second belief and inform them that the FBI does not care, need, want, or even have the capacity to know what people legally do in the privacy of their lives; anything contrary is neither legal, practical, wise, nor ethical. Further, when the FBI uses intrusive investigative techniques such as wiretaps, it first secures legal authorization. And yes, a wiretap is a very powerful means to acquire information and collect data. But if people knew the extraordinary lengths and oversight involved in securing and maintaining a lawful wiretap, concerned citizens might be less concerned. I also add that I suspect the private sector collects far more personal information on people than the government collects, as the private sector does not have the same legal restraints rightfully imposed by the

Constitution and other laws limiting government interference. That said, I do not expect or want the blind trust of citizens in everything the government does; some level of skepticism (not cynicism, as that is damaging to all of us) is healthy. I do, however, seek balance, and I encourage everyone to carefully examine arguments and evidence and draw their own informed conclusions. More lasting, meaningful trust can develop through that very process.

What are some unifying themes in how I approach policing? I have drawn extensively from the Declaration of Independence; U.S. Constitution, particularly the First and Fourth Amendments; and other seminal American documents. At the beginning of each chapter, I also quote one or more of Sir Robert Peel's *Nine Principles of Policing*, which was published in 1829. At various times Sir Robert Peel served as British home secretary and prime minister, and he is widely considered the founder of modern British policing. In fact, his nearly 200-year-old principles predicted much of what are now considered key principles in U.S. policing and elsewhere. These tenets are incorporated throughout the book.

So why did I write this book? Not to assign blame to individuals or any institution, as that practice alone rarely fixes problems. A propensity to find fault too often limits communication and widens the distance among us. However, demanding accountability and responsibility is not the same as assigning blame, as the former approach is forward-looking and constructive. Yes, the focus here is on police—but citizens must reflect upon their own attitudes, practices, and misunderstandings in a fair and honest manner. In short, I want to provide sensible, informed guidance to help shape constructive dialogue, understanding, and practices among police and their communities—or, better stated, among communities and their police.

Whether you are a college or police academy student, law enforcement official, community leader, or concerned citizen, I hope you reflect upon what I share. Above all else, let us seek justice and promote the public good.

References

U.S. Department of Justice. (2008, October 3). *Joint statement of Attorney General Michael B. Mukasey and FBI Director Robert S. Mueller on the issuance of the attorney general guidelines for domestic FBI operations.* https://www.justice.gov/archive/opa/pr/2008/October/08-opa-890.html

Introduction

In 2011, while still chief division counsel of the Norfolk, Virginia Federal Bureau of Investigation (FBI) office, I developed and taught an upper-level undergraduate course about law enforcement and the U.S. Constitution as an adjunct faculty member in the Department of Sociology and Criminal Justice at Old Dominion University. The course in part reflected my deep convictions about relationships among law, policing, and the community. To generate classroom discussion, I provided to students a short handout in which I shared six observations about effective policing borne out of my personal belief and experience. They were:

1. Law enforcement officers must strive to build relationships with the public—those whom they protect and serve. Law enforcement officers must always demonstrate their commitment to the rule of law and the pursuit of justice.
2. Even in circumstances in which law enforcement officers are exercising lawful authority, officers should strive to treat members of public with dignity and respect. They must always be professional, no matter how difficult that may seem.
3. Persuasion and understanding are among the most effective traits a law enforcement officer can use in solving crime or promoting public safety in everyday, nonconfrontational interactions with members of the public.
4. Law enforcement actions and investigative activities should typically be proportional to a perceived threat or danger, as well as its immediacy.
5. In conducting police activities that implicate Fourth Amendment search-and-seizure citizen protections, a warrant is a nearly failsafe option to protect the integrity of the investigation and prosecution of crime. Similarly, obtaining warrants tends to promote public trust.
6. Whether from a constitutional or societal perspective, a law enforcement officer's actions will be judged by their reasonableness in the face of existing threats or dangers.

Eight years later, after I had retired from the FBI and joined the Old Dominion University as a full-time faculty member, these convictions became a springboard for writing this book. Before joining the faculty full-time, I taught other relevant courses, including one about law and social control that provided an opportunity to more formally explore other legal, sociological, and policing materials, including Sir Robert Peel's 1829 *Nine Principles of Policing*. His genius is clear in the concise, insightful principles, tenets that stand the test of time. I was not surprised when I later learned that Sir Robert Peel was a hero of former New York City Police Commissioner William J. Bratton. As you read these chapters, you will note that I often pair Peel's principles with foundational American writings, from the Declaration of Independence to the Bill of Rights to Dr. Martin Luther King, Jr.'s incomparable *Letter from Birmingham Jail*, where you the reader may find some congruence among them all. The book expands upon these and related points.

Searching for Common Ground consists of 10 chapters. Each chapter is subtitled and begins with at least one of Sir Robert Peel's nine principles, along with quotes from other sources. These introductory quotes may fuel personal reflection or group discussion. At the end of each chapter are discussion and review questions that are suitable for individual or group work.

Chapter 1, "Police Work Is Different: *Public Trust Is Easy to Lose, Hard to Regain*," provides historical background and context of modern policing in the U.S., including its relationship to slavery and racism, and an overview of policing's unique nature and diverse demands. Although public expectations of policing have changed markedly over time, sometimes in response to social and economic forces, what has not changed is policing's "monopoly" over the use of coercive power on behalf of the state. To be clear, this power need not be a bad thing when it is used wisely. We are now at another crossroads where many people, communities, and legislative bodies question whether the existing paradigm of policing demands incremental or radical revision, embodied, for example, in the call to "defund police." The remainder of the book provides a platform for examining and sometimes reimagining the role of police in the context of law, sociology, history, and other factors.

Chapter 2, "The Importance of Positive Police-Citizen Interactions," examines the importance of all police-citizen interactions, especially those in which police exercise power and authority, because nearly every act of policing speaks about the person who is behind the badge and gun, who in turn represents the larger organization. Attitudes toward police are shaped, and often quickly, in these encounters great and small. Citizens, of course, also carry preexisting beliefs about police to each encounter, and there are significant racial and partisan divides that must be acknowledged and addressed. Moreover, through their work police can play a key role in promoting and acting upon desirable and shared values and beliefs, such as the importance of the rule of law, the dignity of every human being, or the equal protection of law, values and principles that support a healthy democracy.

Chapter 3, "Cultivating a Culture of Law and Justice: Values Inform Police and Community," reviews the nature of governance and the importance of placing restraints on the exercise of power. The chapter begins by highlighting the importance of civic education in the pursuit of the common good, individual happiness, individual rights, and, of course, justice. This values-driven approach should be an integral part of police training, police practice, and community-building dialogue. In this context there is also a focus on why the exercise of First Amendment rights matter to citizens and police. In sum, sound police practices, coupled with necessary limits imposed on police, should embody principles and values expressed in the Constitution and other seminal American writings. Police must never forget that people possess certain inalienable rights. Police, in short, must serve and protect the people in a manner that does not unreasonably or gratuitously impede upon their inalienable rights.

Chapter 4, "A Social Contract Between Police and Community," examines why the role and rule of law must be part of a social contract between police and community to better promote a society in which both fundamental rights and community safety are preserved. Readers are introduced to the concepts of legal and social controls and their contributions to security, rights, and freedom. The continued viability of the social contract between "We the People" and the "Leviathan" of government relies in part upon a deep-seated commitment to understanding and upholding the rule of law. Police academies and departments must consistently inculcate the rule of law and its values. Police must demonstrate their commitment to it in every interaction with the public. In turn, communities, schools, churches, and other institutions are encouraged to promote the rule of law as fundamental to their security, rights, and freedom, part of a collaborative effort that serves the common good. This culture, in which police honor rights and act with restraint, must embody constitutional values and other foundational American writings. In their mission police must always uphold justice. When properly performed, police work promotes a more just, civil, and trusting society.

Chapter 5, "Making Choices: Police Discretion and Effective Policing," examines the power and significance of police discretion in preventing, detecting and investigating crime, and why citizen discretion can play a key role in supporting these efforts. Discretion in exercising police authority is an intrinsic form of power, and it is a necessary and important aspect of police work when used lawfully and wisely. But discretion begins with an officer's recognition that *there are* choices, big and small, that matter in the work of policing and a community's perception of policing. How an officer exercises discretion speaks loudly to those affected.

Chapter 6, "General Police Powers to Search and Seize Under the Fourth Amendment," identifies what legal restraints guide and limit police when they search and seize persons, places, and things—all of which are Fourth Amendment constructs that limit the coercive power of police. The central message is that police must comport with the requirements of the Fourth Amendment. The Fourth Amendment and its standards relating to reasonableness, warrants, and probable cause stand as bulwarks against unjustified government intrusions into the lives of citizens. Consider what the U.S. Supreme Court said in *Brinegar v. U.S.* (1949), about probable cause, a burden of proof imposed on police that restrains certain intrusive actions: It "safeguards citizens from rash and unreasonable interference with privacy and from unfounded charges of crime. ... [It also)] seeks to give fair leeway for enforcing the law in the community's protection." This chapter also recounts a former officer's deep concerns about police abuse of power, graphically based upon his personal experiences.

Chapter 7, "Use of Force Against Citizens," tackles the most widely reported, serious, and consequential actions by police, namely the use of force and deadly force. The chapter begins by examining the general nature of state power and the grave consequences when state power is left unchecked, and then recounts one former police officer's account of abuse of power. An officer uses force—typically as a form of physical coercion—to gain compliance to a lawful order, protect himself or someone else, or perform other legitimate law enforcement functions. Like many intrusive police activities, the use of force should honor and comport with the Constitution and its values. The use of force should never be gratuitous, arbitrary, or unjustified; it should be used for the right reasons. And it is likely if not inevitable that an officer's choice of force—whether to stop, arrest, or use deadly force—will one day be scrutinized by judge, jury, press, or community. An officer's words and actions should reveal to outsiders that force was used to achieve a lawful purpose and in a manner reasonable under the circumstances. An officer's failure to do so will result in significant personal and professional consequences.

Chapter 8, "Facing the Legacy of Racism, Bias and Inequality with Clarity, Purpose and Action," examines the powerful impact of racism, bias, and inequality from a legal, historical, and practical sense in the context of policing. This chapter explores the continuing legacy of racism, bias, and inequality and their impact on police work and community grievances. Recent events have only underscored the need for self-awareness and change. Police must face these realities with candor, clarity, purpose, and action. Together with communities, police must rewrite the script in a manner that equally honors and secures the rights of *all* citizens, recognizes historical wrongs, and supports safe communities.

Chapter 9, "Evaluating Police Strategies, Tactics, and Militarization: The Importance of Caution," reviews the wisdom and efficacy of police overreliance on military strategies, tactics, and equipment in domestic policing. The nation's founders had clear misgivings about the role of the military in domestic affairs. This chapter also examines competing visions of a "warrior" versus a "servant" mindset in policing practices. There are public consequences to the strategies, tactics, equipment, and, above all, mindset that police adopt. At a minimum, the Constitution, federal law, and various reports and analyses point to the need for caution and self-awareness in following trends toward the militarization of police. Such trends are unlikely to strengthen community trust. Our nation's history is instructive, too.

Chapter 10, "Procedural Justice, Character, Professionalism and Accountability Contribute to Community Trust" provides a broad roadmap for strengthening community-police relations. No one approach is a panacea. Community policing, for example, offers a vision that is designed to promote community trust, but is it enough to ensure community safety and security? Moreover, there are limits to what police can do to serve their communities effectively and efficiently; their inherently coercive powers do not always make police ideal community builders. The ideal if limited role of police should be actively and openly examined. That said, personal character, professionalism, and accountability in policing are always helpful, as they stand behind the implementation of procedural justice, community policing, and other practices that are designed to create a culture of trust and mutual responsibility. Embracing procedural justice in nearly all serious police-citizen encounters is especially effective in building or maintaining community trust—for procedural justice respects the letter and spirit of the law, and it is the right thing to do.

Most readers, even the harshest critics of law enforcement officers, may agree that policing, when properly performed, is a very difficult profession and an important one. Some might echo the words of Bryan Stevenson, civil rights attorney and author of *Just Mercy: A Story of Justice and Redemption*, during a Fresh Air interview by David Bianculli on National Public Radio on August 21, 2015:

> [W]e need law enforcement officers who are committed and brave and dedicated and hardworking and smart. If I had three professions I would double the salaries of, one would be teachers, the second would be police officers and law enforcement, and the third would be social workers because I think they play a critical role in a society as devastated by dysfunction and drugs and racism and bias and poverty as our society. ... So that's always been clear to me that we need people performing these roles in our society who are uncorrupted by the

cynicism, who are not distracted by bigotry and bias against the poor, [and] people of color. ...

I hope all readers will broach topics addressed in this book with open minds.

References

Bianculli, D. (2015, August 21). *One lawyer's fight for young Blacks and 'Just Mercy.'* *Fresh Air*, NPR. https://www.npr.org/2015/08/21/433478728/one-lawyers-fight-for-young-blacks-and-just-mercy

Brinegar v. U.S., 338 U.S. 160 (1949). https://supreme.justia.com/cases/federal/us/338/160/

Peel, R. (1829). *Nine principles of policing.*

Chapter 1

Police Work Is Different

Public trust is easy to lose, hard to regain

Image 1

Peel Principle 2: The ability of the police to perform their duties is dependent upon public approval of police existence, actions, behavior, and the ability of the police to secure and maintain public respect.

The Legacy of Slave Patrols and Policing

To adequately address some of the most pressing issues facing police requires facing an uncomfortable truth: that for centuries racism has been deeply embedded and sanctioned in the law, culture, and practice of policing, no matter how noble and important the calling is to society. As noted by W. Marvin Delaney in his book *Black Police in America* (1996), American policing in the South did not follow the British model but was based "on a model related to the existence of slavery and racial oppression" (p. 2). That is not to say that policing in the North has escaped all censure. It has not.

1

First, consider slave patrols, which have been described by many scholars as an early form of American policing. Beginning in the colonial America, Black slaves, the bulk of whom lived in the South, resisted and often revolted against their oppression. Many of course fled. In response, "groups of white men organized into slave patrols in the southern colonies. These slave patrols are generally considered to be the first 'modern' police organization in the country" (Engel, 2002, p. 1053). In fact, the size of the slave patrol in Charleston, SC, in 1837 exceeded any northern city police force at the time (Engel, 2002, p. 1053). These patrols commonly consisted of three to six men on horseback armed with guns, ropes, and whips. As Sally Hadden writes in her book *Slave Patrols: Law and Violence in Virginia and the Carolinas* (2001), "A mounted man presents an awesome figure, and the power and majesty of a group of men on horseback, at night, could terrify slaves into submission. ..." (p. 121). The following is a North Carolina slave patroller's oath from 1828:

> I [patroller's name], do swear, that I will as searcher for guns, swords, and other weapons among the slaves in my district, faithfully, and as privately as I can, discharge the trust reposed in me as the law directs, to the best of my power. So help me, God (Hadden, 2001, p. 78).

Invoking God's help in support of this "work" is a stark reminder of a benighted past.

In some places, slave patrolling was deemed a "civic duty" in which fines could be imposed if the duty was avoided. In other places, patrollers were paid for their work. Slave patrolling commonly included "enforcing curfews, checking travelers for a permission pass, catching those assembling without permission, and preventing any form of organized resistance" (Hansen, 2019).

Another stark reminder of police brutality, endangerment and subjugation of Black people in U.S. history is the 1921 Tulsa Race Massacre, a massacre that has only begun to gain the nationwide attention it deserves. This massacre by white mobs, sparked by accusations that a 19-year-old Black male assaulted a 17-year-old white female, left hundreds of Black people dead, and thousands displaced from an area that included what was once America's wealthiest Black business district. Most notable in this tragedy was the Tulsa Police Department's active support of white mobs, some of whom the department deputized and provided arms.

In his book *The Condemnation of Blackness* (2011), Harvard historian Khalil Gibran Muhammad examined how Black people have been criminalized throughout U.S. history. Dr. Muhammad reviewed parallel yet contrasting historical narratives of policing in the North and South. Both narratives share a common denominator: the police use of brutal force to control Black Americans. Reviewing the failures of attempted police reforms by police over the past century, Dr. Muhammad remains, at best, skeptical. During a National Public Radio interview on July 8, 2020, he stated that it is time to recognize that:

> [P]olice officers and police agencies are incapable of fixing themselves ... and so the question that has to be asked in the wake of George Floyd—and I think the question is being asked and answered by more white people than I've seen in my lifetime is—do white people in America still want the police to protect their interests over the rights and dignity of Black and, in too many cases, brown, Indigenous, and Asian populations in this country?

In the context of their communities and society, police departments must assess and answer the critical question posed by Dr. Muhammad. As noted later in this book, police departments are encouraged to address all forms of racism and bias, overt or implicit; it is unwise for departments to simply wait for legislative or outside regulatory fixes and oversight, which often fall short of aspirations. Instead, police departments must lead by identifying and implementing effective internal measures in hiring, training, mentoring, and leading in a manner that promotes greater accountability, transparency, and equality in enforcing the law and protecting the rights of all Americans. But more history next.

The Development of Modern U.S. Policing

An understanding of the development of modern policing in the U.S., particularly in the North, also recognizes the historical influence of policing in England. Before modern police forces existed in England, the maintenance of social order was the responsibility of local communities, often comprised of groups bound by kinship or neighborhood or in some manner bound in service to the English monarchy. Early practices that imposed social order were commonly informal, relational, and less professionalized. They also existed in a rural, agriculture society. Beginning in about 1750, the Industrial Revolution overturned the existing social order. Manufacturing and the centralization of labor, finance, and commercial interests in urban areas led to social and economic dislocation and change. The United Kingdom's population tripled in the next hundred years (1841Census.co.uk, 2021; Office of National Statistics, 2015). Population density in urban areas soared. In these conditions, unpaid amateurs were no match for newly emerging crimes and criminals and soaring crime rates. Changes in policing were inevitable, including the establishment of a paid, organized, and easily identifiable police force, although many citizens also resisted these changes, fearing increased costs and governmental overreach into their private lives.

In England, the emergence of a paid, professional police force acting at the direction of the state was led by Sir Robert Peel, appointed in 1812 as chief secretary for Ireland, where there was widespread agrarian violence by a group known as the *banditti*. To address the violence and social disorder, Peel established the Peace Preservation Force, which sought to suppress and prevent violence and rampant crime by exercising more coercive powers. Peel's success in Ireland led him to take "law enforcement out of the hands of amateurs and plac(e) it in those of the professionals" (Chriss, 2013, p. 117). What followed during the next decade was the enactment of the Metropolitan Police Act 1829. The act "established a full-time, professional, and centrally organized police force for the greater London area under the control of the Home Secretary" (U.K. Parliament, n.d.). So instead of "small and disorganized parish forces," there emerged a group of uniformed constables under central leadership that "embodied a new style of policing" (U.K. Parliament, n.d.). The success of this London-based Metropolitan model led to the passage of more laws, such as the Municipal Corporations Act 1835 and the County Police Act 1839, which established paid and professionalized police forces throughout the country. Like Peel's earliest police force, these powers not only responded to new crimes and rising crime numbers but also sought to *prevent* crime and keep order in the streets. Police forces thus grew dramatically, so that by 1851 there were about 13,000 police in England and Wales (U.K. Parliament, n.d.). By most accounts, the transformation was successful. In many ways, the U.S. followed England's model.

Two early forms of policing in the American colonies in the seventeenth and early eighteenth centuries were, as Dr. Gary Potter (2013a) described, both "informal and communal." One was the watch system, which was:

> ... composed of community volunteers whose primary duty was to warn of impending danger. Boston created a night watch in 1636, New York in 1658 and Philadelphia in 1700. The night watch was not a particularly effective crime control device. Watchmen often slept or drank on duty. While the watch was theoretically voluntary, many "volunteers" were simply attempting to evade military service, were conscript forced into service by their town, or were performing watch duties as a form of punishment. Philadelphia created the first day watch in 1833 and New York instituted a day watch in 1844 as a supplement to its new municipal police force (Gaines, Kappeler, & Vaughn, 1999, as cited in Potter, 2013a).

In addition to the watch system was a system of constables or officers, "usually paid by the fee system for warrants they served." Constables also performed non–law enforcement functions, "including serving as land surveyors and verifying the accuracy of weights and measures" (Potter, 2013a). However important these practices were, they were hardly a reliable means of addressing emerging crime and maintaining social order within a community.

Beginning in Boston in 1838, in response to some of the same crime problems that plagued England, major American cities began setting up paid, organized police forces. By 1866, New York City, Philadelphia, Detroit, and Cleveland had established such police forces, and by 1880 "most major American cities had done likewise" (Chriss, 2013, p. 118). These early police forces grew increasingly and necessarily into more formalized, bureaucratic, and specialized units. However, these police forces did not limit their attention to criminals. One historian noted:

> Police dispensed welfare; jails and prisons housed the insane; jails sometimes held more witnesses than offenders awaiting trial. During the first two decades of the twentieth century, the focus of the system began to sharpen. As a result, demands for organization responses to crime became more closely tied to the actual rates of crime because the system no longer attended to problems that were not related to crimes (Monkkonen, 1983, p. 126).

In the nineteenth century, police corruption and brutality were common. Police too often failed to serve and protect the public or the public good, especially among those who lacked power or privilege. Police, for example, were instrumental in union-busting and advancing the interests of the monied class. As Dr. Potter (2013b) wrote, corruption should come as no surprise because police were under the control of local politicians such as the political party ward leader, who often appointed the police executive in charge:

> The ward leader, also, most often was the neighborhood tavern owner, sometimes the neighborhood purveyor of gambling and prostitution, and usually the controlling influence over neighborhood youth gangs who were used to get out the vote and intimidate opposition party voters. In this system of vice, organized violence and political corruption it is inconceivable that the police could be anything but corrupt (Walker, 1996). Police systematically took payoffs to allow illegal drinking, gambling and prostitution. Police organized professional criminals, like thieves and pickpockets, trading immunity for bribes or information. They actively participated in vote-buying and ballot-box-stuffing. Loyal political operatives became police officers.

They had no discernable qualifications for policing and little if any training in policing. Promotions within the police departments were sold, not earned. Police drank while on patrol, they protected their patron's vice operations, and they were quick to use peremptory force.

Scholars have defined three, sometimes four, eras of policing in the United States. The first, running from the 1830s to the 1920s, was the *Political or Political Spoils Era*, alluded to above, which stood for a time when policing was locally controlled and marked by corruption and other glaring shortcomings. Policing itself was designed to meet the broad needs of citizens, although it was beholden to political leadership. In the second, the *Reform Era*, running from the 1920s to the 1960s, policing became more centralized and professionalized, and there were efforts to root out police corruption. Policing and police structures became at least ostensibly nonpartisan and legalistic—a civil service of sorts—and this tradition has continued. There were other changes. For example, August Vollmer, the first police chief of Berkely, CA, commonly referred to as "the father of modern policing," ushered in the advancement of technology, training, and education in policing. Moreover, efforts to professionalize policing have not since abated, even if they have been uneven and not always embraced throughout the United States.

The third, the *Community Policing/Problem-Solving Era*, running from the 1970s to the present, coupled crime control strategies with collaborative efforts between police and local communities to achieve safer neighborhoods. Police became multitaskers or generalists serving a diverse community (Chriss, 2013, p. 239). For example, police departments might assign community policing officers dedicated to rebuilding frayed relationships through nontraditional law enforcement activities aimed at improving the quality of life and encouraging the community to work with officers. It remains a dominant paradigm in policing. The third era also reflects how community expectations have changed.

The fourth and present era, the Homeland Security Era, arose in response to the terrorist events of September 11, 2001. The Homeland Security Era did not displace the Community Policing Era. In fact, facets of both eras continue to exist. In response to 9/11 and the widespread fear of terrorism, the Homeland Security era has seen growing specialization in emergency preparedness, intelligence analysis, security, and counterterrorism. Aligned with these developments, police agencies have collected more data and intelligence, believing that this will help them prevent and respond to traditional crimes, acts of terror, or other real or perceived threats. Likewise, private citizens have been asked to become increasingly responsible for public safety. For example, with little guidance people are commonly asked to report "suspicious activity" to designated police and intelligence agencies. Vigilance is a recurring theme in promoting safety and security. However benign, this mindset can also promote fear.

Furthermore, much has been reported and debated about mass data collection by law enforcement authorities. Modern proactive technologies, such as facial recognition, license plate readers, closed-circuit video capture of public and private spaces, and access and collection of publicly available data in social media, have changed the landscape of traditional policing. However effective these tools are, many see them as threats to civil liberties.

To be clear, each new police era did not break from the past; each era left legacies in policing culture, practice, and tactics, including remnants that continue to affect citizens and communities. Moreover, policing practices in the U.S. are not monolithic, and neither are people's beliefs about police. In every era, there has been a split among citizens who view police in positive, even heroic, terms and citizens who in varying degrees view police as brutal, corrupt, or racist. A fixture in recent years has been a debate about the degree to which police should serve as community caretakers, more closely resembling the earliest forms of policing in which their role was diffuse. Some argue that police cannot and should not become community caretakers, as this distracts police from their mission of fighting crime. However, others argue that police must first and foremost "serve and protect" and that fighting crime is but one face of community protection.

Throughout modern American history, one attribute of policing has remained unchanged—what stands behind police is the coercive power and authority of the state. When wielded rightly and lawfully, that power and authority can promote freedom and individual rights and better ensure public safety and security—the common good. When police power is compromised, it threatens the very foundations of democracy.

The Dangers of Police Compromise: A Look at History Elsewhere

Despite real progress over time, all eras have been marked by varying degrees of police abuse of authority. A grave danger arises when domestic policing, *as an institution*, abuses its authority and becomes detached from promoting such values as justice and the rule of law. This can happen when policing becomes deeply politicized and unhinged from democratic values and principles. The process of police compromise can begin subtly, even ostensibly harmless, but dangers arise when citizens surrender rights and police are given excessive power to promote professed goals of security and safety under some vague notion of law and order. This is a dangerous bargain.

Recall what happened in Germany in the 1920s and 1930s when civilian police were slowly co-opted by the Nazi government, described more fully below. Civilian police agencies contributed to the state-sponsored extermination of about 6 million European Jewish citizens and millions of people belonging to other groups. Rather than stand as a bulwark in support of the rule of law and the public good, police were part of the very evil that marked Nazi Germany.

The steady, corrupt expansion of police power in Nazi Germany was fateful. With the permission of United States Holocaust Memorial Museum (2021), I quote excerpts from an article on its website (June 2, 2021) about the development of the German police state:

> After Adolf Hitler became chancellor on January 30, 1933, he worked to turn Germany into a dictatorship under his sole control. To do so, the new government reoriented Weimar Germany's previously democratic organizations and institutions to serve Nazi ideals. This meant eliminating constitutional rights and protections for individuals. It also meant inserting Nazi ideology into all aspects of life. This process is known as Nazification.
>
> The Nazis believed that the police would have a particularly important role to play in the new Germany. Therefore, almost immediately after Hitler's appointment, the Nazis sought to take over and transform Germany's police forces. ...
>
> In early 1933, the Nazis used a variety of measures to free the police from the constraints of the Weimar constitution. They simultaneously encouraged the police to target Nazism's political opponents, namely Social Democrats and Communists. On February 17, 1933, Nazi Hermann Göring issued a decree to Prussian policemen instructing them to work with Nazi paramilitary organizations and to treat political enemies ruthlessly. The decree clearly stated that policemen would not be punished for shooting a Communist, and, in fact, they might even be disciplined for failing to do so.
>
> A few days later, on February 22, the Nazis began deputizing members of the SS, SA, and Stahlhelm (a nationalist veterans' organization) as auxiliary policemen (Hilfspolizei) in many German states. In Prussia alone, 50,000 armed paramilitary men patrolled alongside policemen. These auxiliaries brutally arrested and beat political opponents, interning many of them in makeshift concentration camps. Typically, auxiliary policemen wore their paramilitary uniforms with a white armband.

"German Police in the Nazi State," *Holocaust Encyclopedia*. Copyright © by United States Holocaust Memorial Museum.

The most important step in the process of Nazifying the police came after February 27, 1933, when an arson attack destroyed the German Reichstag (parliament building) in Berlin. Hitler responded with the Reichstag Fire Decree, which suspended civil rights and most legal protections in Germany. It also expanded the power of the police. This decree, which remained in force until the downfall of the Nazi regime, laid the foundation for Germany to become a police state.

Read this passage again. What is clear is that police have immense authority to protect and support a community. The reverse is also true—the police, if compromised, may become instruments of tyranny or totalitarianism. And so, in any free, open, and democratic society, police must remain public servants, subject to checks and balances, limited in authority, committed to fact-finding and justice, never to become instruments of state oppression. This is both a hope and expectation, never presumed.

Today there is no shortage of nations in which police do not promote justice or the rule of law, who do not "serve and protect" the people. Rather, they serve the narrow interests of those who disdain democratic forms of government. Such totalitarian or tyrannical governments are commonly referred to as *police states*, hardly a good connotation for the word *police*. Unfortunately, a *police state* is widely understood as a coercive, unjust, and authoritarian state. The mingling of *police* and *state* to express a term of contempt is no surprise, as the exercise of power, authority, and force *are* inherent in many policing responsibilities, even when they are legitimate and justifiable. Again, some police actions are necessarily coercive—think of a valid arrest based on a court-authorized warrant. But when empowered by tyrants or totalitarian figures contemptuous of guideposts, accountability, the rule of law, or the pursuit of justice, police may become instruments that endanger the common good. Any move toward empowering such abuse must be recognized, called out, and resisted.

But why do police play such a vital role in society? How is policing different?

Policing is Different

Dr. Egon Bittner, former chair of the sociology department at Brandeis University, wrote a fascinating paper titled *The Functions of Police in Modern Society*. In it he explored popular conceptions of police work in which he identified three traits of character "commonly perceived as associated with police work ... that constitute in part the social reality within which the work has to be done" (Bittner, 1970). A summary follows. Even if the reader does not fully agree with Dr. Bittner's descriptions of police work, at least consider them.

Character Trait 1: Police Work Is a Tainted Occupation

First, Bittner (1970) described police work as a "tainted occupation," a character trait rooted in history and mythology in which police were "feared and despised even by those who ostensibly benefitted from their services" (p. 7). As Bittner explained:

> Because they are posted on the perimeters of order and justice in the hope that their presence will deter the forces of darkness and chaos, because they are meant to spare the rest of the people direct confrontations with the dreadful, perverse, lurid, and dangerous, police officers are perceived to have powers and secrets no one else shares. Their interest in and competence to deal with the untoward surrounds their activities with mystery and distrust. One needs only to consider the thoughts that come to mind at the sight of policemen moving into action: here they go to do something the rest of us have no stomach for! And most people naturally experience a slight tinge of panic when approached by a policeman, a feeling against which the awareness of innocence provides no adequate protection. Indeed, the innocent in particular typically do not know what to expect and thus have added, even when unjustified, reasons for fear (p. 7).

Police interventions elicit strong and sometimes complex reactions, and I suspect many of us share this response. Even as an FBI agent, I reacted when the blue lights of a squad car were directed at me; my reaction abated only when I could fully identify myself to police.

Among some people, that "fear and fascination" may also house an underlying suspicion "that those who do battle against evil cannot themselves live up fully to the ideals they presumably defend" (Bittner, 1970, p. 7). In that situation, a citizen might find "satisfaction" in a belief that *police are no better than anyone else*, one very common among those who question traditional forms of authority. Justified or not, this belief can undermine the legitimate work of policing. This view is fueled by real examples of police abuse. Consider the beating of Rodney King and resulting riots in Los Angeles in 1991, the "Ferguson Unrest" prompted by the police killing of Michael Brown in 2014, and the police killings of George Floyd, Breonna Taylor, and others. To state the obvious, police must account for suspicions among communities of color, victimized groups of gender identity, and other groups. Police must be *trained and mindful* that these doubts, these suspicions, persist among many communities.

Character Trait 2: Police May Need to Act Against Others When They Enforce the Law or Protect the Community

Second, Bittner (1970) wrote that "police work is not merely a tainted occupation" (p. 8). It is work that often requires police to intervene against others, often proactively. Policing is not a passive or merely cerebral undertaking. As Bittner noted:

> It does not take great subtlety of perception to realize that standing between man and man locked in conflict inevitably involves profound moral ambiguities. Admittedly, few of us are constantly mindful of the saying, "He that is without sin among you, let him cast the first stone …," but only the police are explicitly required to forget it. The terms of their mandate and the circumstances of their practices do not afford them the leisure to reflect about the deeper aspects of conflicting moral claims. Not only are they required to proceed forcefully against all appearances of transgression but they are also expected to penetrate the appearance of innocence to discover craftiness hiding under its cloak (p. 10–11).

Police *are* called upon to "proceed" against others, and that includes enforcing unpopular or vague laws and ordinances, often without the benefit of unambiguous evidence of guilt. Consider, too, the challenge and potential for abuse when police are called upon to enforce such vague crimes as disturbing the peace, loitering, or harassment (and consider the individual so accused). When legislators enact criminal laws without clearly describing the prohibited conduct, challenges against the enforcement, prosecution, and public support of the law are sure to follow. And sometimes criminal laws are hopelessly outdated. Many states, for example, never decriminalized homosexuality until 2003, when the U.S. Supreme Court effectively decriminalized it at a national level. See *Lawrence v. Texas*, 539 U.S. 558. Remember who enforced such laws.

Enforcement of nearly *any* criminal law (a "transgression") requires some level of coercive force by police against another. Enforcement may be triggered by crimes committed in police presence or crimes for which outstanding arrest warrants already exist—in which an officer simply finds an individual believed to be identical to the one named in the warrant. In this environment, police rarely have time either "to reflect about the deeper aspects of conflicting moral claims" that may exist or "to penetrate the appearance of innocence" (Bittner, p. 9) to discover what may hide beneath. For example, someone arrested may quickly and often falsely proclaim their innocence and demand their release, but police must nevertheless act in a manner that "penetrates the appearance of innocence" (p. 9). Police cannot accept all such proclamations of innocence at face value. That would be foolish.

Character Trait 3: The Deployment of Police Services May Have Unwonted Impact on Various Groups

Bittner's (1970) third character trait of police work relates to the deployment of police services "that reflects a whole range of public prejudices" (p. 10). For example, if a police chief decides to deploy resources where crime is most serious, there may be a disproportionate impact on an affected community, one commonly associated with racial or ethnic concerns. Consider the challenge as posed by Bittner:

> [I]n and of itself, the fact that someone is young, poor, and dark-complexioned is not supposed to mean anything whatsoever to a police officer. Statistically considered, he might be said to be more likely to run afoul of the law, but individually, all things being equal, his chances of being left alone are supposed to be the same as those of someone who is middle aged, well-to-do, and fair-skinned. In fact, however, exactly the opposite is the case. All things being equal, the young-poor-black and the old-rich-white doing the very same things under the very same circumstances will almost certainly not receive the same kind of treatment from policemen. In fact, it is almost inconceivable that the two characters could ever appear or do something in ways that would mean the same thing to a policeman. Nor is the policeman merely expressing personal or institutional prejudice by according the two characters differential treatment (p. 10–11).

In reading this excerpt, be cautious about relying upon Bittner's initial reference to statistics; this is a complex area of analysis and data (see, for example, Cooper & Smith, 2011) where scholars continue to collect, interpret, and argue over what the data mean. More helpful are Bittner's observations about how police will not treat equally two groups, the young-poor-black and old-rich-white, under the very same circumstances. This is a common reality no matter how one views a police officer's underlying motives. Ignoring this reality will neither fix anything nor promote trust.

Conclusion

In one sense, police most clearly symbolize security and order as law *enforcers*, although in a larger sense they must serve the public good. History has shown the grave consequences of the abuse of police power. For example, the sustained history of police abuse of Black people in America, from the legacy of slave patrols onward, undermines the noble role of police as law enforcers who serve the public good—the good of *all* citizens. In the interests of promoting justice, this history must be acknowledged and addressed in the context of police training, culture, and action.

In a broad sense, the just enforcement of law is fundamental to a democratic society to the extent that enforcement effectively protects people *and* preserves their rights. Where police are respected, citizens take comfort in believing that police will serve their community in myriad ways: Police officers will step in and address dangers; police will find and arrest wrongdoers; police will otherwise protect the innocent; police will, in short, serve and *protect* their community.

Perhaps it is no coincidence that studies have shown that two prime motives among aspiring law enforcement officers are to help people and solve problems—both of which embody a like sense of mission and purpose. I can attest to the sense of purpose that most law enforcement officers share. That said, the difficult realities of daily police work challenge such noble aspirations. The unusual challenges and demands of police work require a closer look. As I have often told students, police work is not easy, and it is not for everyone, although it can be an extraordinarily rewarding vocation. Acknowledging these special challenges of policing will not ensure community trust, but it can promote balance, perspective, open-mindedness, and some reframing of the issues and encourage some level of mutual respect so often lacking in public discourse. In other words, this effort may help community and police find some common ground.

Review Questions

1. In an early form of policing, constables performed duties unrelated to traditional law enforcement. Do you believe police should perform a wider range of responsibilities beyond enforcing the law for the public? If so, what duties are appropriate?
2. What would a society look like without a centralized, trained police force? How would order and security be kept in a large, modern, and diverse society?
3. Do you agree that police work is different, that it is unlike most other occupations? Compare police work with some other occupations. How are they alike and not alike?
4. What does Dr. Bittner mean by policing being a "tainted occupation"?
5. Find a vague local ordinance, state, or federal law and describe the challenges in enforcing and prosecuting such a regulation. Why might the public support for enforcement be lacking? What are the potential consequences to police and community alike?
6. Find a contemporary example of a country where police have been co-opted by a tyrant or totalitarian form of government. What does that society look like from the perspective of rights and freedoms or safety and security?

7. Is it possible to end the use of force and coercion in police work or reduce its use? If so, how?
8. Find an example of how the deployment of police services may have adverse or beneficial consequences to a community.

References

1570–1750 estimated population (n.d.). 1841Census.co.uk. https://1841census .co.uk/1570-1750-estimated-population/

Bittner, E. (1970). *The functions of police in modern society: A review of background factors, current practices, and possible role models.* National Institute of Mental Health. https://www.ncjrs.gov/pdffiles1/Digitization/147822NCJRS .pdf

Chriss, J. J. (2013). *Social control: An introduction* (2nd ed.). Polity.

Cooper, A., & Smith, E. L. (2011, November). *Homicide trends in the United States, 1980–2008. Annual rates for 2009 and 2010.* U.S. Department of Justice, Office of Justice Programs, Bureau of Justice Statistics. https://www.bjs.gov/content/pub/pdf/htus8008.pdf

Delaney, W. M. (1996). *Black police in America.* Indiana University Press.

Engel, R. S. (2002). Police: History. In Dressler, J. (Ed.), *Encyclopedia of crime and justice* (2nd ed., Vol. 3, p. 1053). Macmillan Reference USA.

Hadden, S. (2001). *Slave patrols: Law and violence in Virginia and the Carolinas.* Harvard University Press.

Hansen, C. (2019, July 10). *Slave patrols: An early form of American policing.* https:// lawenforcementmuseum.org/2019/07/10/slave-patrols-an-early-form-of-american-policing/

Monkkonen, E. H. (1983). The organized response to crime in nineteenth- and twentieth-century America. *Journal of Interdisciplinary History, 14*(1), 113–128.

Muhammad, K. G. (2011). *The condemnation of Blackness.* Harvard University Press.

Office of National Statistics (2015 July 6). *UK Population Estimates 1851 to 2014.* https://www.ons.gov.uk/peoplepopulationandcommunity/populationand-migration/populationestimates/adhocs/004356ukpopulationestimates-1851to2014

Peel, R. (1829). *Nine principles of policing.*

Potter, G. (2013a). *The history of policing in the United States.* Eastern Kentucky University. https://plsonline.eku.edu/sites/plsonline.eku.edu/files/the-history-of-policing-in-us.pdf

Potter, G. (2013b). *The history of policing in the United States, part 1.* Eastern Kentucky University. https://plsonline.eku.edu/insidelook/history-policing-united-states-part-1

U.K. Parliament. (n.d.). *Metropolitan police.* https://www.parliament.uk/about/living-heritage/transformingsociety/laworder/policeprisons/overview/metropolitanpolice/

United States Holocaust Memorial Museum. (2021, June 2). *The Police in the Weimar Republic.* https://encyclopedia.ushmm.org/content/en/article/the-police-in-the-weimar-republic?parent=en%2F6413

Image Credit

IMG 1: Source: https://commons.wikimedia.org/wiki/File:Police_group_portrait_Bury_St_Edmunds_Suffolk_England.jpg.

Chapter 2

The Importance of Positive Police-Citizen Interactions

Image 2

Peel Principle 7: The police at all times should maintain a relationship with the public that gives reality to the historic tradition that the police are the public and the public are the police; the police are the only members of the public who are paid to give full-time attention to duties which are incumbent on every citizen in the intent of the community welfare.

From the casual to coercive, each police-citizen encounter matters; each encounter is a challenge and an opportunity. To most citizens, police officers represent the most common face of government, and that first or second encounter may shape a citizen's trust and respect. Consider also the context of many police-citizen encounters. Given the nature of an officer's work, most encounters occur because something happened—an officer responds to a speeding violation, a report of domestic abuse, a missing child, a traffic fatality, or some heinous crime scene. The possibilities are endless and often physically and emotionally demanding. Couple that with the fact that family, friends, neighbors, or casual observers might watch and record such interactions. Moreover, police often wear body cameras, and closed-circuit television from any number of locations may permanently capture images from heroism to brutality. Like it or not, officers are in plain view, and people judge them. And the speed of sharing what people see is swift. When police and their squad cars' flashing lights appear at the scene of an incident, that is news, and in the era of social media, news spreads quickly, often without the benefit of factual accuracy, perspective, or reflection. And bad news travels more quickly and widely than good. Impressions are formed. This is a simple reality for police officers and a challenging work landscape for anyone.

Even encounters—good or bad—not in public view may be consequential and long remembered by those against whom police action is directed. Suppose, for example, an officer tightens an arrestee's handcuffs beyond what is a necessary restraint, inflicting intense and sharp pain. That experience will not be forgotten. On a personal note, I still remember an encounter I had as a college student in 1977 with a police officer in a small, rural Illinois town along Route 47. The officer had stopped my car while I was en route to the University of Illinois in Champaign-Urbana. The officer never clearly explained why he had stopped me, although he treated me like I had committed a crime—but no, the officer was not physically abusive. I knew I had not committed a crime or stored anything relating to a crime in my green 1974 Pinto Station Wagon, and I said so, although the officer conducted a warrantless search of my car. In retrospect, perhaps the officer honestly believed, however mistakenly, that he had legal justification to conduct a warrantless search. In later years I learned that police may search a vehicle without a warrant provided they have probable cause to believe something related to a crime may be concealed in the vehicle (this is a simplified explanation). But I will never know his justification; that is unimportant now. I only recall that he had said something about how I met a profile, which in retrospect I find amusing—I was a moderately long-haired, clean-shaven, clean-cut, wide-eyed, polite kid transporting textbooks, groceries supplied by Mom, and golf clubs in the back seat of my Pinto. Yes, I may have consented to the search. I do not remember. Whatever the officer's justification, I felt relieved after he released me, yet I seethed as I drove away. I have never forgotten my sense of helplessness and frustration in being stopped and wrongly accused of wrongdoing—perhaps this is a universal reaction. My experience also underscored the effect of even relatively minor encounters with police, especially when their words or actions seem unjustified or unreasonable. To be fair and transparent, I've since enjoyed excellent professional relationships with local, state, and federal law enforcement officers through my Federal Bureau of Investigation (FBI) career and beyond. Time and experience have given me a fuller, more mature appreciation of police work. But my memory of that day remains, perhaps because it was tied to my confusion, fear, and anger about what happened, even though it was a relatively insignificant event.

Just as an officer's unprofessional conduct may leave a lasting negative impression, so, too, may an officer's act of respect, restraint, professionalism, or kindness be long remembered and shared with others. In almost any interaction with citizens, police inevitably reveal their values—where lasting impressions are formed. These police-citizen interactions may provoke anger and distrust or, better, garner trust and respect. Such interactions are rarely uneventful or quickly forgotten. They matter.

In their interactions with the public, officers might take note that emotions fuel and influence memory. In a study published in 2007, Dr. Tony W. Buchanan concluded that:

> Emotion has long been known to influence what we remember. On the basis of the reviewed literature, it is clear that emotion can exert effects at the time of encoding, during retrieval search processes as well as during the experience of recollection. Models of affect and memory have described the situations in which emotion can influence cognition and, more specifically, memory retrieval (p. 776).

While police cannot be expected to master the science of emotion and memory, their training and investigative experience inform them of the fallibility of memory, as well as the influence of emotion on witness recollection. In performing their myriad responsibilities, a self-disciplined, professional officer who treats individuals with dignity and respect (and like virtues) is less likely to elicit a threatening and emotionally explosive response from others or leave them with negative and potentially inaccurate memories of their experience. That said, what do most police-citizen encounters look like?

Consider some statistics about the nature and frequency of police contacts reported by the Bureau of Justice Statistics, based on 2015 data. The U.S. population ages 16 and older were listed as 253,587,400. A total of 53,506,941 of the 253,587,400 persons—about 21.1%—had some form of contact with police—no small number itself. Now consider what precipitated each such contact with police. As you examine the numbers, be mindful that cumulative contact figures listed first (e.g., 10.8%) are exceeded by individual subtotal figures (8.6 + 2.4 + 1.1 + 1 = 13.1%) because respondents may have attributed more than one reason for a given police contact.

Police-initiated contact made up 10.8%, broken down as follows:

- *Traffic stop of driver: 8.6%*
- *Traffic stop of passenger: 2.4%*
- *Arrest or other: 1.1%*
- *Street stop: 1.0%*
- *Traffic accidents: 3.1%*

Resident-initiated contact made up 10.7%, broken down as follows:

- *Reported possible crime: 6.7%*
- *Reported noncrime: 3.5%*
- *Block watch: 0.9%*
- *Other: 1.0%*

What can be learned? More than 27 million police-initiated contacts involved at least some clear exercise of police authority, from traffic stops to arrests to street stops. A slightly smaller number, still more than 27 million, represented resident-initiated contacts, more than half of which involved reporting crime. No matter what led to each reported police-citizen contact, most of the circumstances were highly charged, at least from the citizen's perspective. Fair or not, impressions are shaped in these emotionally charged encounters.

It is also instructive to examine public attitudes toward police. The results from a 2016 Cato Institute national criminal justice survey are helpful. The following are sample findings, along with my commentary:

- Unsurprisingly, there are racial and partisan divides in calculating how favorably various groups view police, but no one group is truly "anti-cop." In fact, no single group wants to reduce the number of police officers in their communities, and most believe officers have "very dangerous jobs" (Ekins, 2016).
- There are significant gaps among racial groups in how favorably they view the harshness of police tactics, including the use of lethal force. For example, 73% of Black people believe police are too quick to use lethal force, compared to 54% of Hispanics and 35% of Whites. On a very unscientific note, I have observed similar differences in initial perceptions expressed by my diverse body of students when I raise the use of deadly force by law enforcement officers. The survey also reveals similar partisan divides, as 80% of Republicans, compared to 63% of Democrats, believe that police use deadly force only when necessary. Misperceptions and misunderstandings about the proper use of deadly force have far-reaching and dangerous consequences for all (Ekins, 2016).

- There is clearly a gap among racial groups in their high confidence that their local police departments treat all racial groups equally—Black people 31%, Hispanic people 42%, and White people 64%. These differences cannot be minimized. And roughly two-thirds of all polled say police conduct racial or ethnic profiling through motor and pedestrian stops because these officers believe that these groups are "more likely than others to commit certain types of crimes." Varying majority percentages of all groups oppose racial profiling (Ekins, 2016).
- Nearly half of all Americans (Black people 61%, Hispanic people 61%, and White people 46%) believe that "most officers think they are above the law." Similarly, nearly half (Black people 64%, Hispanic people 51%, and White people 43%) believe police are "generally not" held accountable for misconduct. Although these troubling numbers represent perceptions, they cannot be discounted, and they will be addressed elsewhere in the book, particularly Chapter 4, about the role and rule of law (Ekins, 2016).
- An intriguing overall finding is that Americans across all groups generally have higher personal expectations of being treated equitably by their local police departments than their overall expectation of everyone being treated equitably by the criminal justice system. In reviewing the findings, the writer correctly observes, "It is more important for people to believe the system is fair—even to other people—for the police to have legitimacy" (Ekins, 2016).
- Perhaps to no one's surprise, "only 40% of individuals who have personally or vicariously experienced verbal or physical abuse from officers have a favorable view of the police compared to 70% among those without negative experiences. In sum, abuse at the hands of an individual officer—whether individually or vicariously experienced—may be internalized and help explain differences in favorability toward the police" (Ekins, 2016). Discourtesy and disrespect, including abusive language and actions, shape perceptions; the numbers show it. Police must be cognizant of these findings.
- Significantly for both community and police, groups "who feel less favorable toward local law enforcement are less certain they would report a crime they witnessed" (Ekins, 2016). Unreported crime serves no one well. All lose.

So how *should* police treat citizens, and likewise, how *should* citizens treat police? The same as I would like to be treated? Within that context, many might add "with dignity and respect" or other values that appeal to our better nature. The act of policing, as noted earlier, is in part an expression of values and a moral undertaking. But if values can help the dynamic between police and community, how are values critical to effective policing established and practiced?

Values are developed from childhood; they are not given birth at a police academy, although values can be clearly stated and reinforced there. In their search for recruits, police departments are acutely aware that some past deeds of misconduct are toxic to nearly any healthy police culture. Consider, for example, how important honesty and integrity are in the work of any police department employee—whether an employee is an evidence custodian, file clerk, street officer, Special Weapons and Tactics (SWAT) member, or command officer. From the inception of the recruitment process, to the selection of police candidates, to their training at the police academy, to the work performed by all police staff in the community and the courtroom, police must adhere to key values. There are moral and legal consequences when certain character traits are ignored. For example, suppose that a police department minimized the behavior of a police academy candidate who had repeatedly misrepresented to police recruiters personal background information that the police already knew was false or misleading. What police department values are conveyed to that candidate and others if they are still accepted into the police academy? That lying is OK? That actions have no consequences?

Now consider training. Police academy training clarifies and shapes specific values, but relying solely on training to develop character and a solid value system is risky. That said, specific values—such as honesty and integrity—can be reinforced through training and augmented by experience, including that which recruits observe among all police staff. To be sure, the promotion of an organization's core values does not immunize police from other influences, such as harsh or dispiriting experiences arising out of their personal lives or work. Police and citizens alike are human, but the moral hazard is that police, possessing remarkable power and authority, can more easily abuse their status, especially when they become disaffected or lack the character, training, and tools to do the hard work of the job.

Another concern indirectly related to the formation and practice of values is when officers develop a bunker mentality, an "us-versus-them" attitude. In that mindset's worst manifestation, police view the community as "the other" or, worse yet, "the enemy." When that mentality is joined by explicit or implicit racism, the mix is more toxic and divisive. The us-versus-them view dehumanizes others, including those in a community who may support the legitimate role and mission of police. That same mindset also dehumanizes the officers themselves. Nothing good comes of it. A 1988 National Institute of Justice report noted that in policing, there is "the strong belief among many police officers that they stand as the front line of defense against community lawlessness reflecting what is often a rather narrow definition of order ... within which the police operate. These beliefs can easily become the prevalent values of the (police) force" (p. 1). This defensive perspective does little to strengthen police-citizen relations, let alone better promoting policing. Rather, it promotes widespread fear and distrust.

What are some police values that—if practiced—are critical to a healthy police culture? Most seem obvious. Consider a real example of published core police values. Using the acronym *PRIDE*, the core values of the Virginia Beach Police Department (n.d.) provide:

> **Professionalism** ... in our actions, conduct, and job performance. Constantly striving towards ever-rising standards.
>
> **Respect** ... for all citizens, each other, and for differing points of view, regardless of age, race, gender, appearance, individual beliefs, or life-styles.
>
> **Integrity** ... truthful and honest, deserving of trust. Ethical. Being guided by the concept of fundamental fairness in everything we do. Doing what is right.
>
> **Dedication** ... to the organization, each other, our families, and the citizens we serve. Unquestionable work ethic.
>
> **Excellence** ... in everything we do. Seeking to improve and excel, always.

However, these values, if not enforced or promoted by police, are hollow.

Most police departments also use a code of ethics, which often includes values similar to the following (ACE Electoral Knowledge Network, 2021):

- respect for the constitutional and civil rights of all persons;
- obeying the laws of the country and the regulations of the police department;
- impartial and professional behavior and action; not allowing personal feelings, prejudices, animosities or friendship to influence a decision;
- being honest and not using the office for personal or partisan benefit, refusing personal rewards and gratuities for official conduct;
- respecting the confidentiality of the office and the information gathered on citizens;
- enforcing the law courteously and appropriately;
- not intimidating citizens or suspects, using self-restraint and watching out for the welfare of others;

- never using excessive force or violence;
- compassion and fairness; and
- cooperating with all legal agencies in the pursuit of justice.

How an organization conveys values and underlying ethics need not be limited to pedagogical lectures, practical problems, or study guides. It is useful to consider unfamiliar experiences that have emotional heft. In 2000, for example, the FBI began requiring new agent and analyst trainee classes to visit the United States Holocaust Memorial Museum in Washington, DC. Why? To help them understand "how incomprehensible evil can take hold through individual and institutional acts of moral surrender" (FBI.gov, 2019). Later, in 2014, new FBI trainees began visiting the Martin Luther King, Jr. Memorial, also in Washington, DC, in an effort "to ensure they understand the FBI's past mistakes on civil rights—including its surveillance of Dr. King—and embrace its civil rights mission" (FBI.gov, 2019). Yes, it is important to acknowledge and learn from past and continuing mistakes and wrongs, such as racism, sexism, or xenophobia. This deepens understanding and empathy. Nearly every community, together with its police department, can find those who can recount personal experiences or historical artifacts to underscore key values or the dangers of retreating from these values. These experiences can be deeply moral, humbling, and memorable.

If I were to name a bedrock "value" essential to the culture of any law enforcement organization that professes democratic values, I would single out respect for and adherence to the **rule of law.** That said, however, as important it is to promote the rule of law—and it truly is—conveying this as a standalone value seen simply as rigid conformance to law is not sufficient, as other values such as equality and fairness may seem equal to or more important among some communities. Police departments and their value systems do not exist in isolation—no matter how wise or aspirational they are. Communities, neighborhoods, schools, community organizations, families, and other entities obviously hold their own, and it is especially useful to identify and build upon those that are shared.

Under the right circumstances, police and community groups can discuss what they value most in the context of police-citizen relations and what they are most concerned about. An officer, for example, may find opportunities in neighborhood or school settings. Over time police may learn more about the communities they serve and vice versa. What are police concerned about? What are communities most concerned about? Do police values mirror family, peer, community, or neighborhood values? Do they sometimes clash? How are they alike? These questions and conversations can help develop relationships with those they serve and protect. It may be something as simple as discussing the value of respect and exploring what respect means in everyday life. Participants are encouraged to be curious, imaginative, and open-minded. Do not discount the opportunity for an authentic, honest dialogue. There are also tools, such as moral reframing, that make it possible for police and communities to find places of common ground and growth.

Because of the nature of their work, police are uniquely situated to demonstrate to their community—rich and poor alike—a commitment in real time to share their norms and values. In a sense, their work may reveal aspects of what we value as a greater community and nation and how we might govern ourselves in a democracy.

Police and community alike must resist thinking of themselves strictly as opposing factions, unwilling or unable to identify any shared narrative, any common ground. In a diverse society, this is no easy task, but to establish stable, mutually beneficial relationships, it is necessary. When differences arise between police and community members—and they will—police and citizenry must be able to point to or draw from a reservoir of some common identity, some shared values and ideals, some common commitment to justice, that strengthens trust and promotes the common good.

In demonstrating values in the real world, how police do their work truly matters, as their interactions impact a community's sense of safety, well-being, and even sense of personal freedom. Yes, even freedom, as the spectrum of lawful police activities is not limited to terminating another's physical freedom through stops, frisks, or full custodial arrests. More common are ordinary types of interactions, some casual or informal, such as officers engaged in fact-finding or community-building efforts. Police actions may also promote and protect the exercise of various freedoms, such as when police provide needed security while civil protesters exercise their First Amendment rights safely in a public forum. Without appropriate security, protests can become dangerously confrontational, so in a very real sense police actions may *support* the exercise of First Amendment rights—and make no mistake, this can be very difficult work. Through it all, community members are watching, and the oft-cited police motto "to serve and protect" is not an empty phrase. When police fail to serve and protect, the consequences to society may be grave. There is no lack of historical proof.

In fact, recent history has reminded us that when nations begin moving away from a more open, free, and democratic society toward a more coercive political state, civilian police are often first co-opted—sometimes gradually, sometimes rapidly. Chapter 1 referred to what happened in Nazi Germany. The more recent clash between police and hundreds of thousands of protesters in Hong Kong is also instructive, if not alarming. What first prompted the clash between Hong Kong citizens and police was a controversial extradition bill that could send Hong Kong residents charged with crime to mainland China to be tried there. The extradited

Hong Kong residents would thus be subject to China's authoritarian judicial system—and its coercive power. Ostensibly, the extradition bill was intended to prevent Hong Kong from becoming a haven for fugitives from China—at least according to Hong Kong's chief executive, Carrie Lam. But opponents in Hong Kong feared that the bill would erase the city's judicial independence and expose Hong Kong to China's flawed judicial and criminal justice system. To Hong Kong citizens, these developments threaten traditions, protections, and rights long enjoyed by them. On December 19, 1984 Great Britain and China signed a treaty, the Sino-British Joint Declaration, that described how Hong Kong would be governed after July 1, 1997. That treaty marked the end of British rule and gave Hong Kong a 50-year transitional period, beginning in 1997, in which Hong Kong citizens would retain much of their freedom and autonomy before becoming fully subject to Chinese rule in 2047. That said, the extradition bill was viewed by most Hong Kong citizens as an early step to surrendering Hong Kong's autonomy to China well before 2047. Hongkongers have long tasted freedom and rights, which, once enjoyed, are not lightly surrendered. More recent events relating to new Beijing-imposed national security laws have only worsened such concerns.

Possessing broad, legitimate powers and responsibilities, police interact with community in wildly changing circumstances. They respond to drunk or reckless drivers, abusive partners, con artists, corrupt politicians, drug-addled parents, mass murderers, and even domestic and international terrorists. They witness what is best in people, but they also may see and respond to what is worst. No matter what distinctions we make of criminal conduct, police observe conduct that can be described as sobering at best. When interacting with the accused, how might a police officer respond to this broad spectrum or human behavior, understanding that an officer is neither judge nor jury? Will standards suffer when the accused has committed child abuse or rape or murder? Will rage cloud judgment and professionalism? Will the officer act as judge and jury in some manner? Or act with restraint and self-discipline? Within the rule of law? With justice, equality, and fundamental fairness in mind? And who is watching? Anyone. That *anyone* may become a vocal critic or unabashed supporter. Add to this the likelihood that a police-citizen encounter—behavior representing the good, the bad, and the ugly—is recorded by police themselves or by community witnesses for posterity.

Officers, in short, "perform" on the public stage under intense scrutiny. As Shakespeare wrote in *As You Like It*, "All the world's a stage, and all the men and women merely players: they have their exits and their entrances. ..." Famed twentieth-century sociologist Erving Goffman cited Shakespeare in developing theories of social action that examined, among other things, how individuals want to present themselves most favorably to others. Officers, like their fellow citizens, are "merely players," but their stage is played out on a moral landscape important to people and their government. Their undertaking, rife with making decisions in the context of this moral landscape, is formidable, and the potential for abuse or public misunderstanding or distrust is great. Goffman (1956), while not referring specifically to police, wrote "As performers we are merchants of morality" ("The Presentation of Self in Everyday Life" p. 156). How true for police work! Moreover, if officers, as merchants of morality, misbehave or abuse their authority, the public will notice, and they will care. The press, in performing their vital public role, knows this; that is why police misconduct is *always* newsworthy.

Given these circumstances, what *external* legal, regulatory, and ethical standards guide police in their interactions with citizens? Officers are both empowered and limited by law in how they perform their duties, whether officers are federal, state, or local. But more generally, officers also take an oath. Oaths vary among police departments; one oath promulgated by the International Association of Chiefs of Police states:

> On my honor, I will never betray my badge, my integrity, my character or the public trust. I will always have the courage to hold myself and others accountable for our actions. I will always uphold the Constitution, my community, and the agency I serve, so help me God (*Developed by the IACP Committee on Police Ethics, 2000,* https://www.vachiefs.org/oath_of_honor).

An appointed federal officer in the federal civil service takes the following oath:

> I do solemnly swear (or affirm) that I will support and defend the Constitution of the United States against all enemies, foreign and domestic; that I will bear true faith and allegiance to the same; that I take this obligation freely, without any mental reservation or purpose of evasion; and that I will well and faithfully discharge the duties of the office on which I am about to enter. So help me God. 5 U.S. Code Section 3331 (Oath of Office, 1966).

What do these oaths share? All officers swear to uphold the Constitution, and state and local officers must also swear to uphold binding state and local laws.

These oaths impose lofty standards and important responsibilities on police. Behind the performance of such responsibilities, which sociologist Max Weber explained in his 1919 lecture "Politics as a Vocation" (1919), lies the power of the state, which Weber defined as a "human community that claims the monopoly of the legitimate use of force within a given territory." The key, of course, is the *legitimate* use of such coercive power and physical force.

Institutions and individuals holding coercive power elicit strong reactions, including awe, respect, concern, fear, and sometimes contempt. In fact, the mere presence of police affects others, but when police use their coercive powers or are perceived to use them unwisely, there are consequences. Coercion may also be indirect, too, such as overarching police surveillance. Individuals representing the political spectrum take issue with the perceived abuse of police power. Police have been called pigs or racist or worse, and FBI agents have been called "jackbooted government thugs" or worse. These heated responses to real or perceived police abuses of power and authority exist. Police must account and prepare for them.

No one disputes that police hold considerable coercive power when they interact with citizens, as they are afforded almost unequalled lawful authority to carry out a broad range of responsibilities. The effective exercise of such power relies on the extent to which police are trusted. As such "any excessive use of that authority, abuse of power, or failure to fulfill their duties can erode public trust and reduce or destroy their credibility within the communities they serve" (U.S. Department of Justice, 2008, p. 7). Fair or not, each officer represents the entire agency in their interaction with the public, and that has consequences.

Review Questions

1. Do you believe that policing is a moral and value-ridden undertaking? Why or why not?
2. Have you or someone you know ever had a memorable encounter (even for a traffic ticket) with a police officer? Describe what happened, how you (or someone else) were treated, and what your reaction was. Could the officer have handled the encounter differently? How so?
3. What five qualities do you value most in police? Justify each.
4. Should civilian law enforcement officers at the local, state, or federal level have more or less autonomy from government officials? Why or why not? What are the dangers or benefits? Give examples.
5. Find another example of police in the U.S. or elsewhere who have been co-opted by the government in a manner that is detrimental to citizens. Describe what happened and the harm to citizens.
6. Find another police or law enforcement oath on the web. If you were the chief, what would you do to ensure that officers abide by the letter and spirit of the oath?

References

ACE Electoral Knowledge Network. (2021). *Code of conduct for law enforcement.* https://aceproject.org/main/english/ei/eie12c1.htm

Buchanan, T. W. (2007, September). Retrieval of emotional memories. *Psychological Bulletin, 133*(5), 761–779. https://www.ncbi.nlm.nih.gov/pmc/articles/PMC2265099/

Ekins, E. (2016, December 7). *Policing in America: Understanding public attitudes toward the police. Results from a national survey. Results from the Cato Institute 2016 Criminal Justice Survey.* Cato Institute. https://www.cato.org/survey-reports/policing-america

FBI.gov. (2019, March 13). *'Remember this day': National September 11 memorial and museum visit added to FBI agent and analyst training.* https://www.fbi.gov/news/stories/911-memorial-visit-added-to-agent-and-analyst-training-031319

Goffman, E. (1956). *The Presentation of Self in Everyday Life.* Anchor.

Oath of office, 5 U.S.C. § 3331 (1966). https://www.law.cornell.edu/uscode/text/5/3331

Peel, R. (1829). *Nine principles of policing.*

U.S. Department of Justice. (2008). *Building trust between the police and the citizens they serve: An internal affairs promising practices guide for local law enforcement.* Office of Community Oriented Policing. https://www.theiacp.org/sites/default/files/2018-08/BuildingTrust_0.pdf

Virginia Beach Police Department. (n.d.). *Mission statement and core values.* https://www.vbgov.com/government/departments/police/chiefs-office/Pages/mission-statement.aspx

Wasserman, R. and Moore, H. National Institute of Justice. (1988, November). *Values in Policing* (Perspectives in Policing, 8). U.S. Department of Justice, Office of Justice Programs.

Weber, M. (1919). *Politics as a Vocation* [Lecture]. Free Students Union, Bavaria.

Image Credit

Chapter 3

Cultivating a Culture of Law and Justice

Constitutional values inform police and community

Peel Principle 5: Police seek and preserve public favor not by catering to the public opinion but by constantly demonstrating absolute impartial service to the law.

> "Justice is the end of government. It is the end of civil society. It ever has been and ever will be pursued until it be obtained, or until liberty be lost in the pursuit." James Madison, Federalist No. 51

> "The life of the nation is secure only while the nation is honest, truthful, and virtuous." Frederick Douglas, speech on the twenty-third anniversary of emancipation, Washington, D.C., April 1885

Civic Learning, the Constitution, and Justice

When I began writing this book, retired Supreme Court Associate Justice Sandra Day O'Connor announced that she had been diagnosed with Alzheimer's disease. In a public statement, Justice O'Connor explained that soon after she retired, she committed herself to advancing civic learning and engagement. She explained why:

> I feel so strongly about the topic because I've seen firsthand how vital it is for all citizens to understand our Constitution and unique system of government and participate actively in their communities. It is through this shared understanding of who we are that we can follow the approaches that have served us best over time—working collaboratively together in communities and in government to solve problems, putting country and the common good above party and self-interest, and holding our key governmental institutions accountable (O'Connor, 2018).

Justice O'Connor's message expressed beliefs I have long held in both my Federal Bureau of Investigation (FBI) career and now as a university lecturer, namely how vital it is to understand the Declaration of Independence, our Constitution, and other seminal American writings; to work collaboratively in communities and government to solve problems; to put country and the common good first; to hold key government institutions accountable; to address wrongs openly and honestly to effect sensible, just and sustainable change; and, to borrow Jefferson's words, to promote life, liberty, and the pursuit of happiness. Justice O'Connor acted on her beliefs when she established iCivics, an online program dedicated to teaching core principles of civics to middle and high school students. This approach should inform and guide the relationship between police and community.

I sometimes ask my college classroom students to identify what they believe are their shared values or norms, or what defines the United States as a sovereign nation and people. I am often met with silence, and sometimes bewilderment. Eventually students identify freedom, consumerism, individualism, or economic opportunity, but there is little consensus. In fact, Americans rarely voice what values, principles, or norms bind us, or what gives meaning to the word *patriotism* beyond flag-waving or reciting the Pledge of Allegiance or, more recently, "making America great" without explaining what exactly that means. On their face, these examples may sound laudable, but they are vague, and in this time of intense partisanship and invective, many Americans question, fairly, what if anything defines us as a people and nation. What students shared may be important, but not because it make us uniquely American. And this nation is more than a wealth-seeking people sharing a land mass protected from foreign enemies by its armed forces. It was founded on principles and values that deserve more explanation.

This perspective considers writings and expressions that underscore certain principles and values, such as the Declaration of Independence, the U.S. Constitution, Dr. Martin Luther King, Jr.'s *Letter from Birmingham Jail*, and other uniquely American writings and speeches that continue to define and shape this nation. They express such ideals as the rule of law, freedom and liberty, equality, checks and balances, the pursuit of the common good, the inherent dignity of every person, individual happiness, individual rights, and, of course, justice. This values-driven approach should be an integral part of police training, police practice, and community-building dialogue.

James Madison, fourth U.S. president and drafter of the U.S. Constitution, wrote that "a people who mean to be their own Governors, must arm themselves with the power which knowledge gives" (J. Madison, personal communication, 1822, Aug. 4). In a similar vein, former President John F. Kennedy delivered a speech in 1963 at Vanderbilt University in which he said, "Liberty without learning is always in peril, and learning without liberty is always in vain." People "who mean to be their own governors" must possess some basic understanding of the Constitution and other influential American writings, understanding that is critical to both their freedom and the establishment of good governance. Similarly, knowledge and respect for constitutional values should be deeply embedded in all aspects of police training, not simply in such practicalities as what constitutes a lawful police "search" or "seizure" in the context of the Fourth Amendment of the U.S. Constitution. True, these Fourth Amendment practicalities are important in ensuring that police are trained to properly collect evidence that can be used to prove in court that someone committed a crime. But there is more. The knowledge of rights and responsibilities gained by their study and practice can affirm, protect, and help unify a sovereign people in their relationship to government. And more specifically, they inform and guide how police, as instruments of government, should go about the work of policing when police interact with the community.

Consider too the ultimate purpose of government and how it informs policing. In James Madison's famous *Federalist No. 51* (1788), he wrote that "*Justice* is the end of government. It is the end of civil society. It ever has been and ever will be pursued until it be obtained, or until liberty be lost in the pursuit" (emphasis added). Almost 200 years later, Dr. Martin Luther King, Jr., quoted these same words in his *Letter from Birmingham Jail* (1963), words borne out of Dr. King's personal experience, suffering, and wisdom. In defining justice, Dr. King advocated a natural-law philosophy, one grounded in morality, in right and wrong, in just laws. A just law, he explained, is a "man-made code that squares with the moral law or the law of God" (King, 1963). King advocated for the moral responsibility of obeying just laws to promote order in civil society. But he also he argued that "one has a moral responsibility to disobey unjust laws" (King, 1963). In the letter, Dr. King quoted Saint Augustine, an early Christian theologian and Neoplatonic philosopher from Numidia, who wrote that "an unjust law is no law at all." It takes little effort to find examples of unjust laws. For example, beginning in the 1890s, Jim Crow laws embodied "unjust laws" because they promoted and enforced segregation and disenfranchised Black people. As instruments of government enforcement, police enforced such ignoble laws, sometimes brutally. That is a legacy, one not easily forgotten. And to return to Madison's point, it can hardly be said that Jim Crow laws promoted any sense of justice; if "justice is the end of government," the passage and enforcement of Jim Crow laws failed this test.

Similarly, behind society's acceptance of any law and its successful enforcement by police is some belief that justice is being served. The most widely accepted principle of justice, defined by Aristotle more than 2,000 years ago, is that "equals should be treated equally and unequals unequally" (Velasquez, 2018). A more contemporary explanation might be this: "Individuals should be treated the same unless they differ in ways that are relevant to the situation in which they are involved" (Mintz, 2016).

That said, police enforce a broad range of laws, the vast majority of which *are* just laws, such as those that criminalize murder, rape, or assault and battery, or other crimes commonly characterized as malum in se. The "justice" or "justness" of some laws and local ordinances is less clear, such as loitering, public intoxication, simple possession of marijuana, or laws requiring annual car inspections; this is not to say these laws are manifestly *unjust.* Sometimes the frequency and manner in which these laws are enforced and prosecuted may raise legitimate concerns about the administration of justice, concerns that address the equal treatment of individuals. An independent judiciary, however, serves at least one vital though imperfect check on potential police abuse in enforcing law and administering justice. As Justice Felix Frankfurter wrote in *McNabb v. United States* (1943):

> A democratic society, in which respect for the dignity of all men is central, naturally guards against the misuse of the law enforcement process. Zeal in tracking down crime is not in itself an assurance of soberness of judgment. Disinterestedness in law enforcement does not alone prevent disregard of cherished liberties. Experience has therefore counseled that safeguards must be provided against the dangers of the overzealous as well as the despotic. The awful instruments of the criminal law cannot be entrusted to a single functionary.

A principal theme of this book is this: How police serve, protect, and enforce the law—or even interact with the public—should reveal a mindfulness and respect for the Constitution and its values. According to Oregon police officer Richard Goerling and Brian Shiers, a facilitator from UCLA's Mindful Awareness Research Center, mindfulness training helps police respond to what a community seeks from police, such as treating others with respect and using necessary restraint in carrying out police duties. An underlying knowledge of constitutional principles and values—and the mindfulness to apply them in the work of policing promotes a civic and civil relationship between police and communities. Police should emphasize these civic values and principles in training, and make them a vital part of public discourse and the execution of their duties.

Calling attention to these values and principles need not be some lifeless exercise; after all, the Declaration of Independence and the Constitution are about power and relationships, freedom, responsibility, and more. They are about we the people, how *we* govern ourselves, and how *we* rely upon or limit the role of government. No single group drives the formation, understanding, or application of constitutional principles or values. *We* are all stakeholders. And when these values are manifest in how police perform their public duties, much good can follow.

The opening of the Declaration of Independence (1776) lays a foundation:

> We hold these truths to be self-evident, that all men are created equal, that they are endowed by their Creator with certain unalienable Rights, that among these are Life, Liberty and the pursuit of Happiness. —That to secure these rights, Governments are instituted among Men, deriving their just powers from the consent of the governed, —That whenever any Form of Government becomes destructive of these ends, it is the Right of the People to alter or to abolish it, and to institute new Government, laying its foundation on such principles and organizing its powers in such form, as to them shall seem most likely to effect their Safety and Happiness. Prudence, indeed, will dictate that Governments long established should not be changed for light and transient causes; and accordingly all experience hath shewn, that mankind are more disposed to suffer, while evils are sufferable, than to right themselves by abolishing the forms to which they are accustomed.

In the Declaration, Thomas Jefferson set forth "self-evident" truths: that all people are created equal and that they possess certain unalienable rights, among them life, liberty, and the pursuit of happiness, rights not bestowed by nation or sovereign.

These words speak to the inherent dignity of *all* people, people who possess, who are all entitled—equally—to certain unalienable rights, so "endowed by their Creator" (Jefferson, 1776). People who are *created* equal and endowed with certain unalienable rights are deserving of respect ab initio. Cynics could point to the hypocrisy of Jefferson and other architects of a new nation who owned slaves; some founders acknowledged their hypocrisy and the monstrosity of slavery, but others did not. Yes, at this point cynics could dismiss the power and substance of the Declarations of Independence and other writings, but that would deny their promise, their hope of expanding equality, fairness, due process, and the dignity of *all* people. Such cynicism is neither wise nor useful. In fact, as noted in this chapter, the very victims of slavery and the evils of racism have generously cited principles and values embodied in the Declaration of Independence, the Constitution, and other uniquely American writings. They are sources of strength and common ground for all.

The Declaration of Independence describes the relationship between "Governments, instituted among Men" that derive their "just powers from the consent of the governed," namely a sovereign people who hold certain *preexisting* unalienable rights. The Declaration also states that government *not* based on the consent of the governed could be justifiably overthrown—that is, people have the right to alter or abolish government when it fails to secure their consent. Whether a government succeeds or fails in its task to serve the people, the Declaration makes clear that the end of government is one that lays its foundation "on such principles and organizing its powers in such form, as to them (the people) shall seem most likely to effect their *Safety* and Happiness" (emphasis added). Note how Jefferson valued not just the underlying dignity of all people, but how he assumed, rightfully, that people valued their safety, a vital duty of government in general and the police in particular.

After independence was fought for and achieved, a new nation sought to establish a sustainable form of government that protected these principles and unalienable rights to form a more perfect union and shape a national identity. An inherently challenging task, it required the drafting of a constitution for a sovereign people. Madison also understood that a sovereign people, including the government of the people, must respect and obey the Constitution: "My idea of the sovereignty of the people is that the people can change the constitution [sic] if they please, but while the constitution exists, *they must conform to its dictates*" (1788; emphasis added). The Constitution still exists.

The U.S. Constitution, ratified in 1787, and the Bill of Rights, ratified in 1791, together still exist, having survived roughly 230 years—and through a civil war, no small feat. The U.S. Constitution stands as the oldest living constitution composed in a single document and the second oldest if one includes the Republic of San Marino's constitution, based on a series of six books written in Latin in 1600, known as *Statutes of 1600*. The U.S. Constitution and its amendments created "a more perfect union" that now guide and limit all federal, state, *and local police activities*—and thus deserve our attention.

Consider the preamble of the U.S.:

> We the People of the United States, in Order to form a more perfect Union, establish Justice, insure domestic Tranquility, provide for the common defense, promote the general Welfare, and secure the Blessing of Liberty to ourselves and our Posterity, do ordain and establish this Constitution for the United States of America.

"We the People"—not the government, judges or lawyers, special interest groups, the wealthy, or the powerful, but the people. The preamble is personal and direct. It represents a challenge, a reminder that "we" are the people, both as individuals and as a community, who value not just our personal interests, but something greater than ourselves. We value our safety, our security, our welfare, and our liberties, not just for ourselves but for future generations. To attain these goals, "We the People" established the Constitution for the United States for all. This American promise cannot be attained solely through the pursuit of selfish goals—it must honor and protect the rights of all. The core values of the preamble speak of democratic governance, a limited but effective government, justice, and liberty.

Notably missing in the Constitution's preamble is the value of *equality*. The reason is clear. As first ratified, the Constitution's greatest flaw was the protection of the institution of slavery. As Berkeley Law Dean and constitutional scholar Erwin Chemerinsky explained, the protection of slavery was embodied in several parts of the Constitution:

> Article 1, Section 9, prohibits Congress from banning the importation of slaves until 1808, and Article 5 prohibited this from being amended. Article 1, Section 2, provides that, for purposes of representation in Congress, enslaved black people in a state would be counted as three-fifths of the number of white inhabitants of that state. Article 4, Section 2, contains the "fugitive slave clause," which required that an escaped slave be returned to his or her owner (Cohen, 2019).

Only through and after a civil war did one nation begin to confront slavery and racism in the fateful shortcomings of the Constitution, and to move toward principles of equality in post-Civil War amendments, examined more fully in Chapter 8.

In short, police words and deeds should embody a continuing commitment to the Constitution preamble's core values and, of course, to equality. But citizens themselves play a critical role. James Madison identified in his oft-cited *Federalist Paper No. 51* (1788) the inherent tension between the government and the governed—the freedom-seeking people of a new nation:

> The great difficulty lies in this: you must first enable the government to control the governed: and in the next place oblige it to control itself. A dependence on the people is, no doubt, the primary control on the government; but experience has taught mankind the necessity of auxiliary precautions.

Good governance depends on an *informed* people who serve as a check on government abuse. Good governance also relies on informed officials who carry out their responsibilities consistent with the law. Both are essential.

Constitutional Limits on Government

The Constitution, which established the government, also placed limits and restraints on it. As agents of government, police are and must be subject to limits and restraints. Unfettered police action, even in pursuit of some notional public good such as national security or even public safety, can be tyrannical; unrestrained police action is also the hallmark of failed or oppressive governments. Unrestrained police action, moreover, subverts the rule of law. In the U.S., *all* police—federal, state, and local alike—must conform to certain constitutional standards. The Fourth and First Amendments of the Bill of Rights provide examples of two such restraints.

The Fourth Amendment recognizes that the "right of the people to be secure in their persons, houses, papers, and effects, against unreasonable searches and seizures, shall not be violated. ..." The Fourth Amendment commands that all government searches and seizures of the people must be "reasonable"—a standard that should serve as a bulwark against arbitrary, excessive, or otherwise unreasonable government searches or seizures.

For example, suppose that police identify a violent criminal gang. In their investigation of gang members, police may want to search all gang member homes for evidence of crime and contraband. But such a broad, sweeping approach, one lacking legal standards or judicial oversight, can promote overzealous, arbitrary, and even capricious conduct by police. The Fourth Amendment imposes limits on whether and how police lawfully search, seize, take or otherwise interfere in the property and privacy rights of people they are sworn to protect and serve, including wrongdoers. When police scrupulously abide by these limits, the community recognizes that police not only *enforce* the law—as police *are* uniquely authorized to use *force* (a power indeed) under appropriate circumstances—but also uphold and defend the Constitution as they perform their duties. An officer's act of searching, seizing or using force are only tools to perform her duties—a lawful means to achieve lawful ends. Through this lens, police and citizens may find common ground. Communities expect police to be law abiders, upholders of the law, in their role to serve and protect, not to behave as power-asserting government officials flouting the law. Good policing, subject to Fourth Amendment restraints, is an integral part of good governance. The Fourth Amendment's role in limiting police activities will be explored in greater detail in later chapters.

Another amendment defining the relationship between government and the people is the First Amendment. The First Amendment provides:

> Congress shall make no law respecting an establishment of religion, or prohibiting the free exercise thereof; or abridging the freedom of speech, or of the press; or the right of the people peaceably to assemble, and to petition the Government for a redress of grievances.

The founders recognized the value of promoting a freer, robust, and open civil society. The language of the First Amendment was clearly directed at Congress and its law-making efforts. The First Amendment guarantees that, among other things, when Congress proposes a law, it must consider whether a law establishes a religion, prohibits the free exercise of religion, or abridges the freedom of speech or the press, the right of people peaceably to assemble, or the right to petition the government for a redress of grievances. In a series of significant decisions, the U.S. Supreme Court applied First Amendment standards to other state and local *law-making* bodies, not just Congress, as well as to *actions and practices* of all government and government officials in the performance of their official duties.

The most recognized exercise of First Amendment speech and assembly rights in which police are engaged, involve acts of protest or demonstration. Preserving and protecting such acts are vital to a free and democratic society. As stated in *Keeping Faith with the Constitution*, freedom of speech furthers "both individual dignity and collective democratic activity" (Liu, Karlan, & Schroeder, 2009, p. 15). The challenge to effective yet constitutional policing is no more evident than when there is a huge public outcry against real injustices, such as the nationwide protests sparked by the deaths of Eric Garner, Breonna Taylor, and George Floyd. The deep and visceral reactions provoked by these and other events must be given a safe voice and place. Yet police cannot ignore and must address real and imminent threats to individual and community safety and property. This is no easy task. There are publicly available resources to guide police, such as an IACP publication "Community-Police Engagement: Agency Considerations Checklist for Civil Demonstration Response."

The checklist is designed to ensure "officers engage in valuable dialogue and maintain order." Communities and law enforcement alike must appreciate the extraordinary importance and uniquely American protection of all manner of expression.

Congress has revealed its commitment to preserving First Amendment activities in laws that often escape public attention but greatly impact various government agencies. One such example is an important and complex federal law that establishes a code of fair information practices that govern certain federal executive branch agencies. The law, known as the *Privacy Act of 1974* (1974) specifically regulates how certain executive branch federal agencies, including the FBI and other federal law enforcement agencies, collect, maintain, use, and disseminate information about individuals—the people—that are maintained in their "system of records." Notably, the Privacy Act of 1974 provides in part that any federal agency subject to the act, such as the FBI, shall:

> ... maintain no record describing how any individual exercises rights guaranteed by the First Amendment unless expressly authorized by statute or by the individual about whom the record maintained or unless pertinent to and within the scope of an authorized law enforcement activity[.]"

A federal agency's "system of records" are records 1) that are under the control of that agency and 2) from which such information is retrievable by the name of the individual or by some identifier assigned to the individual. The undeniable message directed to covered federal agencies is this: Do not maintain records on how individuals exercise their First Amendment rights unless there is a lawful reason to do so, such as another law that expressly permits it, or unless it is pursuant to the scope of some authorized law enforcement activity. If covered federal agencies lack lawful justification to maintain such records, they risk violating federal law. Thus, a covered federal agency's random, arbitrary, or unwarranted collection of such records is not only unwise, but also possibly illegal. In my former capacity as an FBI chief division counsel, I often cautioned agents to think carefully about what they collect and preserve as permanent FBI records about individuals—do not collect and maintain gratuitous records describing the exercise of individuals' First Amendment rights unless there is a legitimate law enforcement reason to do so.

How might a covered federal agency violate the Privacy Act of 1974? Suppose an African immigrant (Citizen A) has just gained U.S. citizenship; she has taken pride in her knowledge of the liberties she now enjoys as a citizen, including her right to express views that differ from stated U.S. policy. Exercising this right, Citizen A submits an editorial to a local newspaper, which publishes it. Her editorial harshly—

even inaccurately, perhaps—criticizes the U.S. government's treatment of detainees at Guantanamo Bay. An FBI intelligence analyst reads the editorial and, without further reflection and without establishing any connection to an "authorized law enforcement activity" (or national security or intelligence activity), places an electronic copy of the article, including the writer's (Citizen A) name, into an FBI file. Citizen A later files a Freedom of Information Act (FOIA) with the FBI. An FBI search of its system of records reveals the existence of this published editorial within an FBI file, which is then included in the FBI's response to Citizen A's FOIA request. Under these circumstances Citizen A may assert that the FBI's inclusion of her editorial in its system of records represents a potential violation of the Privacy Act of 1974. Why? Presuming that the FBI included her name and other personally identifiable information about her in connection with her editorial, it had collected and retained expressions of First Amendment activity that bear no apparent relationship to the FBI's authorized criminal investigative or national security responsibilities. Remember, people are free to disagree with government policy—which is itself a very good thing. In this hypothetical situation, the FBI may have violated the Privacy Act of 1974. This is how the system really works, and in a real sense the Privacy Act discourages deliberate or careless government collection, retention, and dissemination of activities that implicate the First Amendment. Our country is better for it.

Another federal statute that refers to the First Amendment, 18 U.S.C. § 112, criminalizes certain acts committed against foreign officials, official guests, and internationally protected persons—foreign diplomats, for example. Understandably, certain crimes committed against these officials are serious matters, as they may adversely affect diplomatic relations. Prohibited acts include intimidation, coercion, threats against a foreign official or guest in the performance of that individual's duties, or harassment. Significantly, subparagraph (d) of this federal criminal law also states, "Nothing contained in this section shall be construed or applied so as to abridge the exercise of rights guaranteed under the First Amendment to the Constitution of the United States" (Protection of Foreign Officials, Official Guests, and Internationally Protected Persons, 1948). Given the language of 18 U.S.C. § 112, suppose Citizen B stood across the street from the Russian Embassy in Washington, D.C., carrying a sign that read, "The Russian ambassador is a stooge of Putin, and Putin is a threat to the world—get the Russians out of our country!" And suppose the Russian ambassador passes the protester, who simply calls out the ambassador by name and then recites the wrongs of the Russian government. On these facts *alone* it would be at best unwise to arrest Citizen B for a violation of 18 U.S.C. § 112 when Citizen B is simply exercising First Amendment rights.

Yet another federal law, the Animal Enterprise Protection Act, 18 U.S.C. § 43, prohibits acts of violence and threats involving "animal enterprises" that use or sell animals or animal products for profit, food or fiber production or research or other options (Animal Enterprise Protection Act of 1992, 1992). A broadly written law, it refers to animal enterprises, which include zoos, animal shelters, furriers, slaughterhouses, and university research facilities that use animals for testing, and more. Animal enterprises often draw the attention of a range of animal rights activists. Some activists express their opposition through lawful protest protected by the First Amendment. Some, however, commit crimes of violence or property damage to express their opposition to an animal enterprise's treatment of animals. When animal rights groups or individuals commit such acts, such as setting fire to an animal shelter, they are subject to arrest and prosecution. By contrast, dissent expressed through speech or peaceable assembly or other forms of communication is protected; dissent expressed through violence or damage to property is not. That said, when laws criminalize conduct that implicates, chills, or somehow restrains First Amendment activities, they will be reviewed by courts for their constitutionality. Laws must not punish lawful, protected First Amendment activities. In fact, the Animal Enterprise Protection Act's rules of statutory construction, clarify that nothing in this section "shall be construed to prohibit any expressive conduct (including peaceful picketing or other peaceful demonstration) protected from legal prohibition by the First Amendment to the Constitution" (Animal Enterprise Protection Act of 1992, 1992).

First Amendment protections give space to and a release for citizens to address politically sensitive or profoundly divisive issues openly. But sometimes expression itself can drift toward violence, and sometimes forms of expression can obstruct expression by others or invite or even incite violence. Consider, for example, activities in which protestors obstruct people entering certain businesses or facilities. One such federal crime that protects certain acts of dissent but prohibits others is the Freedom of Access to Clinic Entrances Act of 1994 (FACE). Signed into law in 1994, FACE "federally criminalized acts of obstruction and violence towards reproductive health clinics" (FACE, 1994). "The law was a reaction to the increasing violence toward abortion clinics, providers, and patients during the 1990s" (Nunez-Eddy, 2017). The First Amendment is repeatedly cited in FACE, including in its rules of statutory construction, which state that nothing in this act "shall be construed to prohibit any expressive conduct (including peaceful picketing or other peaceful demonstration) protected from legal prohibition by the First Amendment to the Constitution" (FACE, 1994). In short, FACE addresses a politically divisive issue in a manner that criminalizes obstructive and violent behavior but also ensures that those who exercise First Amendment rights can do so without fear of punishment. It takes little imagination to appreciate the challenges police face in enforcing such laws.

There are other federal laws that explicitly protect First Amendment rights; moreover, state constitutions and laws often likewise reinforce First Amendment protections. What seems clear is that First Amendment rights and protections are valued because freedom of expression serves not only the individual but also the common good. Individual, community, and national interests are at stake. The freedom to think, pursue, and speak the truth—even to vent—in our public and private must be valued and protected. These rights, these freedoms, when encouraged, protected, and exercised, empower all. One eloquent phrase borne out of the exercise of these rights is the opportunity to "speak truth to power," a phrase invoked first by Quakers and later by civil rights activists. If individuals cannot speak truth to power, our American experiment has failed.

Consider these dynamics when police support the right of citizens to peaceably and safely assemble and air their beliefs and grievances in a variety of forums. Police here promote and serve the common good; their actions, properly performed, acknowledge the inherent dignity and respect of people and their rights. Conversely, when police inhibit First Amendment freedoms, such as police officers who wantonly clubbed protestors at the 1968 Democratic National Convention in Chicago, the promise of protecting and serving is lost, and for many, so is trust. The importance of First Amendment–protected protests and suitable police responses to it could be a difficult but important conversation among community and police, preferably at a time when emotions do not run high (see Chapter 10 concerning difficult conversations). Police should not resent lawful efforts by organizations such as the American Civil Liberties Union (ACLU) to preserve the First Amendment rights of protesters; likewise, the ACLU should respect lawful efforts by police to protect people and property when protests occur. As Sir Robert Peel noted, the police are the community, and the community are the police. They can share common ground.

In George Orwell's *Nineteen Eighty-Four* (1949), beleaguered main character Winston stated, "Freedom is the freedom to say that two plus two make four. If that is granted, all else follows" (p. 77). Freedom to speak the truth, freedom to speak truth to power, freedom to assert that truth embodies an objective reality, one apart from party or from ideology or bias. Freedom of speech also supports individuals or groups who want to tell others, including the government, what they do not want to hear. Recall Ferguson, MO, in 2014 when protestors took to the streets to protest the killing of an 18-year-old unarmed Black man, Michael Brown, Jr., and then when the accused officer was not indicted by a grand jury. As Kayla Reed said in an NBC News story that aired in 2019, about five years after the incident, "I think the Ferguson uprising gave people a lot of courage to use the tool of protest." The unrest in Ferguson was one of many events marked by expressive, irate conduct about police abuse, especially among Black communities. The angry protests sparked a necessary dialogue about police activities, a dialogue that continues and influences how police train and perform their duties and how communities perceive the important and challenging work of police. This dialogue can serve as a platform to examine, practice, and promote constitutional values and principles that strengthen the relationship between communities and the police who protect and serve them.

Police have been fairly accused of too often overreacting to protected First Amendment activities by Americans. Historical and contemporary examples abound. An illuminating 2020 ProPublica project analyzed police response to a host of protests in various major cities. Experts were asked to watch videos showing officers using tear gas, pepper balls, and explosives on protesters. All too often police actions appeared to escalate confrontations. The videos and analysis are instructive (Buford, Waldron, Syed, & Shaw, 2020). Students viewing these videos in my classroom observed what often appeared to be police overreaction to protest activities; yet students also acknowledged the inherent challenges police face in response to angry protesters.

Police critics might fairly acknowledge that police response to First Amendment activities is an imperfect science; their tactics and actions are easily subject to hindsight. The limited information available to police before a protest coupled with the vagaries of human behavior make planning and response challenging; training and preparation, however, are vital in ensuring better outcomes. Their job is much harder when protests are spontaneous.

Following are some sample questions and considerations in evaluating police preparedness in responding to First Amendment activities.

1. Have police officers (and city officials) been trained in basic First Amendment principles and the people's rights to demonstrate?

Activities protected by the First Amendment are not always self-evident to citizens or police alike. While police are called upon to protect the exercise of First Amendment rights by groups and individuals, police must also enforce laws that protesters may intentionally or unintentionally break in their protest activities. At stake are public safety concerns for protesters, counterprotesters, the general public, and the private sector. Given these stakes, police departments are strongly encouraged to provide First Amendment legal training to officers and to otherwise have access to legal counsel.

Police must remember a cardinal principle: The *content* of protester beliefs and related speech is largely protected from government regulation. Police may find speech uttered by protesters unwarranted, ill-informed, unfair, foolish, "un-American," or repugnant; that is irrelevant. Police and other governmental officials should not play favorites. The fact that protesters shout their hatred for police, American foreign policy, or another cause should not factor in formulating an appropriate police response. However, speech that directly incites violence or law-breaking is *not* protected by the First Amendment.

What may protesters lawfully do? Protesters generally have the right to hold signs, distribute papers or leaflets, collect petition signatures, and conduct similar activities in protected areas (see the second point below) as long as they do not unreasonably disrupt or endanger others, such as causing traffic jams or forcing others to accept leaflets. For example, police may arrest protesters who block vehicles on public roads or who impede pedestrian traffic when a permit is otherwise needed. Similarly, the First Amendment does not protect speech by protesters that is *combined* with unlawful activities, such as protesters disobeying or interfering with lawful police orders. Moreover, police may and often *must* in the interests of public safety arrest those who engage in violent or threatening forms of protest—acts that typically are crimes per se, such as malicious destruction of property or assault and battery. Likewise, police *may* lawfully arrest or fine those who engage in acts of civil disobedience, namely unlawful nonviolent forms of protest.

2. Governments may impose reasonable time, place, and manner restrictions when protests are held on public property.

Governments, for example, may require permits for marches on public sidewalks, streets, or rallies in most public parks and plazas. Governments may also require some advance notice of a protest, measured in days not weeks, unless demonstrations are in response to a breaking-news event. Some activities do not require a permit, such as a small rally in a public park. There are other such activities. Consider legal guidance.

The remaining questions and concerns should be addressed by each department.

3. Have police leadership and city officials (e.g., mayor, city manager) exchanged views on a) the role of citizen protest and b) the nature and the expectations of police response?
4. Do mutual aid plans exist if police and government resources are taxed beyond capacity? Who pays for those services?
5. If protesters adopt tactics for which police have not trained, how will police respond? How will police and government officials respond to a prolonged protest?

Many questions are worthy of public and private discussion. For example, what do citizens or communities expect of police who are respond to various forms of protest, and how will they react to the choices police make? Can there be greater communication and transparency between police and community? If so, how might this happen?

In short, sound police practices should reflect principles and values articulated in the Constitution and other seminal American writings. Government officials, especially police, must honor and remember that people possess certain unalienable rights. In the performance of their mission to serve and protect, police must also promote justice. Although police alone do not establish justice, as law enforcers within the context of a criminal justice system, they are central to its pursuit and realization. When properly performed, police promote a more just, civil, and trusting society. When they fail, society suffers.

Review Questions

1. Do you think Americans should be expected to know more about civics in general? If so, how might this be done? Were you satisfied with your civics education? Will such knowledge create more responsible and active citizens?
2. Should police be required to learn more about the U.S. Constitution, especially the First and Fourth Amendments of the Bill of Rights? If so, how will this make them better police officers?
3. According to Dr. King, laws should be grounded in morality. What did he mean? Do you agree, or is there a better approach? Other than what is cited in the chapter, provide examples of just and unjust laws.
4. Find a sample police academy curriculum on the web (see, for example, the Dallas Police Academy's basic training curriculum; link in reference list). Look at hours of instruction dedicated to each topic. Provide any observations and insight about what you believe are its strengths and weaknesses.
5. Have you participated in a protest? If so, what do you remember? Were you fearful and, if so, fearful of what? Were police present?
6. Go online and find an example of a police response to a protest. What was the protest about? What did you observe about police and protesters? Were there counterprotestors? If you were a police chief, what directions would you give to police covering the protest?
7. The Supreme Court has permitted governments to enact reasonable time, place, and manner restrictions on those planning to protest, such as registration requirements and other limits as to where a protest on public property may occur and for how long. Do you believe any such limits are appropriate? Why or why not?

References

Animal Enterprise Protection Act of 1992, 18 U.S.C. § 43 (1992). https://www
.govinfo.gov/app/details/USCODE-2011-title18/USCODE-2011-title18-
partI-chap3-sec43

Buford, T., Waldron, L., Syed, M., & Shaw, A. (2020, July 16). *We reviewed police
tactics seen in nearly 400 protest videos. Here's what we found.* ProPublica. https://
projects.propublica.org/protest-police-tactics/

Cohen, A. (2019, September 17). *Constitution's biggest flaw? Protecting slavery.*
Berkeley News. https://news.berkeley.edu/2019/09/17/constitutions-
biggest-flaw-protecting-slavery/

Dallas Police Department. (n.d.). *Basic training curriculum.* https://dallaspolice
.net/joindpd/Shared%20Documents/DPD%20Basic%20PO%20Course%20
Curriculum%20-%207-9-18%20-%20MASTER.pdf

Frankfurter, F. (1943). McNabb v. United States, 343 (318 U.S. 332).

Freedom of Access to Clinic Entrances Act of 1994, 18 U.S.C. § 248 (1994).
https://www.justice.gov/crt/statute-18-usc-248

Jefferson, T. (1776). *The Declaration of Independence.*

Kennedy, J. F. (1963, May 18). Remarks in Nashville at the 90th anniversary
convocation of Vanderbilt University [Speech] https://www.jfklibrary.org/
archives/other-resources/john-f-kennedy-speeches/vanderbilt-university-
19630518. Vanderbilt University, Nashville, TN, USA.

King, M. L., Jr. (1963, April 16). *Letter from Birmingham Jail.*

Liu, G., Karlan, P. S., & Schroeder, C. H. (2009, September 15). *Keeping faith with
the Constitution.* American Constitution Society.

Madison, J. (1788, February 8). *Federalist No. 51: The structure of the government must
furnish the proper checks and balances between the different departments.* https://
guides.loc.gov/federalist-papers/full-text

Mintz, S. (2016, December 20). *What does it mean to be a fair-minded person?* Ethics
Sage. ethicssage.com/2016/12/what-does-it-mean-to-be-a-fair-minded-per-
son.html

Nunez-Eddy, C. (2017, May 25). Freedom of Access to Clinic Entrances
Act (1994). *Embryo Project Encyclopedia.* http://embryo.asu.edu/han-
dle/10776/11517

O'Connor, S. D. (2018, October 23). *Former Supreme Court Justice Sandra Day
O'Connor's letter on dementia diagnosis.* USA Today. https://www.usatoday
.com/story/news/politics/onpolitics/2018/10/23/sandra-day-oconnor-
dementia-alzheimers-letter-statement/1738512002/.

Orwell, G. (1983). *Nineteen Eighty-four.* United States: Houghton Mifflin
Harcourt.

Peel, R. (1829). *Nine principles of policing.*

Privacy Act of 1974, 5 U.S.C § 552a (1974). https://bja.ojp.gov/program/it/privacy-civil-liberties/authorities/statutes/1279

Protection of Foreign Officials, Official Guests, and Internationally Protected Persons, 18 U.S.C. § 112 (1948).

Richards, J. (2019, August 10). *Five years after the Ferguson, Missouri, police shooting of Michael Brown Jr., residents still seeking change.* NBCNews.com. https://www.nbcnews.com/news/us-news/five-years-after-ferguson-missouri-police-shooting-michael-brown-jr-n1040226. Suttie, J. (2016, May 18). How mindfulness is changing law enforcement. *Greater Good Magazine.* https://greatergood.berkeley.edu/article/item/how_mindfulness_is_changing_law_enforcement

U.S. Const., amend. I.

U.S. Const., amend. IV.

U.S. Const., pmbl.

Velasquez, M., Andre, C., Shanks, T., S. J., & Meyer, M. J. (2014, August 1). *Justice and fairness.* Markkula Center for Applied Ethics at Santa Clara University. https://www.scu.edu/ethics/ethics-resources/ethical-decision-making/justice-and-fairness/

Image Credit

Chapter 4

A Social Contract Between Police and Community

Image 4

Peel Principle 3: The police must secure the willing cooperation of the public in voluntary observance of the law to be able to secure and maintain public respect.

> *"I am convinced that the majority of American people do understand that we have a moral responsibility to foster the concepts of opportunity, free enterprise, the rule of law, and democracy. They understand that these values are the hope of the world."*   Richard Lugar, June 15, 2009

"At the heart of the rule of law is the idea that the strength of the law applies—not the law of the strong. ... It also means that everyone is equal in the eyes of the law. ... Our understanding is of a rule of law—not merely a rule by law. This type of rule of law strengthens people's trust in state institutions and their decisions, and thus also fosters social stability in a country."   Federal Chancellor Angela Merkel, speech while receiving an honorary doctorate from Nanjing University, Beijing, June 16, 2016

Importance of Law

Law is part of the fabric of society; a modern society without law and the legal systems that underlie it is unthinkable to most of us. Some form of tyranny or anarchy is a likely alternative in the modern world. In *Two Treatises of Government, Book II* (1689), John Locke wrote about the importance of law and insisted that those who act on the authority of law must not exceed it:

> Where-ever law ends, tyranny begins, if the law be transgressed to another's harm; and whosoever in authority exceeds the power given him by the law, and makes use of the force he has under his command, to compass that upon the subject, which the law allows not, ceases in that to be a magistrate; and, acting without authority, may be opposed, as any other man, who by force invades the right of another.

Yet most of us view law narrowly. We think of lawyers, courtrooms, and disputes played out in real life or dramatized on television and other media—where battles are fought, where there are winners and losers. But there is another perspective on law that reminds us of its sociological dimension—more specifically, how law shapes individuals and society. Laws, for example, establish expectations and provide some degree of predictability in the interactions and relationships among members of a society. Laws protect people from evil and "give citizens a framework within which they can organize their relations with one another in such a manner as to make possible a peaceful and profitable coexistence" (Fuller, 1975). Although sociologists may debate their efficacy, codifying undesirable or destructive behaviors as crimes punishable by the state may deter individuals from committing them. It may also be important to separate, through incarceration, those who commit certain crimes from victims and from the public—although the length of incarceration may be subject to justifiable debate, a topic beyond the scope of this book. This chapter examines law as a form of social control.

Law and Social Control

Law, including criminal laws, and the legal systems that enforce and apply the law act as what sociologists describe as a fundamental type of *social control*. All forms of social control seek to regulate human behavior. Effective social controls of any stripe check incompatible human activities and stimulate more desirable ones. (See p. 23 of James J. Chriss's *Social Control: An Introduction*.) Consider a simple but graphic example. The act of murder is incompatible with a safe and secure society; it is a behavior dangerous to individuals and society, and any impulse behind it must be held in check. One means—but not the only means—to discourage acts of murder or hold murderous impulses in check among individuals within a modern society is to enact a law that makes murder a crime against the *state* subject to severe punishment. This type of social control is known as *legal control*. Legal control is a *formal* means of social control, in that this type of control involves the intervention of outside *third parties*, such as police, prosecutors, and courts. But why are legal controls important?

In *Leviathan* (1651), an extraordinarily influential political and philosophical text, Thomas Hobbes argued that human beings in their original state of nature are selfish, solitary, hedonistic, and brutish. Perhaps some of us have a more charitable view of human nature, but a clear-eyed view of history reveals how often humans, when unchecked by or unaccountable to third parties, behave badly. According to Hobbes, in a state of *natural right*, each person is free to do what is most expedient for self-gratification and self-preservation. Conceptions of just, unjust, right, or wrong are absent—life is ruled by the immediacy of passions, hardly a stable or secure arrangement for those in society seeking some sense of peaceful coexistence (see Chriss, 2013, p. 139). This selfish, anarchic state would seem fickle and dangerous, one doomed to failure. However, Hobbes argued that over time human beings would come to embrace a more rational alternative, natural law, namely "the power to understand that maximization of self-preservation can occur only if social conditions are created in which all others realize that the unbridled pursuit of self-interest will ultimately destroy everyone" (Chriss, 2013, p. 139). Hobbes (1651) believed that the development of *natural law* would avoid "the war of all against all" (p. 148).

Natural law, like the nature of justice, tries to reconcile the competing claims of individual freedom and responsibility. (For a comprehensive analysis, see Lloyd L. Weinreb's *Natural Law and Justice* [1990]). Most classical theorists of natural law asked a basic question:

> [H]ow does one act morally? Or, more specifically, what are one's moral obligations as a citizen within a state, or as a state official? And, what are the limits of legitimate (that is, moral) governmental action (Bix, 2004, p. 63)?

In his famed *Letter from Birmingham Jail* (1963), Dr. Martin Luther King, Jr., reflected on the vital role of natural law and justice. In one of his most quoted statements concerning injustice, Dr. King wrote:

> Injustice anywhere is a threat to justice everywhere. We are caught in an inescapable network of mutuality, tied in a single garment of destiny. Whatever affects one directly, affects all indirectly. Never again can we afford to live with the narrow, provincial "outside agitator" idea. Anyone who lives inside the United States can never be considered an outsider anywhere within its bounds.

Like any member of society, consciously or not, police officers decide how to balance freedom and responsibility in their personal lives; however, as agents of the state, they also inhabit this space in their work among fellow citizens. They must commit themselves to justice and law in their mission to protect and serve.

Three precepts comprise natural law, as summarized by Charles Ellwood (1938):

> human beings must seek peace and observe peace in lieu of actual or potential war;
> human beings must abandon their natural right to whatever to get whatever they want; and
> human beings must keep all promises, or the state of nature will surely return (pp. 116–127).

But how do human beings achieve and maintain this safer, more rational alternative to a state of natural rights? Chriss (2013) summarized Hobbes's solution as this: "[Since] individuals would have trouble consistently abiding by these ideals, they enter into a social contract whereby the state and its agents of formal control are acknowledged as legitimate enforcers of these precepts, as embodied in legal statutes" (p. 139). Enforcement in turn relies on the presence of a government or sovereign holding a monopoly over the use of coercive force to ensure these "promises" are kept; this monopoly might be described as the *Leviathan*. But what does this social contract look like, one in which citizens surrender certain freedoms of choice to government to gain some security and to preserve their essential rights and assume essential duties? And does this "surrender" of certain freedoms of choice really work?

In his book *The Better Angels of Our Natures: Why Violence Has Declined*, Steven Pinker credited "the Leviathan—a government with a monopoly on the legitimate use of force—as a major reducer of violence" (p. 538). He acknowledged that a Leviathan "implements justice at the point of a sword" and that "the law may be an ass, *but it is a disinterested ass* [emphasis added], and it can weigh harms without the self-serving distortions of the perpetrator or the victim" (p. 538). Undoubtedly some will disagree, but "the government's monopoly on force prevents the loser from doing anything about it, and it gives him less reason to want to do something about it, because he is not conceding weakness to his adversary and has less incentive to carry on the fight to restore his honor" (pp. 538–539). In his research, Pinker found that the sheer presence of government brings rates of violence down "from the hundreds of homicides per 100,000 people to the tens" (p. 540). That is no small drop. Pinker added another significant point, one consistent with a central proposition of my book:

> A further drop into the single digits (per 100,000) may depend on something hazier, such the people's acceptance of the legitimacy of the government and social contract (p. 540).

I do not cite Pinker's observations to suggest that a government's monopoly over the use of force is always beneficent. Hardly. As he noted, government "vengeance" in punishing wrongdoers can be excessive and ineffective. Our nation's founders recognized these evils, one of which is expressed in the Eighth Amendment's prohibition against cruel and unusual punishment and excessive fines and bail. And there *is* widespread and justifiable criticism of various law enforcement abuses, but that does not support the notion that government should surrender its monopoly over legitimate force or coercion. Rather, the public ("We the People") should expect and ensure that government, including and especially police, use its monopoly over force fairly, lawfully, and wisely.

Here is an example describing how a state's monopoly over the use of force in modern society plays out. Suppose Neighbor N hears two men outside her home engaged in a heated confrontation. Alarmed, Neighbor (now Witness) N walks to her front porch and observes Perpetrator P shoot Victim V, who is seated in a car parked on the adjoining street. N observes P then flee into a nearby home—believed to be P's residence. N calls 911 and shares what she observed. Police respond swiftly to the scene and find Witness N, who provides a description of P and points out the house that P entered. While other emergency responders attend to V, police gain entry to P's house and find and interrogate P, who claims he shot V in self-defense. While police are inside P's home, P's family members rally to his support, while V's family and friends gather nearby and angrily demand justice on the street outside. Meanwhile, police arrest P, interview witnesses, collect evidence at the homicide site and P's home, and then transport P to their local precinct for further processing. Police also interview and explain their actions to V's family and encourage them to return to their homes. Although emotions run high among V's family members, they eventually accede to police requests. Note that in this scenario Neighbor/Witness N reached out first to police. Moreover, family members used no force to exact vengeance. Instead, they relied on police to investigate the homicide. There was no vigilante justice, no immediate vengeance. But what if police had not been contacted?

In the example above, police investigated the homicide and identified and arrested P, but on what authority? The state, of course—because state law criminalizes homicide—and police are agents of the state formally endued with the authority and responsibility to investigate and solve crimes and arrest those responsible. In these circumstances, the authority of police to intervene did not rely on relationships to Victim V or Perpetrator P. Police were outsiders in that sense. Nevertheless, Neighbor N trusted police enough to report the homicide. Rather than take matters into their own hands, V's family members relied on and trusted police and the criminal justice system enough to believe that police would investigate and support the prosecution of the homicide. So, in this sense, V's family, friends, and community handed over responsibility. They did not direct police actions; police acted independently. That is legal control, a formal type of social control in which people have "surrendered" their "right" to take matters into their own hands, also known as *vengeance*. However, for such legal control to help most effectively—to serve and protect society—there must be some degree of trust that the government, including police, will protect them and preserve their many rights. When trust dissipates, police and community alike suffer. So does justice.

Before we examine another type of social control, consider this: Ideally police would have *prevented* the homicide, however unlikely given the lean facts presented in this example. It would be a tall, complicated, and perhaps unachievable order for an outside agent of legal social control—police—to prevent this crime alone, certainly in a free society. A dystopian, totalitarian, surveillance state might stand a better chance at preventing such acts of violence, but at great cost to individual rights and freedom and with little chance of achieving any real justice. Think of the book and movie versions of *Nineteen Eighty-Four* and *Minority Report* or the reality that exists in North Korea. Perhaps then another type of social control—a second option might be more effective, especially working in conjunction with police and legal controls, in *preventing* this homicide.

This second broad type of social control is *informal* control. Here, neither the state nor an agent of the state is directly involved. Within the realm of informal social control, there is no outside third party that *formally* intervenes, influences, or responds to such "incompatible human activities" as homicide. Law here is not the centerpiece, as it is not about third-party mechanisms of legal control. Although not as legal controls, informal social controls likewise shape and promote behaviors deemed beneficial and prevent those thought injurious to individuals and society. But agents of social control do not rely on any formal power and authority conferred by the state.

What does this look like? Consider some of the many examples of agents of informal social control—parents or guardians, extended family, or neighbors. These agents may stimulate good behavior and regulate or steer behavior away from most human activities that are deemed incompatible with society's aims. For example, parents may raise their child to believe that murder is morally wrong, a violation of religious beliefs, or otherwise a violation of society's norms; in that sense parents want to steer their children away from murderous predispositions or actions that are potentially dangerous to society. Together with other agents of informal social control, parents may insulate children from growing up to believe that murder and other violent acts are acceptable choices to resolve conflict, or to act upon such impulses. But why are informal social controls so powerful?

Informal mechanisms of social control do *not* rely on interventions by formal third parties to prevent, respond to, or otherwise address behavior thought incompatible to a safe and secure society. Instead, informal controls instead rely on *relationships*. Or, as Chriss (2013) wrote, informal controls "consists of all those mechanisms and practices of ordinary, everyday life whereby group pressures to conform are brought to bear against the individual" (p. 56). Our families and friends—those closest to us—represent the most direct forms of informal social control. Less direct but powerful agents of social control include peers, schools, religion, and the workplace. They all serve to regulate human behavior, too, and their influence, as noted above, is based on *relationships*. Relationships pack powerful, longstanding emotional connections among people. At best, their collective influence promotes the development of beliefs and behaviors believed compatible with the aims of a society that values such civic virtues as safety, freedom, and justice.

A related and well-researched sociological concept within the realm of informal social control is that of social capital, defined by sociologist Alejandro Portes (1998) as "the ability of actors to secure benefits by virtue of membership in social networks or other social structures" (p. 24). Social capital has been applied in many ways, but it is partly related to the development of useful ties an individual has among other individuals and groups within a society, such as community organizations, churches, volunteer groups, and others. The ties and membership in social networks supply benefits to individuals, such as job references and other opportunities not otherwise available to them. Police-citizen cooperation often exists where social capital is strong. As Chriss (2013) wrote, the condition of social capital at its best "characterizes citizens as having high levels of trust with regard to their dealings with other citizens, and these mutual sets of obligations create a tapestry of informal control which thereby also facilitates the pursuit of collective goals" (pp. 144–145).

In short, legal social control and informal social control differ in significant ways but are mutually supportive. As noted earlier, many would argue that taken together, informal social controls are more effective than legal controls in modifying behavior deemed harmful to society or stimulating behavior thought helpful to society. No matter—when informal mechanisms of social control also support the aims of formal, legal controls, societies and communities are the beneficiaries. For example, parents, schools, and community leaders may encourage children to respect the law. A child's respect for law is conducive to law-abiding behaviors. Similarly, one can argue that when agents of legal social control support agents of informal social control, communities are stronger and safer. For example, police and other agents of legal control may find effective ways to support parents, schools, and community institutions. There *are* limits—police cannot serve their communities strictly as educators or social workers, and parents, schools, and community institutions cannot serve strictly as agents of police. Police alone cannot erase poverty, inequality, or racism (although police should never tolerate racism or inequality—see Chapter 8, which discusses this topic), but in their efforts to make communities safer, not only in the pursuit of justice but as role models in their interactions with the community, police can help create conditions to address longstanding concerns. By contrast, communities alone cannot realistically prevent, investigate, and prosecute crime. But within that space where support and collaboration are possible, where at a minimum knowledge, understanding, trust, and mutual respect are pursued in thought and action—and where common ground is sought—the common good is served. With these considerations in mind, let us return to legal control.

As Chriss (2013) explained, the linchpin of legal control is the criminal justice system. Criminal justice students are taught that the U.S. criminal justice system is made up of police, courts, and corrections. Each plays a crucial part. As law enforcers, police stand at the gateway for those who are investigated, charged, arrested, and processed through the complex weave of laws, practices, policies, and procedures that exist within a state or federal criminal justice system. Police work, moreover, is subject to oversight by legislators, public officials, courts, police administrators, and, to an extent, a community. Indirectly, their work is also subject to press scrutiny. No matter who is watching police—or judging them—all groups agree that police should "play by the rules" and that by doing so, justice and society are better served. These rules—these laws—include the same laws to which everyone is subject. The "rules" most relevant to policing are those that govern and limit how police collect evidence, testify in court, and respect the rights of those they investigate. But policing and law do not exist in a vacuum. How police abide by, interpret, and apply the law affects those whom they serve—the public. Individuals and communities witness their actions. As gatekeepers to the criminal justice system, police must know, abide by, and respect the law. Any societal hope or trust that legal controls are effective rests upon the assumption that those who enforce the law respect and abide by the law. Some sense of earned trust in the law and legal systems, including the work of police, are preconditions to a healthy, functioning society in which rights, responsibilities, freedoms, opportunities, and justice coexist. And when the criminal justice system is not seen by some as serving these ends, society at large, especially the government—including police, courts, and corrections—must take a hard look at themselves and do something about it.

Law and Its Importance to Police and Community

In *For Common Things: Irony, Trust, and Commitment in America Today* (1999), Jedediah Purdy wrote that law and policy pervade "our lives and affect the possibility of living responsibly" (p. 153). He added that when "we let public talk take on an air of unreality, we are letting ourselves ignore something whose importance we cannot escape" (p. 153). Good governance and the public good rely on some knowledge of and commitment to the law by the people. That includes the public's basic understanding of laws, rights, and principles fundamental to our national identity, as well as an understanding of that part of government that enforces the criminal law—police. While civilian police work touches upon the role of law, the role of law is no less important to the communities that police serve. Purdy (1999) explained that law "depends on both a culture of enforcement among those charged with implementing it, and participation by the citizens who are nominally responsible for making it and inescapably charged with living under it" (p. 159). Ideally, *support of the law is a shared responsibility*. This is an inescapably important consideration in the laws that guide and govern police work.

The role and influence of law are fundamental to policing in society, even if they are not a normal part of public discourse. Communities know that police enforce violations of a multitude of laws and ordinances. Communities also expect, if not always believe, that officers are subject to the same laws and legal controls as everyone else. Communities expect that police will not violate the law—including their rights—when they enforce the law. Most citizens also believe that police *should* fairly and equally enforce the law and promote justice. But what constitutes fair and equal enforcement of the law gets complicated. For example, consider how a community might respond to police when police strictly and uncompromisingly enforce laws that prohibit minor infractions, such as jaywalking or loitering. Not only may strict police enforcement rile the individual cited for these minor infractions, but the community may also object. Alternatively, citizens may object when police *selectively* enforce minor infractions of law. In short, there is more than meets the eye, and the community must recognize the difficulties and ambiguities in effective policing. But for the sake of this analysis, presume that the crimes or ordinances that police investigate and enforce enjoy broad community support—such as crimes that prohibit murder, rape, robbery, theft, fraud, threats of violence, to name a few. Communities demand that police act to prevent, investigate, or prosecute such crimes. Likewise, the community would expect that these same laws apply to everyone—no one gets a pass. And similarly, the community would expect the police to perform their work without violating fundamental individual rights. That said, review more closely a principle fundamental to shared trust between police and community, the rule of law.

Why Individuals and Communities Should Understand and Value the Rule of Law

The rule of law escapes easy definition, but its contribution toward a safe and healthy society is undeniable. At its basic level, the rule of law requires that the law must guide those subject to it—namely *all* members of society. And the belief among a sovereign people that *all are subject* to the rule of law may also reinforce their belief that some sense of justice and equality are sought after and achievable goals of society, even if these concepts are not synonymous (Alcala, 2019). Moreover, the rule of law, when honored, supplies some predictability and stability among a sovereign people, as well as a check on government in its relationship to the people. In this sense people know there are rules—and no individual or class or position of power or authority is exempt. All people are thus answerable to the constraints of law.

For their own self-interest and for the common good, citizens are strongly encouraged to support the rule of law because, as noted by the Judicial Learning Center (n.d.), such a commitment "allows us to live in a civil society in which everyone's rights are respected; where each of us is guaranteed liberty and equality of opportunity." Engraved on the front of the United States Supreme Court Building is the phrase "Equal Justice Under Law," a phrase that embodies an ideal of the rule of law and is "at the heart of our American democracy" (Judicial Learning Center, n.d.).

USCourts.gov (n.d.) describes the rule of law as "a principle under which all persons, institutions, and entities are accountable to laws" that are publicly issued, equally enforced, independently adjudicated, and consistent with international human rights principles. It is fair to say that equality before the law and the rule of law complement one another.

A popular description of the rule of law is that a nation must be a government of law, not men and women. As explained in an American Bar Association article ("What is the rule of law," n.d.)

> Aren't laws made by men and women in their roles as legislators? Don't
> men and women enforce the law as police officers or interpret the law

as judges? And don't all of us choose to follow, or not to follow, the law as we go about our daily lives? How does the rule of law exist independently from the people who make it, interpret it, and live it? The easiest answer to these questions is that the rule of law cannot ever be entirely separate from the people who make up our government and our society. The rule of law is more of an ideal that we strive to achieve, but sometimes fail to live up to.

Without a community's widespread support for the rule of law, it is difficult to plot a path toward safety, security, justice, and other key virtues. The continued viability of the social contract between "We the People" and the "Leviathan" of government relies in part upon a deep-seated commitment to understanding and upholding the rule of law.

Why Police Should Always Respect the Rule of Law

Why should police, as *law enforcers*, understand and embrace the rule of law? What if police do not? What if police believe, at least as part of an occupational culture, that strict adherence to the rule of law undermines its effectiveness? In a 2002 article entitled "Law Enforcement and the Rule of Law: Is There a Tradeoff?" David H. Bayley assessed whether "a strong evidence-based argument can be made to support the proposition that when police violate the rule of law they do more harm than good to their collective, as well as personal, interests." Bayley described among some police an ethos that justifies the need and efficacy to cut corners to promote public safety, such as an aggressive and unlawful practice of stop-and-frisk. Bayley (2002) listed seven factors that encourage police to violate the rule of law and human rights. They are summarized as follows (p. 135):

1. Public safety: The "noble" cause of crime—control through aggressive deterrence efforts
2. Unique empowerment: The unique ability to physically constrain people to protect the public from wrongdoers
3. Public respect: The public is less concerned about due process than crime control
4. Career success: Police are more likely to be rewarded when they achieve "results," such as crimes solved, arrests, citations issued, and more
5. Belonging: Police, as most people, like to fit in and be accepted in their group, and that may mean embracing a culture that deems strict adherence to the rule of law as an impediment to being an effective officer

6. Complexity of the law: When the law, such as laws governing police searches and seizure under the Fourth Amendment, is seen as overly complex and unclear, the law itself becomes suspect in the eyes of police

7. Police personality: Studies show that police tend to be "practical, action-oriented people" who bring closure to disorderly, ambiguous situations

Bayley (2002) then weighed the seven disadvantages of law-breaking, summarized as follows (p. 139):

1. Violating the rule of law contributes marginally to deterrence: Rather, questionable law enforcement practices may be criminogenic.

2. Violating the rule of law reduces enforcement effectiveness: It instead alienates the public who are less likely to aid police efforts.

3. Violating the rule of law weakens the authority of law: The way in which laws are enforced affects perceptions of their legitimacy and the willingness of people to obey them (see also research by Dr. Tom Tyler and others referenced in this book).

4. Violating the rule of law scapegoats the police: Violating the rule of law to make up for various social policy deficiencies over which they have no control leads to them being blamed.

5. Violating the rule of law depresses morale and makes the police job less satisfying: Violating the rule of law puts pressure on all employees to hide what is going on, putting them at risk, and invites outside correction when the law is violated. Accountability practices imposed on police because of rule of law misdeeds makes police work more rule-bound and formalistic, and supervisor-subordinate relations become strained and adversarial.

6. Violating the rule of law wastes community resources: It raises the costs of law enforcement, wasting investments made in prosecutions and diverting funds that might be used for crime prevention.

7. Violating the rule of law places police officers at risk: Police who are caught face personal and professional costs.

After assessing available research, although calling for more, Bayley (2002) concludes that "it is in the interests of police, both individually and collectively, to adhere to the rule of law (p. 147). The rule of law similarly benefits society in a very practical sense—that is, countries with a strong tradition in the rule of law are also wealthier and healthier (Piconne, 2020). It is no leap of faith that police and citizens can find common ground here.

The Social Contract, the Constitution, the Rule of Law, and Policing

In a sense, the U.S. Constitution can be understood as a social contract that binds citizens, communities, and police; also embedded in this contract is respect for the rule of law. The Constitution's preamble says that *the people* ordained and established the Constitution to, among other things, "promote the general Welfare, and secure the Blessings of Liberty to ourselves and our Posterity." To that end police academies and departments must explain and advance the rule of law and constitutional values and principles—and, equally important, display this to the citizens whom they serve and protect. It is not simply a matter of checking a box that requires police officers swear an oath to uphold the Constitution; it is not simply a matter of police training—it never is. It must be fully embraced in police culture. Police must show their commitment to constitutional values and principles in every public interaction, however difficult that may seem. This is their part of the social contract. However, police cannot do it alone. Informal agents of informal social control, including families, schools, and other important social and political institutions, should support the rule of law and its realization in the Constitution. (Those interested in learning more about worldwide efforts to promote the rule of law may refer to the World Justice Project; you can find the link in the "References" section.)

To be sure, the rule of law is not simply an ideal, aspiration, or ideological construct; it stands behind the integrity of each officer and every department, and it is a bulwark against tyranny and oppression—it must be honored. The U.S. does not "own" the rule of law, but its founders embraced its ideals in the Declaration of Independence, the U.S. Constitution, and other key documents. One may argue that the rule of law defines free nations. As nations and as individuals, our allegiance to it best guarantees our freedom. The rule of law has a long history, predating America's independence. According to the Stanford online Encyclopedia of Philosophy, the "heritage of argument about the Rule of law begins with Aristotle (c. 350)" and continues through works of John Locke (1689), James Harrington (1656), Niccolo Machiavelli (1517) and others (Waldron, 2016). In a letter to John Penn on March 27, 1776, examining how laws shall be made, John Adams, a founding father and second U.S. President, also insisted that "good Government ... is an empire of laws" (Adams, 1776).

What is key in police work is that officers must demonstrate commitment and self-discipline, to abide by the law and the rule of law in the execution of their duties, even when citizens do not. Police must not only demonstrate some mastery of the law, including criminal laws, but also faithfully and fairly execute the law in every facet of their duties. Perhaps that is why the Federal Bureau of Investigation prioritizes public corruption investigations at a national level. The meaning is clear: There is a serious threat to society when government officials break the law—as they are not above the law.

Although they differ in meaning, a close companion of the principles embedded within the rule of law is procedural justice. The National Initiative for Building Community Trust and Justice (NIBCTJ) states on its website (n.d.) that procedural justice "focuses on the way police and other legal authorities interact with the public, and how the characteristics of those interactions shape the public's views of the police, their willingness to obey the law, and actual crime rates." The NIBCTJ also describes procedurally just policing, which emphasizes values that police and communities share—shared values based upon a common conception of what social order is and how it should be maintained—and encourages the collaborative, voluntary maintenance of a law-abiding community. Research indicates this approach is effective at producing law-abiding citizens. This makes intuitive sense—people welcome being treated as equals with a stake in keeping their communities safe, as opposed to being treated as subjects of a capricious justice system enforced by police who punish them for ambiguous, if not arbitrary, reasons. These themes are more fully developed later in the book.

Conclusion

The continued viability of the social contract between "We the People" and the "Leviathan" of government relies in part upon a deep-seated commitment to understanding and upholding the law and rule of law. Police academies and departments must consistently inculcate the rule of law and its values. Police must demonstrate their commitment to it in every interaction with the public. In turn, communities, schools, churches, and other institutions are encouraged to insist upon and likewise promote following the law and the rule of law as fundamental to their security, rights, and freedom. This is a collaborative effort that serves, most importantly, the common good.

Review Questions

1. Describe key differences between legal and informal social controls.
2. Consider this scenario: Suppose you and your friends attend the opening night of a much-anticipated movie, and it is a serious drama. During the preview, a group seated behind you begin speaking and laughing loudly, and they continue as the movie begins, interfering with your ability to hear the dialogue or enjoy the movie. You politely ask the group to stop, but they do not, and there are no other available seats.

a. What informal or legal social controls might you or perhaps the theater manager consider next?

b. How might these choices play out? What are the costs and other consequences of each choice?

3. What is the Leviathan?

4. What is the relationship between law and morality? Should all laws have a moral foundation? Why or why not?

5. What does the rule of law mean to you? Should there be greater emphasis on its importance in schools and elsewhere?

6. Find and share an example where the rule of law has been ignored by someone in a position of power in a government. What are the consequences?

7. Review the referenced Brookings Institution article and its underlying research. What are its implications?

References

American Bar Association. (n.d.). *What is the rule of law?* https://www.americanbar.org/advocacy/rule_of_law/what-is-the-rule-of-law/

Alcala, R.T.P., (2019, November). Rule of Law and Human Rights in Military Stability Operations: Clarifying the Military's Role in Rule of Law Development. *Department of Justice, Journal of Federal Law and Practice, 647(4),* 211–228.

Bayley, D. H. (2002). Law enforcement and the rule of law: Is there a tradeoff? *Criminology and Public Policy, 2*(1), 133–154.

Bix, B. H. (2004, January 22). Natural law: The modern tradition. In J. L. Coleman, K. E. Himma, & S. J. Shapiro (Eds.), *The Oxford handbook of jurisprudence and philosophy of law* (p. 61–103). Oxford University Press.

Chriss, J. J. (2013). *Social control: An introduction* (2nd ed.). Polity Press.

Ellwood, C. (1938). *A history of social philosophy.* Prentice Hall.

Fuller, L. L. (1975). *Law as an instrument of social control and law as a facilitation of human interaction. BYU Law Review, 89.* https://digitalcommons.law.byu.edu/lawreview/vol1975/iss1/5

Hobbes, T. (1651). *On the Citizen.*

John Adams to John Penn, March 27, 1776 [electronic edition]. Adams Family Papers: An Electronic Archive, Massachusetts Historical Society. http://www.masshist.org/publications/adams-papers/index.php/view/PJA04dg2

Judicial Learning Center. (2019). *Law and the rule of law.* https://judiciallearningcenter.org/law-and-the-rule-of-law/

King, M. L. K., Jr. (1963). *Letter from Birmingham Jail.*

Locke, J. (1689). *Two treatises of government.* Of Tyranny, Chap. XVII, section 202, Book II.

National Initiative for Building Community Trust and Justice. (n.d.). *Procedural justice.* https://trustandjustice.org/resources/intervention/procedural-justice

Peel, R. (1829). *Nine principles of policing.*

Richards, J. (2019, August 10). Five years after the Ferguson, Missouri, police shooting of Michael Brown Jr., residents still seeking change. NBCNews .com. https://www.nbcnews.com/news/us-news/five-years-after-ferguson-missouri-police-shooting-michael-brown-jr-n1040226

Pinker, S. (2011). *The better angels of our natures: Why violence has declined.* Penguin Books.

Portes, A. (1998, August). Social capital: Its origins and applications in modern sociology. *Annual Review of Sociology, 24,* 1–24. https://doi.org/10.1146/annurev.soc.24.1.1

Purdy, J. (1999). *For common things: Irony, trust and commitment in America today.* Alfred A. Knopf.

Raz, J. (1979). *The authority of law: Essays on law and morality* (2nd ed.). Clarendon Press.

U.S. Const., amend. VIII.

USCourts.gov. (n.d.). *Overview—Rule of law.* https://www.uscourts.gov/educational-resources/educational-activities/overview-rule-law on 1/14/2021

Waldron, J. (2016, June 22). *The Rule of Law.* Stanford Encyclopedia of Philosophy. https://plato.stanford.edu/entries/rule-of-law/#HistRuleLaw.

Weinreb, L. L. (1990). *Natural law and justice.* Harvard University Press.

World Justice Project. (n.d.). *What is the rule of law?* https://worldjusticeproject .org/about-us/overview/what-rule-law

Image Credit

Chapter 5

Making Choices

Police discretion and effective policing

Peel Principle 2: The ability of the police to perform their duties is dependent upon public approval of police existence, actions, behavior, and the ability of police to secure and maintain public respect.

> *"A public officer has discretion whenever the effective limits on his power leave him free to make a choice among possible courses of action or inaction."* K. Davis, *Discretionary Justice: A Preliminary Inquiry (1969)*

The Significance of Police Discretion

Is discretion even important in policing? If so, can an officer's discretion be refined or qualitatively enhanced? The answer to the first question is clear: the very nature of policing invariably requires discretion—that is, policing demands a *choice* of actions or no action at all, within the effective limits of police power. But discretion begins with an officer's awareness that *there are* choices, big and small, that contribute to the effectiveness and quality of policing, where community perceptions are also shaped.

Personality traits, personal values, background, training, experience, to name some, contribute to an officer's choices in any police-citizen encounter. These influences, however, are not static, so in that sense how an officer exercises discretion may also change over time. In fact, it is an underlying premise of this book that *how* anyone makes choices may change—perhaps not dramatic differences, but incremental change in self-awareness, critical thinking, and attitudes—resulting in different and more favorable outcomes. When police use or abuse their legitimate power in a police-citizen encounter, the spotlight is most clearly directed at *their* choices.

Some may argue that too much police discretion is inherently bad, that all police behavior must be rules-driven to ensure the fair and equal distribution of justice. As shown later in this chapter, this belief may be a bit naïve. Yes, police discretion can be harmful when exercised unwisely. But it can also promote justice when police are held clearly accountable for their acts of discretion. Others might argue that police discretion, subject to a system of accountability, is in fact indispensable to justice in that it reduces the influence of selective law enforcement (Pepinsky, 1984). Police are expected to manage human conflict—a complex and demanding task. Tying their hands to too many rules and regulations or otherwise micromanaging them as they navigate this terrain can be counterproductive. Moreover, as Pepinsky (1984) showed, more rules may expand, not contract police discretion (p. 265).

In a broad sense, acts of police discretion should encourage immediate and long-term community compliance with legal authorities. Police need some level of community compliance to be effective; however, voluntary compliance with the law and cooperation with legal authorities cannot be gained solely by unilateral police efforts. A community, in *its* discretion, must decide to trust police enough to provide information to them and work with police in collaborative efforts to address crime and disorder. As Tom R. Tyler, Macklin Fleming professor of law and professor of psychology at Yale Law School, wrote (2011):

> The ability to shape people's behavior is key to the effectiveness of legal authorities since, if the law does not shape the behavior of most people most of the time, the legal system is not effectively fulfilling its social regulatory function (p. 66).

Police and legal authorities must earn community trust, but how? Citing numerous studies, Tyler (2011) found that among other things, police must show a community that it is effective in controlling crime, fairly distributes police services and protection throughout the community, and ensures that "those who break the law are punished" (p. 70). There are also social motivations that "might be tapped to supplement efforts to engage public cooperation" (Tyler, 2011, p. 73), alluded to in Tyler's book and this book.

What understandably attracts most public attention is whether and how officers use coercive force, which are acts of discretion in which stakes are high. Police may be called upon to use coercive force in evolving and volatile situations, such as a stop or arrest, situations in which officers are expected to make sound and justifiable decisions. When an officer uses force, what that officer knows, sees, perceives, and acts upon forms the basis upon which they are judged by others. In abuse-of-force cases, a prosecutor or court may review an officer's decisions and actions by a Fourth Amendment reasonableness standard in conjunction with other relevant federal or state laws. A police department may independently evaluate whether an officer's actions violated departmental policy. Civilian or other external review boards may review the officer's actions from other perspectives. Based upon multiple reviews, an officer may be charged with a crime, sued, fired, or made subject to other administrative action. In short, allegations of police abuse (call it an abuse of discretion) may result in personal, professional, and legal consequences to an officer.

There are other possible consequences when an officer abuses power, such as the exclusion of incriminating evidence in a criminal trial (based on the exclusionary rule), damage to an officer's or department's reputation, public ridicule, and more. There is another side. Individuals *subject* to coercive police action also face a multitude of consequences. Those not treated with some measure of dignity during a coercive police-citizen encounter, such as individuals who are stopped and frisked but never charged or arrested, may deeply resent police. Justifiable or not, those processed and convicted through the criminal justice system face potential incarceration, fines, and related legal costs, in addition to public humiliation, embarrassment, ridicule, and public outrage. The innocent or falsely accused will certainly be especially outraged, and even those rightfully charged may be justifiably incensed by being disrespectfully or wrongly treated. A community in turn may direct its ire at the perceived unfairness or injustice of an officer's or department's decisions and actions or at the criminal justice system itself. Yes, choices that officers make have consequences.

Policing, Stress, Bias, and Neuroscience

As noted earlier in the book, police interact with individuals in widely varying circumstances, from social interactions with community members to potentially violent and sometimes deadly encounters that elicit high stress. Sometimes an officer's unremarkable encounter with a citizen may quickly escalate to a highly stressful one, or an officer may be called away from an uneventful encounter to address a highly stressful one elsewhere. Police must thus remain vigilant given the vagaries of their work, and they must be prepared to perform—"do the right thing"—ethically, morally, and legally under great stress. That said, science has shown that dangerous or threatening events trigger portions of the brain that rely on reflexes, gut feelings, and intuition—very basic survival mechanisms. There is a good evolutionary reason for this. When people perceive a life-threatening situation, they "often go into autopilot, with all energy directed at escaping the threat," according to Rachel Nuwer in a *Scientific American* article (2016). In the article, Nuwer refers to findings by former Seattle Police Chief Norm Stamper, who wrote *To Protect and Serve: How to Fix America's Police*, and Rajita Sinha, director of the Yale University School of Medicine's Stress Center. A reactive response may be triggered "by a tiger emerging from a forest or a man wielding a gun" (Nuwer, 2016). In these circumstances, blood flow in the brain shifts from the regions that support analytic reasoning, cognitive flexibility, and the inhibition of impulses and desires to brain regions that support fast-paced and emotional reactions—sometimes characterized as *fight or flight*. Nuwer writes that general findings about the brain under stress are especially relevant to cops on the beat, referring in part to Stamper's book and research by Dr. Rajita Sinha:

> In experiments performed with actual officers during a video simulation of a confrontation, a team from Vrije University Amsterdam found that shooting accuracy, arrest and self-defense skills and communication all decreased when stress levels are high, and that officers fired more often in a high-anxiety situation on suspects that had already surrendered.
>
> Stamper says many cops operate in a continual state of hypervigilance, as though they are in imminent danger—a feeling that has only intensified in the wake of gun attacks on officers in Dallas, Baton Rouge, La., and New York City. Though vigilance is essential for safe police work, for a hypervigilant officer an action as innocuous as reaching for a wallet may activate the brain's subcortical reactive emotion areas, which leap to the conclusion that the person is going for a weapon. A cop who is vigilant but calm may correctly recognize that the movement is harmless. "A stimulus that might have multiple interpretations for one person could very quickly push another person who is sensitized to threatening scenarios over the edge," Sinha says (Nuwer, 2016).

The findings make clear that training should address the profound role that stress plays to enable police to better perform their difficult jobs in a safe, lawful, and effective manner, especially in high-stress environments. Effective training should include face-to-face approaches that amp up the pressure and complexity of interactions, especially those where police might meet hostility and potential danger. Many officers are already quite familiar with training scenarios that require them to decide whether to shoot or refrain from shooting in response to potential threats—a more singular point of decision-making about whether to use deadly force. However, broader and more sophisticated approaches are needed to address a spectrum of interactions. On a related note, many law enforcement agencies hold police-citizen academies that introduce citizens to the work of their agencies, including real-life demands. Citizens who participate in shoot-vs.-don't-shoot simulations typically have a greater respect for the inherent challenges involved in responding to hostile or potentially deadly encounters.

In both highly stressful and less traumatic encounters, police also bring their own bias and mental conditioning. How a police officer acts or reacts depends on many considerations. To borrow a Fourth Amendment standard used by courts to assess the reasonableness of police actions, police may rely on the "totality of circumstances" to formulate their response, factors that are commonly based on external, observable phenomena; what they have learned from others; and their training and experience. There are less obvious factors. Researchers and scholars in neuroscience, psychology, and other disciplines study how and why people make choices, and their findings consistently reveal the influence of cognitive *biases* and *heuristics*. Their findings challenge any presumption that humans are purely rational in thought and action. In an *Atlantic* story titled "The Cognitive Biases Tricking Your Brain" (2018), Ben Yagoda wrote:

> If I had to single out a particular bias as the most pervasive and damaging, it would probably be confirmation bias. That's the effect that leads us to look for evidence confirming what we already think or suspect, to view facts and ideas we encounter as further confirmation, and to discount or ignore any piece of evidence that seems to support an alternate view.

It is difficult to overstate the pernicious effect confirmation bias has on police work and the reputation of the criminal justice system. The results of such bias can undermine a community's respect for the rule of law and trust in legal authorities. For example, police officers who wrongly presume, consciously or subconsciously, that young Black males wearing hoodies are criminals (or hiding something) may also ignore salient facts that point to perfectly innocent or otherwise nonthreatening behavior. Stereotyping in general and racism in particular sow the seeds of confirmation bias that infects how police act and react. Such potential biases must be identified, understood, and addressed. This important arena has already drawn considerable attention and research, and there are ample subject matter experts who develop or provide training. Any successful approach helps officers recognize and account for bias—be they racist, sexist, xenophobic, or otherwise—in any encounter. That is the hope.

There is yet another variation of bias that may unduly interfere with police decision-making and acts of discretion—heuristics. What is a heuristic?

> A heuristic is a mental shortcut that allows an individual to make a decision, pass judgment, or solve a problem quickly and with minimal mental effort. As humans move throughout the world, they must process large amounts of information and make many choices within limited amounts of time. When information is missing, or an immediate decision is necessary, heuristics act as "rules of thumb" that guide behavior down the most efficient pathway (Psychology Today, 2021).

Police officers encounter, process, and respond to vast amounts of information throughout their days, often in emotionally charged circumstances, where key information may also be missing. Further complicating this is the reality that officers often lack time to carefully analyze and process the information and clearly map out feasible options. Time is sometimes a luxury, especially if a perceived threat poses imminent serious physical harm or death to officers or others. In this context, officers must sometimes use coercive force for their and others' safety. What officers are called upon to do is not suited for navel gazers or couch philosophers. Police work demands wise, intelligent, and often prompt action in an environment where unimpeachable choices are not self-evident. Those who possess the right qualifications and character must also be properly trained.

Police Power and Discretion

The sound exercise of discretion begins in part with an officer's choice to fully and humbly appreciate the inherent power and authority that the position holds and an awareness of the practical consequences and larger impact that their behavior has on individuals and a community. Like it or not, police officers must be role models, even when it does not feel good or when it stands at odds with any impulses to punish those who broke the law or endangered others by their own poor choices. Officers must "protect and serve" in a world where they necessarily confront acts of cruelty or injustice with the accompanying pain, anger, loss, and sorrow that follow. In this landscape, officers must consider their own and others' safety. In short, officers live, work, and try to make a difference in a world where they see the best and the worst of the human condition. Not everyone is up to this task, but those who choose to become officers must have not only the right qualifications, skills, temperament, and values, but also the wisdom to appreciate their own shortcomings and flaws. Police departments must recognize these realities in their hiring, training, and oversight practices.

Although law, rules, and policy directives establish police authority and standards of conduct, they inevitably require officers to understand, interpret, and apply them in real life, often involving ambiguous circumstances; discretion is a part of this process. To be clear, discretion in policing itself is not a bad thing; police cannot and should not be automatons—in a free society, Robocop is not an ideal. An officer who respects the space and freedom of lawful acts of discretion, as well as its potential for their abuse, will better serve and protect. It is a necessary and important function of police work. At the same time, police must appreciate that their choices and actions influence the public perception of police and the consequences to public trust and respect for the law.

What if police were required to rigorously enforce every apparent violation of law? Imagine if officers were *required* to issue a citation to citizens for *every* traffic violation (for example, 57 miles per hour [mph] where the posted speed limit is 55 mph) committed in their presence. Or imagine if officers were *required* to arrest every individual for *every* misdemeanor committed in their presence—including some crimes punishable up to one year of jail or prison time. Loitering, disorderly conduct, trespassing, and similar offenses would thus become a gateway for many into the criminal justice system. But is that wise, just, or humane? Even without considering the ethics or wisdom of such a rigid approach, do the math. Conduct a cost-benefit analysis. Calculate the tax-funded resources required to subsidize more police and police benefits, more equipment, more judicial resources, more corrections resources, and other interventions. Or calculate the social costs. That said, these costs and concerns should not preclude police from issuing citations or from making arrests for low-level crimes. Sometimes a community with an exceptional crime problem may support targeted and limited enforcement practices. But it is never simple; when laws are broken, their enforcement should never be taken lightly. But there are myriad considerations in deciding whether and how to enforce the law. The extremes of neither overly aggressive enforcement nor nonenforcement bode well for community respect for the rule of law, the criminal justice system, or the freedoms and rights guaranteed by the U.S. Constitution. Any practice, even a lawful one, that fuels contempt for legal authorities is self-defeating. Many would argue that the long-running debate about the legalization of marijuana, or at least possession of small quantities, is fueled in part by these same concerns.

Presume then that discretion is a necessary part of policing. Choices matter. For example, an officer's threshold decision to enforce a law has consequences, even in routine matters, and any such decision may be influenced by bias or heuristics mentioned above. A familiar scenario occurs when an officer enforces traffic laws along a busy, long stretch of highway where nearly every vehicle exceeds the speed limit during rush hour, often at speeds that constitute reckless driving. An officer begins by *choosing* locations where to set up and at what vehicle to point a radar gun; perhaps it is near an interstate access point alongside a poverty-stricken neighborhood (that factor alone should not preclude an officer setting up there). Then, based on a radar gun's results and other factors, an officer next *chooses* whether to stop a speeding vehicle. After the traffic stop, an officer requests a driver's license, registration, and proof of insurance. Throughout this process, that officer makes choices. Following a traffic stop, a uniformed, armed, badge-carrying officer *may* lawfully order the driver and all passengers out of a vehicle and *may* promptly ask some questions, even some that are beyond the scope of a traffic violation, the ostensible reason for the traffic stop itself. If a driver's answers seem reasonably suspicious or incriminatory to an officer, an officer *may* prolong the encounter. Meanwhile, during an encounter an officer can (and should, in the interests of safety) view everything that can be seen through the vehicle windows or open doors. Even if officers lack a search warrant or probable cause to believe there is evidence of crime or contraband inside a stopped vehicle, they *may* lawfully ask a driver for consent to search the vehicle. Although a driver's consent must be deemed voluntary to allow the introduction of seized evidence at a criminal trial, this still places a driver in an uncomfortable and legally perilous position. In many states, if a marijuana joint or other contraband is visible, an officer's choices may trigger a series of events that place a driver squarely in the criminal justice system, beginning with an arrest. Even if a traffic stop is otherwise unremarkable, an officer still retains some discretion over whether to cite a driver, what violations to cite, or whether to only issue a warning. Throughout this encounter, driver and passengers alike witness officers' deportment and professionalism—and, in that sense, as officers *choose* how to conduct themselves in their professional capacity. So even in simple encounters, discretion plays an important and lasting role in police work, and in like measure, police discretion contributes to how the public perceives police. Officers must be mindful of this.

Now consider three broad police responsibilities that rely upon police discretion and choice, namely: 1) preventing crime, 2) detecting and investigating crime, and 3) responding to crime or other acts that may be illegal or otherwise threaten the safety of a community. Nearly every decision or action among these broad responsibilities involves acts of discretion.

The Role of Discretion in Preventing Crime

Police and community members likely agree on a truly desirable goal—preventing crime. Most, I suspect, agree on the benefits of crime prevention and reduction: diminishing personal and community fear, increasing social engagement, decreasing violence and personal trauma, and increasing confidence and use of community institutions and public space, as well as business investment and attendant jobs and—perhaps most important—more hope. There are others. But any overly rigid or intrusive approach by police and government can be a threat to civil liberties, which calls attention to finding the right balance between freedom and security. There are two extreme consequences: Unchecked, unrestrained behaviors within a community can be anarchic, while unchecked, unrestrained efforts by police to promote security and order can be totalitarian. There must be some underlying consent among government and its citizens about where that balance lies, a balance that in part should be guided by the values and principles embodied in the U.S. Constitution and related writings.

In this context, preventing crime, terrorism, or other threats to national security often require law enforcement, not just intelligence agencies, to proactively collect intelligence—whether that information is secured from direct observations, records, data, human sources, information volunteered by community members, or ever-increasing public surveillance monitoring involving security cameras and similar devices. In collecting such intelligence, police may use that intelligence to predict and prevent crime. This approach differs from a more reactive approach, which measures success by the speed and success in solving crime or even acts of terrorism, crimes that *already occurred*. But there is no unanimity in identifying what is the best intelligence and data, the methods for collecting it, or the best predictive policing practices supported by this acquired intelligence to prevent or reduce crime. This remains a work in progress among scholars, researchers, and police and an important one at that. In meeting these challenges, police departments must ask questions and exercise sound discretion. A few examples follow.

In some communities, police use intelligence to strategically place officers at known hotspots where crime is common and *likely to recur* (Hvistendahl, 2016). This proactive, predictive strategy may lower crime rates after an initial yield of arrests and criminal prosecutions occur. Increased officer presence at hotspots may also help lower crime rates. However, a community's response to what appears to be an aggressive, if effective, police effort may be less than enthusiastic, although public responses may vary. Another predictive policing model involves generating lists of individuals more likely to commit crime and then targeting them for continued surveillance and investigation. The criteria for compiling that would-be criminals list and the responsive measures taken by police may also provoke debate. There are other variations of predictive models, summarized in the cited RAND Corporation study (2013, p.1–4).

However effective they are, there are also inherent concerns of underlying bias and discrimination in using such predictive models.

Law enforcement agencies cannot be idle in addressing crime and disorder in a community. Simply responding to a crime scene is not enough. Police must *choose* whether to use predictive models and strategies to support efforts to prevent or respond quickly to crime. However desirable any of these choices are in promoting community safety, they are also made within the limits of a budget. Here are some sample questions policymakers may consider:

- Begin by assessing how a department measures its crime problems and how it measures its success in addressing crime. Be prepared to challenge previous police approaches in collecting intelligence and data and how the results are used to formulate police responses, including predictive methods. In doing so, evaluate the best questions to ask as well as the best information and data to collect that accurately assess a community's crime problems.

- In addition to what is available from other agencies or state-sponsored criminal databases, what are other relevant sources or tools of reliable, trustworthy data or indicators about a community's crime problems? For example, what about crime-mapping or other statistical data that identify where crimes have occurred in the community? If used, what crimes or related data should be mapped? And beyond mapping, should police seek anecdotal information directly from community members about what they believe are the most serious crime threats? If so, from whom? Informants? Ordinary citizens? Community, business, church, or other leaders?

- To what extent do anecdotal stories or broader community surveys comport with results supported by solid, reliable data and methods that meet rigorous standards? The wording of this question does not imply that anecdotal stories or surveys of community perceptions are not valuable; they are important, too. But incongruities should raise questions.

- If implemented, have predictive methods based on collected data prevented and reduced crime, or have these efforts merely diverted public attention and drained limited resources to reach uncertain or unattainable outcomes? These are hard and important questions.

- Once a community's most significant crimes are identified, however imperfectly determined, consider the underlying causes of such crimes. For example, why are break-ins, gang violence, fraud against the elderly, internet scams, retail theft, or other crimes the most significant? Police chiefs must consider these and other questions. This is also fertile ground for criminologists and sociologists, whose research findings, if available, might support revising police department policy and training choices.

- Proactive methods need not be limited to traditional police responses but may of course include heightened community outreach or other practices within the means, budgets, and authorities of police.
- Consider a cost-benefit analysis of any approach before and after its implementation. For example, in hotspot policing strategies, have the projected costs increased by adding or reallocating more officers worked? Does the cost justify the gain?
- Even if the most significant crimes are identified, will curbing them make a community safer, will new or other crime problems emerge, or will criminals move elsewhere?

There is rarely a clear roadmap to reach wise, effective, and accurate answers to these questions. Each choice has consequences. But the key is ask the right questions, be open-minded about answers and options, act, and be prepared to revise strategies and tactics based on results.

The Role of Discretion in Detecting and Investigating Crime

Most movies and television dramas do not accurately depict how police investigate crime. In the investigation of crime, police consider many methods and tools, many of which are neither riveting to watch nor conducive to dramatization. Apart from responding to crimes in progress, investigative work is often slower and more laborious than the public appreciates. Physical surveillance (watching people or places in real time) can be long, tedious, and often uneventful. Similarly, police dramas do not depict the actual time it takes for officers or agents to conduct interviews or write up their results, comb through financial records, reach out to colleagues or other agencies for more information, meet superiors, write lengthy affidavits, schedule and meet prosecutors, seek court orders or subpoenas, or appear in court. The underlying work required to successfully secure court orders for invasive or intrusive investigative techniques can be especially painstaking and time-consuming. Some police actions are intrusive if not coercive.

Many intrusive techniques, such as stop-and-frisks, search warrants, and court-authorized wiretaps, implicate the Fourth Amendment and related federal and state statutes. When constitutional and statutory concerns exist, legal challenges may follow. For example, a warrantless search of a vehicle without the consent of a driver may violate the Fourth Amendment and render any seized evidence (and its fruit) inadmissible at a criminal trial if an officer cannot establish that they had probable cause to search that vehicle. As another example, a law enforcement officer may stop—that is, temporarily detain—someone based on a reasonable suspicion of criminal activity. If that same officer reasonably believes that the person stopped may be armed and dangerous, that officer may frisk—pat down—the suspect for weapons. Widespread stop-and-frisk practices are also likely to generate community hostility, even when they pass legal muster (stop-and-frisks will be addressed later in this book). In short, intrusive law enforcement actions—especially those deemed Fourth Amendment searches or seizures—are more likely to be challenged in either the court or the court of public opinion. Each involves choices.

Even choices of physically nonintrusive investigative activities, such as witness interviews, may have consequences, as they may unfairly impugn a witness's or suspect's reputation in a workplace or community. For example, a police officer or Federal Bureau of Investigation (FBI) agent who elects to openly interview a suspect at a suspect's workplace—rather than discreetly at another location—may wittingly or unwittingly jeopardize a suspect's reputation or livelihood. Bosses or coworkers may presume the worst; rumors will fly. Bold investigative acts may also direct public attention to someone who just might be innocent of any wrongdoing. Compounding the problem is when a suspect's identity is leaked to the press during a pending investigation in which no one has yet been formally charged with a crime. Small wonder that the consequences are especially devastating to the innocent. As always, there are consequences in uninformed acts of discretion. A well-known example occurred in Atlanta.

In 1996, Atlanta hosted the Summer Olympics. At the time, Richard Jewel worked as a security guard for AT&T. He was assigned to the games. While on duty shortly before 1:25 a.m. Sunday, July 27, at Centennial Olympic Park, Jewell discovered a suspicious-looking backpack that was later determined to contain a 40-pound pipe bomb spiked with screws and nails. Jewell cleared the immediate area before the bomb exploded in the park, although the blast still killed two and wounded at least 111. While running to cover the blast, a Turkish television cameraman died of a heart attack. Shortly thereafter, then President Clinton denounced the bombing, calling it an "an evil act of terror" and vowing that those responsible would be punished. Jewell undoubtedly saved lives and was initially hailed a hero. The pressure on law enforcement to find the bomber was enormous, and, as will be seen, investigative attention was quickly directed at Richard Jewell.

And after the deadly blast, Jewell embraced his notoriety, perhaps to his detriment. Certain traits also attracted law enforcement interest in Jewell, including the FBI. Soon Jewell became the primary suspect of the Centennial Olympic Park bombing investigation, code-named "CENTBOM" by the FBI. Even more unfortunate, his status as prime suspect was leaked to the *Atlanta Constitution*, which is when his life was forever changed, and not for the better. As national media descended on him, investigators began to realize that Jewell was not responsible. In fact, he was never charged with a crime. But damage to him, his well-being, and his family was done. Although Jewell did later receive a large monetary settlement for his suffering, he died a broken man in 2007 at age 44 following a series of health-related issues. (https://en.wikipedia.org/wiki/Richard_Jewell) Despite all that, I consider Jewell a hero for his actions that fateful day.

The real Centennial Olympic Park bomber was later identified as 29-year-old White male, Eric Rudolph. Rudolph, in fact, committed this and other bombings between 1996 and 1998, fueled by his hatred of abortion, gays, and the government. A survivalist, Rudolph eluded law enforcement officials for years while hiding out in the mountains. He was arrested on May 31, 2003, by police officer J.S. Postell "while [Rudolph was] rummaging through a trash bin behind a rural grocery store in Murphy, North Carolina" (FBI.gov, n.d.). He was sentenced to life without parole (FBI.gov, n.d.).

Is there a lesson from the Richard Jewell tragedy about how law enforcement agencies can make better choices and exercise more informed discretion in conducting investigations? Are there lessons from the many documented wrongful convictions revealed through the Innocence Project (https://www.innocenceproject.org/) and other efforts?

Many, including some former FBI officials, pointed to confirmation bias as a weakness in how the investigation proceeded. This is a teachable moment. In a *Northeastern University Law Review* article entitled "Confirmation Bias and Other Systemic Causes of Wrongful Convictions: A Sentinel Events Perspective" (2019), Dr. Kim Rossmo, a Canadian criminologist and then professor and university chair in criminology, and Dr. Joycelyn Pollock, professor of criminal justice, examined how investigators make decisions and what cognitive biases hamper them. They identified, among others, faulty assumptions, probability errors, and groupthink. While cognitive biases do not represent deliberate decision-making, they are the product of below-conscious, unintentional strategies (Rossmo & Pollock, 2019, p. 811). Rossmo and Pollock noted how confirmation bias "produced problems of poor thinking, logic failures, misjudgment of witness reliability, and flawed evidence assessment." All represent a type of selective biased thinking in the search for evidence, the interpretation of information, and their influence on memory. What suffers is an investigator's failure to pursue the truth logically and relentlessly—an evidence-based approach. Discretion and choice should rely on what is: the facts and circumstances as they are.

A legal concept that, when applied, serves as a check on overaggressive investigation is one that requires investigators to at least *consider* using the *least intrusive* techniques as they conduct a logical investigation. The U.S. Department of Justice (2008) describes how this concept applies to the conduct of criminal and even national security investigations by the FBI in the *Attorney General's Guidelines for Domestic FBI Operations*, I.C.2.a (2008), which states:

> The conduct of investigations and other activities authorized by these Guidelines may present choices between the use of different investigative methods that are each operationally sound and effective, but that are more or less intrusive, considering such factors as the effect on the privacy and civil liberties of individuals and potential damage to reputation. The least intrusive method feasible is to be used in such situations. It is recognized, however, that the choice of methods is a matter of judgment. The FBI shall not hesitate to use any lawful method consistent with these Guidelines, even if intrusive, where the degree of intrusiveness is warranted in light of the seriousness of a criminal or national security threat or the strength of the information indicating its existence, or in light of the importance of foreign intelligence sought to the United States' interests. This point is to be particularly observed in investigations relating to terrorism (p. 12–13).

Although I taught this concept to FBI personnel and applied it to real FBI investigations in my former capacity as chief division counsel of an FBI field office, I have also grown to better appreciate its significance as I have transitioned from an agent to a private citizen who now teaches at a university. Awareness of these pitfalls encourages investigators to think independently and mindfully as they follow the evidence. This may dampen investigative tendencies toward groupthink, a rush to judgment, and other cognitive weaknesses. As a professor and as an FBI division counsel, I also dovetailed this guidance with another belief: Just because an investigative technique might be used lawfully does not mean it is appropriate to use that technique early in an investigation. Investigations are rarely begun with wiretaps and undercover operations, two highly intrusive investigative techniques. Interesting commentary about this topic may be found in a review by Morris Panner (1997).

A final example underscoring the significant role of sound and deliberate decision-making is revealed in federal wiretap laws that govern the use of electronic surveillance, including the interception of telephone wiretaps and electronic transmissions and the use of concealed microphones. These techniques are the most intrusive and invasive available because they authorize the government, pursuant to court order, to contemporaneously intercept the content of private, personal communications. A court-ordered wiretap, for example, authorizes the government to listen to phone conversations to find evidence of criminal activity, subject to many limitations, for up to 30 days, plus any court-authorized extensions. Among other requirements, these laws enumerate what a law enforcement officer must establish before a federal judge will consider authorizing a wiretap. Moreover, Title 18, U.S.C. § 2518(1)(c) (1998) provides in part that each application for a wiretap shall include:

> ... a full and complete statement as to whether or not other investigative procedures have been tried and failed or why they reasonably appear to be unlikely to succeed if tried or to be too dangerous.

This forces investigators to consider other, less intrusive means to collect evidence of crime. This requirement forces investigators to consider a wide variety of choices and to not overlook assorted options. It expects them to think.

The Role of Citizen Discretion

What cannot be overlooked is how individuals and communities perceive and respond to police, the courts, and the law in a variety of settings. Police and community together are stakeholders in this relationship; the choices of one affect the other. The most significant community choices in this context are choices of 1) whether to comply with the law and 2) whether to cooperate with legal authorities, especially the police. As Tyler (2011) stated, "If the law does not shape the behavior of most people most of the time, the legal system is not effectively fulfilling its social regulatory function" (p. 66). In other words, as was also noted earlier in this chapter, decisions by police or judges "mean very little if people generally ignore them, and laws lack importance if they do not affect public behavior" (Tyler, 2011, p. 66). Compliance *is* important, but widespread compliance relies on various attitudes, actions, and conditions among community and police. For example, compliance borne of a fear of police is not a reliable measure of the success of the social regulatory function of law. What accurately measures meaningful citizen compliance is not always clear. A citizen who complies to a police command when facing overwhelming police force in one encounter does not ensure that same citizen will not renege at a future police encounter where the odds look more favorable. For example, arrestees may comply with an armed police officer's orders to raise their hands or kneel with their hands against a wall when facing such overwhelming force. But compliance to such short-term commands and coercive force hardly reveals a suspect's underlying respect for police, the law, or the criminal justice system. If faced with different odds later, that same suspect may not comply (Tyler, 2011, p. 66). Similarly, arrestees who "freeze" in response to a police command may be reacting through their limbic system, not their respect for the police. Long-term, abiding compliance by citizens and community requires more.

Community safety is not a product of police *or* community acting alone. They *are* interdependent. Mark Moore of the Kennedy School of Government at Harvard University delivered a lecture titled *The Legitimation of Criminal Justice Policies and Practices* (1997) that was later published, in which he stated:

> The loss of popular legitimacy for the criminal justice system produces disastrous consequences for the system's performance. If citizens do not trust the system, they will not use it. If citizens do not use the system, the expensive apparatus we have constructed will be largely useless because the system depends fundamentally on citizen mobilization. Moreover, to the extent that confidence in the system is maldistributed, with poor minorities more suspicious of the system than the wealthier majority, the capacity of the system to act fairly is undermined, and with that, its future legitimacy, effectiveness, and capacity to teach what we owe to one another. To the extent that the system is viewed as inefficient or unjust, its ability to mobilize citizens to comply with laws voluntarily will be undermined. Without popular legitimacy supporting criminal justice operations, instead of having a collectively established criminal justice system helping to enforce a widely shared conception of a just moral order, we will live in a world of gated communities, each with its own conception of right conduct, and each enthusiastically excluding citizens of other communities. To avoid this result, we must find a way to restore the popular legitimacy of the Nation's criminal justice system (p. 55).

It is unlikely that any one specific measure taken to strengthen police legitimacy, and with it a community's *choice* to cooperate, can succeed without public trust. Public trust rests upon many factors. Facile, packaged answers will not likely survive the realities of policing. That said, Dr. Moore's phrase about the need for "a widely shared conception of a just moral order" resonates with primary themes raised throughout this book. When minorities clamor for justice, justness, or fairness in policing practices, or when there is widespread cynicism about criminal justice system, there is work to be done. Official inaction in response to what a community perceives is wrong will not foster respect or promote finding more common ground in values and outlook. Similarly, people and communities must decide whether to embrace legitimate attempts by police to further their common interests in safety and security.

Review Questions

1. Create a scenario involving police taking official action against a citizen. Identify whether and how discretion plays a key role.
2. Do you believe police have too much or too little discretion? Explain your position and give examples.
3. Define and distinguish *bias* and *heuristics*. Give examples of each.
4. Read the *Science* article linked in the chapter. Do you think the findings should help guide what police departments do?
5. Review the referenced RAND Corporation study on predictive policing models. If you were a police chief or a community leader, what might be your takeaway in deciding what and what not to use?
6. What is the purpose of using the least intrusive technique in an investigation? Should the least intrusive technique always be used? Why or why not?
7. Based on what you read, why do people choose to comply with legal authorities or otherwise obey the law? Do you have other suggestions?

References

FBI.gov. (n.d.). *Eric Rudolph*. History. https://www.fbi.gov/history/famous-cases/eric-rudolph

Hvistendahl, M. (2016, September 28). Can 'predictive policing' prevent crime before it happens? *Science*. https://www.sciencemag.org/news/2016/09/can-predictive-policing-prevent-crime-it-happens. doi:10.1126/science.aah7353

Moore, M. H. (1997). The legitimation of criminal justice policies and practices. In J. Q. Wilson, P. Reuter, M. H. Moore, C. S. Widom, & N. Morris, *Perspectives on crime and justice: 1996–1997 lecture series*. https://www.ncjrs.gov/txtfiles/166609.txt). National Institute of Justice.

Nuwer, R. (2016, September 20). Stress training for cops' brains could reduce suspect shootings. *Scientific American*. https://www.scientificamerican.com/article/stress-training-for-cops-brains-could-reduce-suspect-shootings/

Oswald, M. E., & Grosjean, S. (2004). Confirmation bias. In R. F. Pohl (Ed.), *Cognitive illusions: A handbook on fallacies and biases in thinking, judgment and memory* (pp. 79–96). Psychology Press.

Panner, M. (1997). Law Enforcement Intelligence in a Free Society—A Review of the "Attorney General Guidelines on General Crimes, Racketeering Enterprise and Domestic Security/Terrorism Investigations." (https://www.google.com/url?sa=t&rct=j&q=&esrc=s&source=web&cd=&ved=2ahUKEwjzmLO-6mIbxAhXCEVkFHXrRA_sQFjAAegQIAxAF&url=http%3A%2F%2Fwww.law.harvard.edu%2Fprograms%2Fcriminal-justice%2Fag-guidelines.pdf&usg=AOvVaw0VGTwitPTKiFEgWkluIBv4)

Peel, R. (1829). *Nine principles of policing.*

Pepinsky, H. E. (1984). (1984). Better living through police discretion. *Law and Contemporary Problems, 47,* 249–267.

Procedure for Interception of Wire, Oral, or Electronic Communications. 18 U.S.C. § 2518(1)(c) (1998). https://www.law.cornell.edu/uscode/text/18/2518

Psychology Today. (2021). *Heuristics.* https://www.psychologytoday.com/us/basics/heuristics

RAND Corporation. (2013). *Predictive policing: Forecasting crime for law enforcement.* https://www.rand.org/content/dam/rand/pubs/research_briefs/RB9700/RB9735/RAND_RB9735.pdf

Rossmo, K., & Pollock, J. (2019). Confirmation bias and other systemic causes of wrongful convictions: A sentinel events perspective. *Northeastern University Law Review, 11*(2). https://dx.doi.org/10.2139/ssrn.3413922

Stamper, N. (2016). *To protect and serve: How to fix America's police.* Nation Books.

Tyler, T. R. (2011). *Why people cooperate: The role of social motivations.* Princeton University Press.

U.S. Department of Justice. (2008). *The attorney general's guidelines for domestic FBI operations.* https://www.justice.gov/archive/opa/docs/guidelines.pdf

Yagoda, B. (2018, August 7). The Cognitive Biases Tricking Your Brain. The Atlantic. https://www.theatlantic.com/magazine/archive/2018/09/cognitive-bias/565775/.

Image Credit

Chapter 6

General Police Powers to Search and Seize Under the Fourth Amendment

Peel Principle 4: The degree of cooperation of the public that can be secured diminishes, proportionately, to the necessity for the use of physical force and compulsion in achieving police objectives.

> *"The right of the people to be secure in their persons, houses, papers, and effects, against unreasonable searches and seizures, shall not be violated, and no Warrants shall issue, but upon probable cause, supported by Oath or affirmation, and particularly describing the place to be searched, and the persons or things to be seized."*   *U.S. Const., amend. IV*

Understanding the Fourth Amendment as the Primary Check on Police Searching and Seizing

Searching and seizing someone's *"persons, houses, papers, and effects"* (straight from the Fourth Amendment) are key manifestations of the exercise of police power and authority. That's what police often do to collect evidence to prove that a crime or other violation of law is being committed. Examples of police searches and seizures where the Fourth Amendment serves as a check on police conduct—whether these searches and seizures are based on a warrant—include investigative stop-and-frisks, vehicle stops, arrests, searches of home and the seizure of evidence therein, the seizure and search of records and documents—electronic or digital—and so on. If police are to protect and serve the community, it also makes sense for them to investigate past, present and impending crimes (crime *prevention* is perhaps best of all). But let us be clear: The Fourth Amendment protects only against searches and seizures conducted *by the government or under governmental direction.* Surveillance and investigatory actions taken by private persons or entities, such as private investigators, suspicious spouses, or nosey neighbors, do not raise *Fourth Amendment* concerns. The same applies to information and records collected by private companies, such as banks, or mortgage companies, Facebook, or Google—they are not restrained by the Fourth Amendment or, for that matter, the First Amendment. By contrast, Fourth Amendment standards and limits are imposed when those same actions are taken by law enforcement officials or private persons working at the direction of law enforcement. Let us briefly examine some Fourth Amendment standards and limits.

The Fourth Amendment isn't simply a set of rules that police should follow (the how)—rather, the Fourth Amendment recognizes a fundamental right of the people, and it provides guiding principles (the why). Most constitutional scholars point out that the Fourth Amendment did not *establish* the "right of the people to be secure in their persons, houses, papers, and effects, against unreasonable searches and seizures. ..." Rather, this right *already* belonged to the people—it wasn't a gift bestowed to the people by the Constitution or the government. The freedom from unreasonable government intrusion was thought of as a *natural right*, a right so fundamental to liberty that people were entitled to it by virtue of their very existence. When the Constitution was ratified in 1787, the very existence of slavery, of course, pointed to a gross and immoral shortcoming in the realization of this ideal. But absent this fundamental flaw, the vision and principles of the Fourth Amendment and the Constitution were central to promoting good governance. While the passage of the Thirteenth Amendment in 1865 addressed this fundamental flaw, it only brought the nation one step closer to a greater vision of the dignity and liberty of all citizens. Much work remains, and police are part of that effort.

Thus, Fourth Amendment principles are central to the proper exercise of police authority. However, a cursory review of the Fourth Amendment also reveals it is hardly a self-effectuating roadmap to guide police actions. Constitutional scholar Jacob Landynski (1966) wrote that the Fourth Amendment, "as finally drafted and adopted, had both the virtue of brevity and the vice of ambiguity" (p. 42). Look at it again. Do the 53 words of the Fourth Amendment spell out how police must exercise their power and authority in the context of every contact with the public? Of course not. But there are key Fourth Amendment words and phrases in which the Supreme Court has examined their meaning and application that help officers and civilians alike understand the proper limits of police power.

The Fourth Amendment states in part that the people have a *right* "to be secure in their persons, houses, papers and effects, against unreasonable searches and seizures." This right, the Fourth Amendment continues, "*shall* not be violated" (emphasis added). It is a command, and as commonly understood, it serves as a check on the power of the police to seize and search people and their property, homes and effects. Clearly, the drafters were concerned about state power—Great Britain and its monarchy—*abusing* its control over the colonies. Informed by their experiences with the Crown, colonists were enraged by British customs officials and their use of writs of assistance. But what were writs of assistance? We must return to eighteenth-century Colonial America. At the time British subjects complained loudly about the use and abuse of such writs of assistance. These writs were general warrants that British authorities used to enforce revenue laws. But why was that bad? General warrants authorized the bearer—namely British authorities—to enter *any house or other place* to search for and seize "prohibited and uncustomed" goods and to command all British subjects (the colonists) to assist them. General warrants required *no* factual justification supporting their issuance, and they remained in force through the *lifetime* of the sovereign, King George III, and six months after the sovereign's death. Think about it—there were no limits on the time or place when British officials could search and seize "uncustomed goods." And demand support of the colonists themselves. What an invitation to arbitrary and capricious government actions. And when English officials seized "uncustomed" goods pursuant to these warrants or writs of assistance, they were not required to make a record of what exactly was seized. It takes little to imagine that English officials could have abused their unrestrained authority to search for and seize uncustomed goods wherever they chose. It likewise takes little to imagine that colonists were infuriated by this plainly unreasonable use and gross abuse of authority. On its face, the Fourth Amendment ended the issuance and use of general warrants by requiring that warrants may be issued only upon a showing of "probable cause, supported by oath or affirmation, and particularly describing the place to be searched, and the person or things to be seized."

The Fourth Amendment did more; it commanded, as noted above, that people were protected against "unreasonable searches and seizures." Note that the Fourth Amendment protection against searches and seizures by the government is *not* absolute. Rather, the Fourth Amendment protects only against those searches and seizures that are deemed *unreasonable* (see USCourts.gov's *What Does the Fourth Amendment Mean?* [n.d.]). For much of U.S. history, this protection was understood to limit police actions—the searching and seizing—that occurred in the physical world, an understanding that follows the language of the amendment itself—"persons, houses, papers and effects"—physical things. In this context, police might arrest and take custody of your *person*, search your *home*, or seize your *effects*. All these actions would play out if police were to *search* your home, find and *seize* illegal drugs and other evidence, and then arrest you. But in asserting their power and authority, the key question remains: Did officers act lawfully, or did they abuse their power? The Fourth Amendment addresses these questions by establishing checks on the exercise of police powers, even if vaguely so. That is, government searches and seizures must be *reasonable*, and searches and seizures may require a *warrant*. But what is a search or seizure, and when is either unreasonable?

Search and Seizure in Police Work

It is important to define what *search* and *seizure* mean. A Fourth Amendment *search* may occur when police intentionally search or look for something in the physical world (later, we will examine searches in the context of the informational or data world). A Fourth Amendment *seizure* may occur when police intentionally seize, detain, control, or otherwise take something. The Fourth Amendment commands that all such searches and seizures shall be reasonable no matter whether a warrant is required. But when is a search or seizure reasonable or unreasonable within the meaning of the Fourth Amendment? Again, not everything an officer looks for or takes constitutes a *Fourth Amendment* search or seizure. An officer may walk along neighborhood sidewalks or other publicly accessible areas *looking* for possible criminal activity. Such activities do not represent a *Fourth Amendment* search. Similarly, an officer may seize a discarded illegal sawed-off shotgun left on a public park bench; that, too, is not a *Fourth Amendment* seizure. But at what point do police violate someone's personal Fourth Amendment rights? To better understand when someone's rights are triggered by police intrusions, we must turn to what the Supreme Court has written about an individual's right of *privacy*.

As noted above, the Fourth Amendment's reasonableness standard checks police power. As shown below, courts will evaluate the reasonableness of a police search or seizure by examining where it is conducted and how it is conducted. In this analysis, a key question is whether the police have intruded upon someone's personal *privacy*, a term not found in the Fourth Amendment. The notion of privacy, however, has served as a core Fourth Amendment principle by the Supreme Court in more recent times. As Justice Felix Frankfurter wrote in *Wolf v. Colorado* (1949):

> The security of one's privacy against arbitrary intrusion by the police—which is at the core of the Fourth Amendment—is basic to a free society. It is therefore implicit in "the concept of ordered liberty," and, as such, enforceable against the States through the Due Process Clause. The knock at the door, whether by day or by night, as a prelude to a search, without authority of law but solely on the authority of the police, did not need the commentary of recent history to be condemned ... (pp. 27–28).

The Fourth Amendment thus serves as a shield against arbitrary police intrusions—in this case, police intrusion into the privacy of one's home. In fact, the Supreme Court has used the much-quoted phrase "every man's house is his castle" (see, for example, *Weeks v. United States* [1914]). To search someone's home, a place where individual privacy is so highly valued, police must typically secure a search warrant. But the importance of personal privacy arises in other contexts, not just houses.

Privacy protection against government intrusion is central feature of citizenship—and it arises in various contexts at federal and state levels. For example, in *Roe v. Wade* (1973), the Supreme Court held that a woman's right to an abortion fell within the right to privacy, a right earlier recognized in a different context in *Griswold v. Connecticut* (1965). Both court decisions found privacy protections were said to exist within the meaning of the Due Process Clause of the Fourteenth Amendment. In *Roe v. Wade*, the Supreme Court specifically recognized a fundamental "right to privacy" that protects a pregnant woman's freedom to choose whether to have an abortion during certain stages of her pregnancy. That means that laws or governmental actions that contravene certain privacy rights may be found unconstitutional.

In *Katz v. United States* (1967), the U.S. Supreme Court examined the notion of privacy in the context of police actions. The *Katz v. U.S.* opinion explained why and how the Fourth Amendment protects individual privacy and places restraints when governments or their agents—the Federal Bureau of Investigation (FBI), in this case—want to search or seize something in which personal privacy interests are at stake. Remember, the Fourth Amendment does not protect you from your neighbor entering and searching your house without your consent, but it does protect you from *unreasonable government intrusions* into your home. Other laws, such as criminal trespass or breaking and entering, may criminalize what nongovernmental actors do, such as your neighbor. To reiterate, the Fourth Amendment limits only *government* activity, such as a police officer who plans to enter your home and search for and seize evidence in your home or other places. The *Katz v. U.S.* decision established a framework to determine whether and how Fourth Amendment privacy protections apply before police may lawfully search or seize something in which someone has a personal privacy interest. What follows is a summary of the facts and the decision in *Katz v. U.S.*

Charles Katz was a basketball handicapper—a professional bookie—in the 1960s who lived in Los Angeles. Katz placed bets for interstate gamblers and kept a portion of their winnings for himself. But under federal law, interstate gambling was illegal. A clever man, Katz had long avoided detection by using public telephone booths along Sunset Boulevard to conduct his gambling operation. His luck ran out when the FBI learned of his activities and identified the three phone booths that Katz used to take bets. At the FBI's request, the telephone company took one booth out of service. The FBI then placed microphones in the remaining two booths to intercept and record what Katz said that would otherwise be audible if someone were standing alongside him inside the booths. FBI agents were also stationed outside of Katz's apartment. Based on his recorded conversations, the FBI arrested Katz after he was charged in an eight-count federal indictment.

Did the FBI violate Katz's Fourth Amendment rights when it intercepted and recorded Katz's audible *conversations* inside *public* telephone booths? Remember, the Fourth Amendment expressly protects against unreasonable searches and seizures of "houses, papers and effects." But his conversations were communications—no physical property was implicated, and similarly, there was no government trespass on private property. Also, remember, the FBI bugs were installed in *public* payphone booths. So why did the Supreme Court find that the FBI violated Katz's Fourth Amendment rights? The Court explained that the Fourth Amendment protects not only property, but also people. That is, the Fourth Amendment protects an individual from unreasonable government (here, the FBI) intrusions—searches or seizures—when an individual has a reasonable expectation of privacy in what the police seek to search or seize. Since *Katz v. U.S.*, Fourth Amendment protection has been extended to circumstances in which the government searches or seizes anything in which an individual has a reasonable expectation of privacy. In *Katz v. U.S.*, the Supreme Court found that Charles Katz had a reasonable expectation of privacy in what he said aloud as he stood and spoke inside closed public phone booths, recognizing that Katz could see no one around him who could eavesdrop on his portion of the call. The FBI thus needed a warrant—that is, judicial authorization—to nonconsensually intercept his private conversations within the phone booth in which the door was closed and no one was present nearby who could have overheard him.

In *Katz v. U.S.*, the U.S. Supreme Court also explained what the Fourth Amendment does *not* protect, namely what "a person knowingly exposes to the public, even in his own home or office. ..." From a Fourth Amendment perspective, consider the following: Suppose you are now in your home—your "castle," if you will—and you stand before your open living room window that faces a public street. You hold what appears to be an illegal sawed-off shotgun. Anyone, *including* police officers, can see the shotgun from the public sidewalk. Do you hold a reasonable expectation of privacy that protects you from what the police or anyone else can *see*? Of course not. The police may use its observations to secure a search warrant of your house to seize the weapon (illegal contraband) and other evidence, depending on the warrant's express language. You have "knowingly exposed" yourself and your sawed-off shotgun to their view. Similarly, when you "knowingly expose" (or post) something on publicly accessible social media that humiliates, degrades, educates, or, better yet, shows evidence of criminal activity, do you have any Fourth Amendment protection prohibiting the government (or anyone else) from looking at your social media? The short answer is no. Police know that, and so should citizens.

The second section of the Fourth Amendment, the warrant requirement, is also tied to the reasonableness requirement. When someone holds a reasonable expectation of privacy in some place, effects, records, or something else (the place to be searched or persons or things to be seized) recognized by the Court, there is a presumption that police need a warrant before they search or seize, although there are exceptions to the warrant requirement. The Fourth Amendment commands that "no Warrants shall issue, but upon probable cause, supported by Oath or affirmation, and particularly describing the place to be searched, and the persons or things to be seized." The Fourth Amendment does not clearly answer all questions about obtaining and issuing a warrant, such as who may issue a warrant. But what is clear is that no warrant will be issued unless there is a showing of probable cause that is specific to the object of the warrant. At its most basic, before an arrest warrant is issued, police must establish **probable cause** that someone has committed a specific crime. In the same sense, before a search warrant is issued, police must establish **probable cause** that particular evidence of a particular crime(s) will be found in a particular place(s).

Stop-and-Frisk: Proactive Policing and Fourth Amendment Limits

One of the more controversial issues in policing is the use of stop-and-frisk, a proactive police tactic ostensibly designed to allow police to respond to individuals involved in "reasonably suspicious" activity, activity that perhaps falls short of the Fourth Amendment's probable cause standard. Such suspicious activity may reveal impending but nonspecific crime—one in which an officer "observes unusual conduct which leads him reasonably to conclude in light of his experience that criminal activity may be afoot" (*Terry v. Ohio*, 392 U.S. 1 (1968). https://supreme.justia.

com/cases/federal/us/392/1/). This reasonable suspicion standard *falls short* of meeting the probable cause standard that police need to conduct a full custodial *arrest* of a suspect for specific crimes. Where police have only reasonable suspicion that a suspect is somehow involved in criminal activity, should they then be authorized to intervene more coercively to seek additional information that may then establish probable cause to arrest a suspect, and, if so, exactly when and how? Or should officers simply walk away, bide their time for an indefinite period awaiting clearer proof, or wait for the crime to occur and then intervene? And what if the suspicious conduct is indicative of a potentially *violent* crime?

This takes us to the practice of a police-initiated stop-and-frisk, a legally defensible action that authorizes a police officer to take limited action when an officer has reasonable suspicion that criminal activity is afoot. In the context of real-world facts, the U.S. Supreme Court case of *Terry v. Ohio* (1968) laid out what justifies an officer to stop and frisk a suspect. Not only did the court's opinion define the legal standard behind stop-and-frisk, but it also explored how this police practice plays out in ordinary police-citizen encounters. For these reasons, *Terry v. Ohio* deserves review and historical context.

Earl Warren delivered the Court's opinion on June 10, 1968. Fifteen years earlier, while serving as Republican governor of California, Warren had been appointed Chief Justice by President Dwight Eisenhower. Many considered Warren a nonpartisan conservative at the time. Warren had earlier served as a distinguished district attorney and then as California attorney general. His legacy, however, is his work as Chief Justice of the U.S. Supreme Court, from which he retired in 1969. Here is how one legal source described Warren's tenure as chief justice (Oyez, n.d.):

> Warren's position as Chief was one of courage and flexibility in carving new paths. Warren joined the Court in the midst of some of its most important issues—racial segregation in public schools and the expansion of civil liberties. The new Chief proved an effective leader as he brought the Court from division to unanimity in many cases.

In *Terry v. Ohio*, Chief Justice Warren forged a near-consensus (8–1) among the justices at a time when police-citizen interactions were extremely contentious. How so? The decision was delivered during a time of tumultuous social and political unrest in the U.S. that included both peaceful and violent protests against the Vietnam War; the assassinations of Dr. Martin Luther King, Jr., on April 4, 1968, and presidential hopeful Senator Robert F. Kennedy on June 6, 1968; widespread race rioting; and the "police riot" against protesters at the Democratic National Convention in Chicago on August 28, 1968. Although I was a child then and lived near Chicago, I was old enough to dimly sense the social upheaval. So yes, *Terry v. Ohio* was handed down at a time when overt challenges to traditional authority, including police, were commonplace. Although some may disagree with the Court's decision, *Terry v. Ohio* remains a fascinating and instructive read about the interests at stake when police perform their role in protecting the community consistent with the letter and spirit of the Constitution.

Chief Justice Warren began by noting this "case presents serious questions concerning the role of the Fourth Amendment in the confrontation on the street between the citizen and the policeman investigating suspicious circumstances" (Oyez, n.d., p. 1). Below are facts derived or quoted from the opinion (pp. 4–7) because the background facts give context to the court's decision. Relying on the court's holding alone is less informative.

John Terry was convicted and sentenced for carrying a concealed weapon based on two revolvers and some bullets seized from him and a codefendant by Cleveland Police Detective Martin McFadden. At the evidence suppression hearing:

> Officer McFadden testified that, while he was patrolling in plain clothes in downtown Cleveland at approximately 2:30 in the afternoon of October 31, 1963, his attention was attracted by two men, Chilton and Terry, standing on the corner of Huron Road and Euclid Avenue. He had never seen the two men before, and he was unable to say precisely what first drew his eye to them. However, he testified that he had been a policeman for 39 years and a detective for 35, and that he had been assigned to patrol this vicinity of downtown Cleveland for shoplifters and pickpockets for 30 years. He explained that he had developed routine habits of observation over the years, and that he would "stand and watch people or walk and watch people at many intervals of the day." He added: "Now, in this case, when I looked over, they didn't look right to me at the time."

From the entrance to a store 300 to 400 feet away, McFadden continued to observe the men, which only confirmed his suspicions:

> He saw one of the men leave the other one and walk southwest on Huron Road, past some stores. The man paused for a moment and looked in a store window, then walked on a short distance, turned around and walked back toward the corner, pausing once again to look in the same store window. He rejoined his companion at the corner, and the two conferred briefly. Then the second man went through the same series of motions, strolling down Huron Road, looking in the

same window, walking on a short distance, turning back, peering in the store window again, and returning to confer with the first man at the corner. The two men repeated this ritual alternately between five and six times apiece—in all, roughly a dozen trips. At one point, while the two were standing together on the corner, a third man approached them and engaged them briefly in conversation. This man then left the two others and walked west on Euclid Avenue. Chilton and Terry resumed their measured pacing, peering, and conferring. After this had gone on for 10 to 12 minutes, the two men walked off together, heading west on Euclid Avenue, following the path taken earlier by the third man.

McFadden suspected the two men were "casing a job, a stick-up" and believed it was his duty to investigate further. Given the potentially violent nature of what these men were doing, he was also concerned that they were armed. Officer McFadden then followed the two men and saw them stop and meet a third man (Katz) in front of the same store where they had earlier conferred. Based on these observations, McFadden acted—he approached the three men, identified himself as a police officer, and asked for their names. When the men mumbled responses, Officer McFadden grabbed Terry, spun him around so that Terry was between the officer and the others, and, as this happened, he patted down the outside of Terry's clothing. In Terry's left breast pocket overcoat, Officer McFadden felt a pistol, but he was unable to remove the gun. Then Officer McFadden ordered all three men to enter the store in question, keeping Terry between himself and the other. As they entered, McFadden removed Terry's overcoat and seized a .38 caliber revolver from the pocket. McFadden then ordered the three men to face the wall and raise their hands. McFadden next patted down *only* the outer clothing of Chilton and Katz, the third man. Officer McFadden discovered a second revolver in the outer pocket of Chilton's overcoat. After Officer McFadden seized Chilton's gun, he asked the store proprietor to call for a police wagon. Chilton and Terry were formally charged with carrying concealed weapons.

In light of these facts, Chief Justice Warren cited the Fourth Amendment's "right of the people to be secure in their persons, houses, papers, and effects, against unreasonable searches and seizures" and explained that this "right of personal security belongs as much to the citizen *on the streets* of our cities as to the homeowner closeted in his study to dispose of his secret affairs" (Oyez, n.d., p. 9). Chief Justice Warren cited this 77-year-old Supreme Court decision:

No right is held more sacred, or is more carefully guarded, by the common law than the right of every individual to the possession and control of his own person, free from all restraint or interference of others, unless by clear and unquestionable authority of law (*Union Pacific Railway Co. v. Botsford* [1891]).

In a broad sense, the central issue in *Terry v. Ohio* was whether Officer McFadden had the power and authority to act as he did, as his actions—his searching and seizing—were clearly coercive. How did the Fourth Amendment limit or constrain Officer McFadden when he confronted the three men in this manner? Remember that Officer McFadden did *not* have "probable cause," the burden of proof needed to arrest the suspects, but, as the court found, he was justifiably—or reasonably—suspicious of their criminal behavior. Here again is a redacted portion (citations are omitted) of Chief Justice Warren's opinion:

> [W]e must decide whether and when Officer McFadden "seized" Terry, and whether and when he conducted a "search." There is some sugges-tion in the use of such terms as "stop" and "frisk" that such police con-duct is outside the purview of the Fourth Amendment because neither action rises to the level of a "search" or "seizure" within the meaning of the Constitution. We emphatically reject this notion. It is quite plain that the Fourth Amendment governs "seizures" of the person which do not eventuate in a trip to the stationhouse and prosecution for crime—"arrests" in traditional terminology. It must be recognized that, whenever a police officer accosts an individual and restrains his freedom to walk away, he has "seized" that person. And it is nothing less than sheer torture of the English language to suggest that a careful exploration of the outer surfaces of a person's clothing all over his or her body in an attempt to find weapons is not a "search." Moreover, it is simply fantastic to urge that such a procedure performed in public by a policeman while the citizen stands helpless, perhaps facing a wall with his hands raised, is a "petty indignity." It is a serious intrusion upon the sanctity of the person, which may inflict great indignity and arouse strong resentment, and it is not to be undertaken lightly (392 U.S. 1 at p. 17; 1968).

When Officer McFadden approached the suspects, he did three things: 1) He *or-dered* the suspects *to stop*; 2) he *questioned* them about their suspicious behavior to as-sess whether there was probable cause to arrest them for a crime; and 3) he *frisked* them for weapons because he was concerned about his personal safety. Chief Justice Warren examined the justification for all three acts and whether each comported with the Constitution. In his review of the events, Chief Justice Warren considered the totality of facts and circumstances confronting Officer McFadden. Were his actions—his exercise of power and authority—reasonable under the circumstances? Or was Officer McFadden required to have probable cause that a crime was being committed before taking any coercive action at all? Is that where a bright line must be drawn to countenance any coercive seizure or search? Or should the legal standard imposed on police more fully account for the nuance and range of police-citizen encounters?

The court said Officer McFadden's swift actions, based on "on-the-spot observations," could not be subjected to the warrant procedure, in which a judge independently determines whether to issue a warrant based on a probable cause standard. Rather, McFadden had to be "tested by the Fourth Amendment's general proscription against unreasonable searches and seizures" (392 U.S. 1 at p. 20; 1968). In doing so, the court balanced the governmental interest in the intrusion against the constitutionally protected interests of the private citizen. The government's justification for the intrusion must rely on "specific and articulable facts which, taken together with rational inferences from those facts" (392 U.S. 1 at p. 21; 1968), justify that intrusion. An officer's actions must be judged against an objective standard: What were the facts available to an officer at that moment that would "warrant a man of reasonable caution in the belief" that such actions were appropriate? An officer's good faith alone is not enough. Otherwise, people would not be secure in their "persons, houses, papers and effects" but rather at the mercy of unfettered police discretion.

And what are the government interests? "One general interest is, of course, that of effective crime prevention and detection" which recognizes that police, "in appropriate circumstances and in an appropriate manner" (392 U.S. 1 at p. 22; 1968), approach someone to investigate possible criminal conduct even when probable cause to make an arrest is lacking. The court then reviewed all the available facts and circumstances confronting McFadden and said that it "would have been poor police work indeed for an officer of 30 years' experience in the detection of thievery from stores in this same neighborhood to have failed to investigate this behavior further ..." (392 U.S. 1 at p. 23; 1968).

The court next addressed the immediate interest of police officers in assuring themselves that persons with whom they are dealing are not armed with a dangerous weapon. In its analysis, the court said it would be unreasonable to require police to take "unnecessary risks" as they perform their duties and noted the long tradition of armed violence, especially those inflicted by guns and knives by American criminals against police. In addressing this concern, the court stated:

> In view of these facts, we cannot blind ourselves to the need for law enforcement officers to protect themselves and other prospective victims

of violence in situations where they may lack probable cause for an arrest. When an officer is justified in believing that the individual whose suspicious behavior he is investigating at close range is armed and presently dangerous to the officer or to others, it would appear to be clearly unreasonable to deny the officer the power to take necessary measures to determine whether the person is, in fact, carrying a weapon and to neutralize the threat of physical harm (392 U.S. 1 at p. 24; 1968).

Our evaluation of the proper balance that has to be struck in this type of case leads us to conclude that there must be a narrowly drawn authority to permit a reasonable search for weapons for the protection of the police officer, where he has reason to believe that he is dealing with an armed and dangerous individual, regardless of whether he has probable cause to arrest the individual for a crime. The officer need not be absolutely certain that the individual is armed; the issue is whether a reasonably prudent man, in the circumstances, would be warranted in the belief that his safety or that of others was in danger. And in determining whether the officer acted reasonably in such circumstances, due weight must be given not to his inchoate and unparticularized suspicion or "hunch," but to the specific reasonable inferences which he is entitled to draw from the facts in light of his experience (392 U.S. 1 at p. 27; 1968).

And what are those "necessary measures"? The Court allowed police to conduct a limited search of the outer clothing for weapons—a "severe, though brief intrusion upon cherished personal security ... an annoying, frightening, and perhaps humiliating experience ..." (392 U.S. 1 at p. 25; 1968). And when might police consider such an intrusion?

To promote public safety and the interests of police-citizen relations, police must apply *Terry v. Ohio's* legal standards correctly. A police-initiated *stop*—a brief investigative, although coercive, act—must be based upon reasonable suspicion supported by articulable facts and circumstances indicating that criminal activity is afoot. A police-initiated *frisk* for weapons must be based on a reasonable belief that the person stopped may be armed and dangerous. Failure to adhere to these standards is both legally hazardous and damaging to public trust. Officers must also understand the rationale behind the balancing of interests in creating these legal standards. The practice of stop-and-frisk— "an annoying, frightening, and perhaps humiliating experience" (392 U.S. 1 at p. 27; 1968)—must be used judiciously. This practice can be useful in promoting community safety, but it carries significant risks.

When an officer has an objectively reasonable basis to stop someone, whether due to a traffic violation or a more serious crime, that officer's other personal, subjective intentions may not matter. An officer may have multiple *legitimate law enforcement motives* to stop someone. For example, suppose Citizen X is suspected by state police of being a cocaine dealer, but there is currently no outstanding arrest or search warrant for the driver or their vehicle. A state trooper then observes Citizen X driving among a group of unrelated vehicles, all travelling about 12 miles per hour over the posted speed limit. The state police officer may lawfully stop Citizen X's speeding vehicle, but the trooper may also use that stop as a pretext to request Citizen X's consent to search the vehicle. The trooper's ulterior motive to stop Citizen X is perfectly legal provided the trooper has a lawful basis to otherwise stop the vehicle—in this case, speeding. But not all motives are lawful. A police officer stopping someone based solely on race, for example, is never a lawful motive. As Justice Antonin Scalia noted in *Whren v. United States*, 517 U.S. 806 (1996), the Constitution, through the Fourteenth Amendment, "prohibits selective enforcement of the law based on considerations such as race" (p. 813). But "subjective intentions play no role in ordinary, probable-cause Fourth Amendment analysis" (p. 813).

Stop-and-frisks can be misapplied, abused, or overused by police. Officers who fail to abide by the legal standards imposed by the court or use them in a *discriminatory* manner may violate the letter and spirit of the Fourth and Fourteenth Amendments. Police cannot discount the potentially risky racial component of some stop-and-frisk practices. Litigation risks are real, too. Liability exposure and court-ordered sanctions were underscored in a 2013 lower federal court decision that addressed 1) the New York City Police Department's (NYPD) widespread failure to adhere to the legal standards of individualized reasonable suspicion to justify stop-and-frisks and 2) the NYPD's discriminatory application of otherwise legal standards. In this case, *Floyd, et al. v. City of New York, et al.* (2013), U.S. District Court Judge Shira Scheindlin harshly criticized the NYPD because of obvious racial disparities in whom police stopped and searched. This case is more fully addressed in Chapter 8. To be clear, Judge Scheindlin never questioned the practice or legality of stop-and-frisk. Rather, she condemned the police department's *failure to follow the law*. She underscored the importance of the rule of law and the cultural and legal competency needed to apply the law in a nondiscriminatory manner.

Stop-and-frisk practices attract untoward public attention, but community and police share a common goal: public and police officer safety. These same stakeholders may differ in what police practices and tactics bring them closer to these goals. When police tactics are used in an illegal, abusive, or even unprofessional manner, police-community relations suffer. Communities want police to take measures that promote safety and security, but not all measures are equal or acceptable. That said, community resentment builds when any of these circumstances are present:

- Police conduct *illegal* stop-and-frisks, attributable to a lack of legal and practical training;
- Police aggressively pursue stop-and-frisks that target or profile various groups, such as racial or ethnic minorities, that violate the Equal protection Clause of the Fourteenth Amendment—*even when* individual encounters between police and citizens otherwise meet minimum Fourth Amendment standards; or
- Police conduct lawful stop-and-frisks but do so in an unnecessarily or gratuitously harsh or disrespectful manner—this, however, does not imply that police cannot use reasonable force to reach legitimate law enforcement ends.

Given all of these factors, police departments or legislative bodies are free to limit (even abolish) stop-and-frisk policies and practices, even though the practice of stop-and-frisk is constitutionally valid. Alternatively, police departments may provide better legal and cultural or diversity training and practice in the context of real-world applications of stop-and-frisk to gain greater community support. Greater police transparency about certain practices such as stop-and-frisk may also encourage some community buy-in. All choices must carefully balance police and community safety. Perhaps this is another arena where open and necessary conversations between police and community might occur.

What is the central message here? The Fourth Amendment and its standards relating to reasonableness, warrants, and probable cause stand as bulwarks against unsubstantiated or unjustified government intrusions into the lives of citizens—all abuses of discretion. Consider what the U.S. Supreme Court said in *Brinegar v. United States*, 338 U.S. 160 (1949) about probable cause: It "safeguards citizens from rash and unreasonable interference with privacy and from unfounded charges of crime. ... [It also] seeks to give fair leeway for enforcing the law in the community's protection" (p. 176). That "leeway for enforcing the law in the community's protection" is more fully examined later.

About Search Warrants

In conducting criminal investigations, law enforcement officers use various techniques to find evidence, some of which do not implicate Fourth Amendment protections. But when significant privacy or property interests are implicated, such as home searches, the Fourth Amendment may require a court-authorized search warrant.

Law enforcement officers can apply for and obtain search warrants to search for and seize evidence, instruments, contraband, or fruits of crime. An officer typically writes an affidavit. An affidavit, which is a sworn factual statement, must establish sufficient justification to satisfy an independent and neutral judicial officer that probable cause exists to support a warrant. Moreover, officer swear or affirm that the information in the affidavit is true and correct to the best of their knowledge. As the Fourth Amendment provides in part, "no Warrants shall issue, but upon *probable cause*, supported by Oath or affirmation, and particularly describing the place to be searched, and the persons or things to be seized." *Upon a showing of probable cause* to believe that evidence, contraband (inherently illegal things, such as child pornography or heroin), or fruits of a particular crime(s) *(the persons or things to be seized)* exists at a particular place *(particularly describing the place to be searched)*, such as a house, a judge or magistrate may issue a search warrant.

The search warrant, in short, authorizes officers to both **search** a particular place for things **and seize** these items once they are found. In the physical world, it is easier to visualize officers rapidly searching someone's house for illegal drugs, drug paraphernalia, and related documents. The physical search may also reveal physical objects that contain *electronic or digital* records, where the mechanics and application of the Fourth Amendment get trickier because a thorough search of these items at the search location is unrealistic, so that some items are merely searched for, found, seized, but later more fully searched after officers have left the premises. These items might include laptops, cell phones, or cameras. To be clear, officers search those areas where these items might be found in the place described in the warrant, but nothing more. Further searching and analysis of some seized items may continue later.

Now suppose that officers have completed their search and seizure as authorized by the search warrant. They typically leave at the search site a **copy** of the search warrant and an inventory (a list) of what they have seized. After the officers have left, the search authorized by the warrant is over. Officers cannot return if they have forgotten something unless they secure another warrant or lawful consent.

But it is not quite finished. In seizing the items from the site of the search, officers establish and document a chain of custody. The chain of custody is a document that records who seized the evidence and what happened to the evidence (such as a laptop) after it was seized and transported to a law enforcement agency office or another designated location. For example, a laptop may be seized at a home and later transported to a digital forensics lab for further **search limited to what is authorized in the search warrant itself**; the chain of custody must account for all such activity, including all who had access. If nothing else, police and community should know that there are important restraints on searches and seizures performed by police. A further safeguard is the exclusionary rule, which excludes evidence and its fruits that were obtained by police in violation of the Fourth Amendment. Unless there is a judicially recognized exception to the exclusionary rule, any such evidence is rendered inadmissible in a criminal prosecution. According to the U.S. Supreme Court, the exclusionary rule is a judicially created rule designed to safeguard Fourth Amendment rights—and, specifically, to deter police misconduct. The police undoubtedly have considerable power and authority to search and seize, but their actions must comport with the law, especially the Fourth Amendment, as further interpreted by the Supreme Court and lower courts. There are clear checks on their power.

Review Questions

1. Do you trust the government or the police? Why or why not?
2. Describe from personal or professional experience an interaction in which you witnessed someone abuse power and authority. Who was affected? What was their reaction? Did your opinion of that person change, and if so, how?
3. If you were a police officer, would you like your every word and deed recorded? Would this affect how you behave? In what sense? Identify other jobs in which recording is commonplace.
4. Explain why checks and balances on those in power are important. What "checks and balances" limit what you do in your private or professional lives? Do you think it is important that they exist?
5. Do you believe the Fourth Amendment should more clearly spell out what the rights of citizens are against unreasonable searches and seizures? If so, suggest some language. What are the difficulties, if any, of too much detail in the Fourth Amendment?
6. Identify any place or circumstance where you believe that you have a reasonable expectation of privacy against police searches or seizures. When you are inside your car? When you are not in your car? When you are inside your friend's car? When you are in a dressing room? In a public restroom? Consider other scenarios.

References

Brinegar v. United States, 338 U.S. 160 (1949). https://supreme.justia.com/cases/federal/us/338/160/

Floyd, et al. v. City of New York, et al., 959 F. Supp. 2d 540 (2013). https://casetext.com/case/floyd-v-city-of-ny-2

Griswold v. Connecticut, 381 U.S. 479 (1965). https://supreme.justia.com/cases/federal/us/381/479/

Katz v. United States, 389 U.S. 347 (1967). https://supreme.justia.com/cases/federal/us/389/347/

Landynski, J. (1966). *Search and seizure and the Supreme Court: A study in constitutional interpretation.* Johns Hopkins University Studies in Historical and Political Science, Series LXXXIV, No. 1. Johns Hopkins Press.

Madison, J. (1788). *Federalist No. 51.*

Oyez. (n.d.). *Earl Warren.* https://www.oyez.org/justices/earl_warren

Peel, R. (1829). *Nine principles of policing.*

Roe v. Wade, 410 U.S. 113 (1973). https://supreme.justia.com/cases/federal/us/410/113/

Terry v. Ohio, 392 U.S. 1 (1968). https://supreme.justia.com/cases/federal/us/392/1/

Union Pacific Railway Co. v. Botsford, 141 U.S. 250 (1891). https://supreme.justia.com/cases/federal/us/141/250/

Weeks v. United States, 232 U.S. 383, 390 (1914). https://supreme.justia.com/cases/federal/us/232/383/

Whren v. United States, 517 U.S. 806 (1996). https://supreme.justia.com/cases/federal/us/517/806/

Wolf v. Colorado, 338 U.S. 25 (1949). https://www.ravellaw.com/opinions/c34166c7ed01440746a3a344ff55c3cf

U.S. Const., amend. IV.

USCourts.gov. (n.d.). *What does the Fourth Amendment mean?* https://www.uscourts.gov/about-federal-courts/educational-resources/about-educational-outreach/activity-resources/what-does-0

Image Credit

Chapter 7

Use of Force Against Citizens

Image 7

Peel Principle 6: Police use physical force to the extent necessary to secure observance of the law or to restore order only when the exercise of persuasion, advice and warning is found to be insufficient.

Peel Principle 8: The police should always direct their actions toward their functions and never appear to usurp the powers of the judiciary by avenging individuals or the state, or authoritatively judging guilt or punishing the guilty.

Concerns About the Coercive Power of Police

The relationship between people and their governments has a troubled history, marked by governments that assert ever greater control over people. A virulent form was captured in George Orwell's famed novel *Nineteen Eighty-Four* (1949). In the book, "Big Brother"—the state—sought ever greater physical and thought control over the individual and all aspects of society. Power served no noble or virtuous or civic purpose. Control itself *was* the goal, and it suffocated the human spirit. It was coercive and manipulative. It was control at any cost—imprisonment, torture, doublethink, lies that must be believed—that "two plus two equals five" (p. 77). It was a paradigm that described a relationship between government and people founded on brute power, not on moral, just, legal, or legitimate authority in which some level of trust exists between people and government.

The exercise of power and authority arises in the context of other relationships, too—personal, professional, gender-based, class, racial, institutional, citizen-state, cultural, and other forms. These relationships involve the holder asserting some form of control or dominance over another. Even when power and authority are legitimate, the risk of abuse is a constant. A child knows this when a parent abuses parental authority; an employee knows this when a supervisor abuses workplace authority; a soldier knows this when a commanding officer issues orders unwisely or abuses a position of authority.

Similarly, in a functional democracy, citizens understand that police carry legitimate powers and authorities that justify a broad spectrum of interventions, from crowd control to the use of deadly force, but they are acutely aware of their potential abuse. In this context, no matter how coercive, police authority and power should be understood from many perspectives—by police *and* by those they serve, namely the community, comprised of diverse races, ethnicities, and other distinctions. When police better understand and respect the perspectives of diverse community groups and backgrounds and community groups better understand the functions and perspectives of police, the two will less likely be at odds.

Legitimate or not, police conduct invites public scrutiny, and nearly any act, but especially a coercive one, can elicit strong public sentiment. Public reactions range from respect and even admiration to fear and outright hatred. This is especially true for those subjected to coercive police authority; those who witness it, including fellow officers; and those who learn of it from others. Although not all assertions of police authority are demonstrably coercive, even noncoercive acts may invite public resentment. And to be clear, the *denial* or suppression of fundamental freedoms and rights is also an exercise of authority and power. That might be represented by police denying protesters their right to peacefully exercise their First Amendment speech and assembly rights. In short, assertions of power, especially ones deemed abusive, are consequential. Violent protests, revolution, and even war are responses to acute or longstanding abuses of power. America's history attests to this. Our nation's founders resented powers exercised by King George III and the British Parliament. Thomas

Jefferson, Benjamin Franklin, John Adams, and others catalogued these abuses in the Declaration of Independence.

This is not to suggest that the exercise of government power is always wrong or unjust; its exercise can be proper and often necessary. All expressions of just and legitimate authority involve some exercise of power. Those who hold it might well consider its exercise as a *privilege, not a right*. Use it wisely and cautiously, because its unjust, cruel, or even uninformed use can be deemed abusive, oppressive, and destructive.

History has revealed that the exercise of unchecked state power, at its worst, is often brutal and dehumanizing and a danger and rebuke to the true dignity of human beings. The countless victims of Nazi Germany are proof. A contemporary example of unchecked state power exists in North Korea. According to the Human Rights Watch 2019 report on North Korea:

> North Korea remains one of the world's most repressive states. In his seventh year in power, Kim Jong-un—who serves as chairman of the States Affairs Commission and head of the ruling Workers' Party of Korea—continues to exercise almost total political control. The government restricts all civil and political liberties, including freedom of expression, assembly, association, and religion. It also prohibits all organized political opposition, independent media, civil society, and trade unions.
>
> The government routinely uses arbitrary arrest and punishment of crimes, torture in custody, and executions to maintain fear and control over the population. The government and security agencies systematically extract forced, unpaid labor from its citizens—including women, children, detainees, and prisoners—to build infrastructure, implement projects, and carry out activities and events extolling the ruling Kim family and the Workers' Party of Korea (WPK).

Under Kim Jong-un's tyrannical rule, government agencies such as the Ministry of People's Security impose pervasive control, supported by other organs of state that actively spy on citizens using a vast surveillance and informer network (see the 2019 BBC News story link in the "References" section). In addition to the physical and emotional toll such controls exact on North Korean citizens, their personal privacy, freedoms, and opportunity are victims.

Is this an avoidable outcome? What curbs the destructive accretion of state power? What protects citizens from abuse of state power and moves a nation toward such "self-evident truths" as equality and "life, liberty, and the pursuit of happiness"?

The establishment of a system of government "of the people" and "for the people" is one option, within which viable checks and balances on the exercise of government power exist. Checks and balances rely upon the division of power, just and enforceable standards, the rule of law, and some form of accountability, to name a few key ingredients that must be imposed on institutions of government and their agents.

Why are checks and balances effective? They limit government overreach and abuse. Just as important, checks and balances account for the fallibility of human nature—they are an acknowledgment that governments and their agents may exploit or abuse whatever powers are conferred on them unless they are answerable to other people or institutions. The U.S. Constitution is a case in point, in which branches of government are designed to serve as a check on one another. Perhaps one of the most brilliant and lasting legacies of James Madison was his insistence on the need for a system of checks and balances. As he wrote in *Federalist No. 51* (1788):

> It may be a reflection on human nature, that such devices [checks and balances] should be necessary to control the abuses of government. But what is government itself, but the greatest of all reflections on human nature? If men were angels, no government would be necessary. If angels were to govern men, neither external nor internal controls on government would be necessary. In framing a government which is to be administered by men over men, the great difficulty lies in this: you must first enable the government to control the governed; and in the next place oblige it to control itself.
>
> A dependence on the people is, no doubt, the primary control on the government; but experience has taught mankind the necessity of auxiliary precautions.

Madison had no illusions about relying on the better nature of people to secure successful governance. Modern history suggests that governance in which fundamental rights are secured must be founded on some form of voluntary structure and agreement that binds government and people. But within this complex relationship, checks on the exercise of power are essential. One branch of government may serve as a check on the exercise of power by a government and its leaders. The structure of government itself may serve as a check on overreach by any one branch. Enforcement of the rule of law may serve as a check on the ambitions of any would-be tyrant. Similarly, checks may serve to protect the tyranny of a majority over a minority. Police officers and citizens alike might recall an impulse that partly drove Britain's North American colonies toward independence. As Joseph J. Ellis noted in *Founding Brothers: The Revolutionary Generation* (2000), "The original 'spirit of 1776' was an instinctive aversion to political power of any sort ..." (p. 9). Then and now, defenders of the Constitution "have saluted it as a sensible accommodation of liberty to power, and a realistic compromise with the requirement of a national domain" (Ellis, 2000, p. 9).

By contrast, unchecked power is a hallmark of totalitarianism, where power and control are ceded by government and people are expected to obey their leaders. In circumstances where the machinery of state is unencumbered by checks and balances on power, it is wishful thinking (if not delusional) to believe that out of this imbalance of power wise or just governance will follow. Rather, checks, balances, and accountability are preconditions to the establishment of legitimate authority and to the protection and potential realization of fundamental rights and liberties for all people. Their absence invites misuse and abuse, especially among those not fit to wield the power that accompanies legitimate authority. When the holder of power carries a badge and gun, it is especially important to appreciate this dynamic. To be specific, police departments and their officers who do not understand and respect these checks on the exercise of power can damage public trust and, with it, a police department's reputation. Police authority is not a license for unchecked power. Moreover, one rogue officer can scar public trust.

As agents of government, police hold diverse roles that enable them to lawfully regulate, investigate, respond to, and control aspects of what people do—all are manifestations of power and authority. Many police roles are unremarkable and unchallenged by the public, such as when an officer directs drivers around a crash site or oversees traffic at an intersection where a stoplight has malfunctioned. But an officer's exercise of authority can be more direct, personal, and intrusive, even when used legitimately. When police, in their official capacities, search, seize, or use force, they execute unmistakable powers, *powers not held by ordinary civilians*. If these powers are abused, they are understandably a source of friction between police and citizens. To be deemed just and legitimate, these powers must be subject to constitutional, statutory, regulatory, and other limits. Similarly, there must be accountability over how power and authority are exercised. Only certain U.S. military personnel share similar power, but their authority and power are directed at foreign adversaries and are highly circumscribed and prohibited if directed at civilians in the U.S. The military engages the enemy; police protect and serve the people. The people are not the enemy.

The U.S. Constitution and federal and state laws impose limits on intrusive, coercive actions by police. In many circumstances, police must secure independent judicial authority before taking certain intrusive actions. For example, the Fourth Amendment's warrant requirement establishes a clear preference that police secure a search warrant before entering and searching someone's home. When police lack legal authority, public trust suffers. If you are in your private residence, imagine your reaction to police officers who forcibly enter unannounced and without a warrant at 6 a.m. Trust and confidence in police do not grow out of these circumstances.

Even the *lawful* exercise of police authority can be performed in a manner that promotes or undermines public trust. Something as routine as an officer's traffic stop can partly shape and inform individual and community opinion about the proper exercise of police power and authority. A person stopped for a minor speeding violation confronted by an overly aggressive officer will not forget the officer's demeanor. Good and effective officers know that in *any* situation, police have an arsenal of options that promote greater respect for their authority. They know, for example, that self-control, professionalism, and even humility promote public trust. Anyone who has viewed North Little Rock Officer Tommy Norman's website (http://www.officer-tommynorman.com/) or his videos may note how effectively he demonstrates kindness and humor in his interaction with the community. When I share a sample of his videotapes in the classroom, students invariably appreciate his approach. Obviously, kindness alone does not make for successful policing. And obviously, these videos featuring Officer Norman represent only a thin slice of the range of police-citizen interactions—all are noncoercive—but they underscore the value of treating people with kindness, dignity, and respect whenever possible. Moreover, wise officers know that more physically coercive and forceful acts, even when justified, are often best used as a last resort. Even when force and coercion are justified, they should be used reasonably (more about Fourth Amendment "reasonableness" as a legal and professional imperative will be addressed later).

One Officer's Account of Abuse of Power

Police are not angels—they are humans. Some officers have abused and will abuse their power. No manner of vetting police recruits or departmental training will eradicate all abuse, but these practices can minimize its occurrence. Perfection in all police-citizen encounters is also unattainable. But all who want to carry a badge and gun must recognize the consequences of abuse of power on citizens *and* fellow police officers. It demeans and degrades all. Read this personal account by former Baltimore Police Department Officer Larry Smith (Smith, 2018), who became deeply disillusioned by police abuse of power. Even if his account represents only one perspective, and even if some may challenge his observations and perceptions, Smith provides real insight at what the abuse of power by police looks like. Note, too, the chasm he describes between police and citizens. As you read his account, do not presume that what former Officer Smith describes represents universal police norms or practices; that is neither fair nor informed. Police and police departments are not monolithic in principles or practices; personnel, training, police cultures, and other circumstances vary. Just as police officers who demonize or demean a neighborhood, a culture, a race, or an ethnicity do great and untold harm, citizens who demonize *all* police serve no one well. Such attitudes perpetuate stereotypes and disillusion good officers who are unfairly maligned. Demonization and stereotyping rarely lead to addressing, let alone resolving, concerns that divide people and police. There *are* countless examples of professionalism, heroism, integrity, and like qualities among police and police departments. What Smith recounts is not one. Nevertheless, consider what might be learned from his account.

> I am frequently asked why I became a cop, but I never seem to have a satisfactory answer. I was an only child in a single-parent home and was ... introverted growing up. ... [T]here were no other cops in my family. ... Being a police officer seemed like a job that paid relatively well, and most departments did not require anything more than a GED. After learning that Baltimore was hiring officers and that their process moved fast, I applied in mid-March of 1999 and was hired on June 21, 1999. I resigned in July 2017, a little more than a year after being diagnosed with PTSD [post-traumatic stress disorder] and spending 10 days in a mental health facility, the cumulative result of 18 years of experiences.
>
> Making the transition from civilian to cop was overwhelming. I wasn't accustomed to exerting any type of authority, and now, after six short months, I was given the power to take away someone's freedom and the instruments to take someone's life. At the police academy, we were taught the basics of the job: driving, firearms training, report writing, and self-defense tactics. The academy did not teach us the fundamental difference between power and authority or how to judiciously apply either.
>
> I remember being intimidated when I first hit the street as a patrol officer and began responding to 911 calls. I [was] expected to intervene in a variety of situations, from neighbors arguing over loud music to domestic assaults. I had to learn on the job to use my power as a police officer to take control, and then, if needed, issue lawful commands or effect an arrest. The challenge was realizing when I was crossing the line and abusing my power by ordering people to do things that weren't lawful.

Larry Smith, "I Was a Cop for 18 Years. I Witnessed and Participated in Abuses of Power," *Medium.* Copyright © 2018 by A Medium Corporation. Reprinted with permission.

One summer, I arrested a man on the Fourth of July. I don't remember why I arrested him, but I can remember taunting him about having his freedom taken away on Independence Day. That was funny to me at the time. In the Special Enforcement Team (SET), a unit I belonged to from 2006 to 2008, we were often encouraged to "clear corners"—our supervisors didn't want groups of people hanging out on the street, especially during summer. I would usually walk up to a group of men on the sidewalk and order them to move. Many times, this wasn't a lawful order. If they balked at my order or began to argue, I would threaten them with arrest for loitering. Fearing arrest, many people would comply. The other members of my unit used the same tactics, and as a group we pretty much just bullied our designated patrol area.

I began to feel less like a cop and more like a member of an occupying army.

Eventually, this style of policing began to eat away at me. In 2008, after several run-ins with my supervisors over what I felt was unjust and heavy-handed policing, I was kicked out of the SET unit and sent back to patrol. Policing institutions often punish officers who don't conform.

The abuse of power spread into my private life as well. Prior to becoming a police officer, I had never been pulled over. In fact, I had never interacted with the police at all except once when I worked in retail and had to call them for a shoplifter. As a cop, I was pulled over, off-duty, at least a half-dozen times for speeding, and each time I flashed my badge and identification and was let go without so much as a warning. Cops refer to this as "professional courtesy." ...

I became an internal affairs detective in 2013 and became privy to other, more nefarious ways cops used and abused their power. It was a common problem for cops to stalk former romantic partners. ... They used criminal databases to look up tags of cars parked in front of their former lovers' homes or ran a de facto background check on their new partners. One well-documented case is Lieutenant Brian Rice, the supervisor who initiated the foot chase of Freddie Gray that led to Gray's arrest and, ultimately, his death. Prior to his involvement in the Gray case, Lieutenant Rice had been stalking and threatening his ex-girlfriend for well over a year. The police were called multiple times for his threats of violence—none of which resulted in his arrest.

After Freddie Gray's death, the Department of Justice investigated the Baltimore Police Department [BPD] and released a scathing report detailing the rampant abuses of power and constitutional violations by its officers, including the use of excessive force, illegal stops and searches, and the targeting of African Americans for enforcement. That report and subsequent consent decree didn't deter an entire unit of cops from curtailing their own criminal behavior.

The Gun Trace Task Force (GTTF), a group of elite cops tasked with targeting violent offenders and getting guns off the streets of Baltimore, used their power to rob and steal, not just from citizens but also from the police department itself in the form of thousands of dollars in fraudulent overtime. They also resold guns and drugs back onto the streets. In March 2017, seven members of the unit were arrested on federal charges of robbery, theft, and selling drugs. All are now serving federal prison sentences. During the trials of two GTTF detectives, Daniel Hersl and Marcus Taylor, there was testimony that the members of the unit didn't fear internal affairs and that a deputy commissioner coached them through a fatal shooting to avoid punishment.

In Baltimore, after the death of Detective Sean Suiter, who was scheduled to testify before a grand jury the day after he was killed as part of the federal investigation into the GTTF, the BPD effectively locked down the entire Harlem Park neighborhood where the incident occurred while they conducted their investigation. Officers were told to turn off their body cameras as they conducted searches of citizens in the area and checked identifications of people trying to enter their own neighborhood. This was unchecked power at its worst. The death of Detective Suiter remains unsolved and shrouded in controversy.

In the final years of my career in the BPD, I struggled with trying to process the memories I had collected and the terrible things I saw as a cop. My head felt like a storage unit crammed full of old damp boxes. I never realized failing to properly process memories like these could cause PTSD. When you're a cop, there isn't always time to stop and think about something horrible you've just witnessed or been through, and with the exception of being involved in a shooting, the department didn't readily offer up any mental health evaluations to its officers. ... Mental health is also stigmatized in policing, and officers are reluctant to admit they're having problems and typically suffer in silence.

It wasn't just the blood and guts I was struggling with. I eventually began to realize all the work and energy I was putting into arresting people, usually for petty crimes, was having no positive impact on the city as a whole. And I realized I had lost all empathy for anyone or anything. Crime seemed just as bad as when I first started. Drugs were still being sold. People were still being shot. Murdered. All I was doing was helping to feed the machine of institutionalized oppression. I could arrest drug addicts all day long if I wanted to. Who did that help? What crime did that solve?

I chose to remain silent about the struggles I was having and attempted suicide for the first time in April 2016. I was briefly hospitalized in a local emergency room, where a psychiatrist diagnosed me as having PTSD. I thought it was something only combat veterans could get and never considered it could happen to cops. When I informed the department of my diagnosis, I was told that PTSD wasn't considered a work-related injury or illness, so any treatment was my responsibility to bear.

After about a year of stops and starts with various therapists and medications, I attempted suicide a second time, in June 2017. That was when I decided to voluntarily check myself into a mental health facility. I figured if I did it on my own, at least I'd have sort of control of the situation. I wound up staying for 10 days. I was evaluated and placed on medications for depression and anxiety. I also underwent several rounds of electroconvulsive therapy.

After I was released, I decided I had to leave not only the BPD but policing altogether, or it would kill me—if I didn't kill myself first. I realized that policing and police departments as institutions don't care about their officers. They care about justifying their own existence and protecting their budgets. I was just a number to them. My badge number, my sequence number, my unit number. Easily replaceable (Smith, 2018).

Smith's account is provocative. It may anger police who believe they are being unfairly maligned, and it may fuel the anger of those who have witnessed police abuse. But this account also opens a window for understanding and a platform for further discussion. Smith writes of power and the abuse of authority, the denial of basic freedoms, unlawful acts by police, coverups, and other malignancies in his former department. He raises questions about the nature and quality of police training as well as police practices. What also struck me from his account above was this: "At the police academy, we were taught the basics of the job: driving, forearms training, report writing, and self-defense tactics. The academy did not teach us the fundamental difference between power and authority or how to judiciously apply either" (2018). Understandably, a law enforcement academy must dedicate a great deal of time to the "how" of the job, but not at the expense of the why, including a greater appreciation and understanding of the proper exercise of police power and authority, and why there are checks and restraints. Such training should not end at the academy; it should be part of police culture. Perhaps the most important check on the exercise of police power and authority is the Fourth Amendment of the U.S. Constitution.

Fourth Amendment Use-of-Force Standards

Officers use *force*—typically a form of physical coercion—to gain compliance to a lawful order, protect themselves or someone else, or perform other legitimate law enforcement functions. The use of force should never be gratuitous, arbitrary, or unjustified; it should be used for the right reasons. And it is likely if not inevitable that an officer's choice of force—whether to stop, arrest, or use deadly force—will one day be scrutinized by judge, jury, press, or community. An officer's words and actions should reveal to outsiders that force was used to achieve a lawful purpose and in a manner reasonable under the circumstances. For example, an officer may use force to restrain and handcuff a resistant suspect. Once handcuffed, however, a suspect no longer poses the same threat to an officer. That said, an officer's subsequent actions must be guided by what force is appropriate or otherwise reasonable to achieve another law enforcement objective, such as transporting a suspect to a police station for booking. An officer's actions are always defined and circumscribed by their lawful purposes. If an officer's physically coercive force directed against a suspect is perceived as vindictive or gratuitous, critics may rightfully argue that such force is unreasonable, potentially violating the bellwether reasonableness standard of the Fourth Amendment. An officer's choices have significant personal and professional consequences.

Consider this scenario. It is near the end of Officer Brown's day shift. As she is driving her patrol car toward precinct headquarters, Officer Brown sees John cross Main Street. Officer Brown knows there is an outstanding arrest warrant for John for attempted murder, and she knows that John is also a convicted felon. Officer Brown steps out of her car and approaches him. As she closes the distance, they make eye contact. Officer Brown orders John to stop and states that he is under arrest. John sees the gun and badge and flees, so Officer Brown chases John through a busy intersection and into a residential neighborhood. Despite Officer Brown's repeated commands to stop, John keeps running; moreover, Officer Brown cannot tell whether John is armed. Finally, Officer Brown closes the distance and tackles John, and they struggle, all while Officer Brown is concerned that John may wrest her service weapon from her. Officer Brown ultimately gains physical control and handcuffs John. Chances are Officer Brown would be angered and exhausted by John's flight and resistance and flooded with adrenalin. Officer Brown also knows she must resist the urge to punish him after gaining custody and control over John because he is now compliant. Any punitive action by Officer Brown, whether she strikes a handcuffed John or deliberately slams his head on her patrol car's door frame as he is placed in her squad car, is not legally justifiable. In either instance, there is no legitimate law enforcement purpose in her deliberate actions; venting one's rage is not a lawful purpose. Officer Brown must limit her response to maintaining custody and control of John to protect herself and others. Officers such as Officer Brown must restrain their very human impulses, and this takes training, knowledge, self-awareness, self-discipline, understanding, and character. This is not work suitable for most people.

Whether to use force at all and, if so, what force to use are critical decisions police officers make every day. Officers' *failures to use enough or too much force* may endanger themselves or others. Suppose John, wanted for attempted murder, begins charging toward Officer Brown after she orders him to stop. As Officer Brown withdraws her weapon, John continues charging at her. Her prospects are grim as she clearly faces an imminent threat. John may take away her weapon and use it against her and others if she does not react decisively. By contrast, an officer may rashly resort to use deadly force without a reasonable belief that an imminent threat exists. Suppose instead that a subject readily complies with an officer's commands, but the officer still fires her weapon. Most circumstances are more ambiguous, and choices are always not self-evident, especially when they must be made in a split second in tense and rapidly changing environments. To guide and inform officers in whether and what level of force is appropriate, police departments may establish a force spectrum, better known as a *use-of-force continuum,* ranging from mere officer presence to the use of deadly force, with the understanding that any use of force must be reasonable and appropriate to the situation at hand. Officers must always consider whether their actions are reasonable under the circumstances and, in the same sense, whether they further a legitimate law enforcement purpose. This is how officers will be judged by Fourth Amendment standards. Police department *policies* may further constrain the level of force deemed best, but their policies must meet or exceed baseline Fourth Amendment *legal standards.* An officer's conduct may violate stricter police department policies yet still comport with Fourth Amendment standards.

The National Institute of Justice's Office of Justice Programs (2009) has provided an example of a use-of-force continuum:

- **Officer presence: No force is used. Considered the best way to resolve a situation.**
  - The mere presence of a law enforcement officer works to deter crime or diffuse a situation.
  - Officers' attitudes are professional and nonthreatening.
- **Verbalization: Force is not physical.**
  - Officers issue calm, nonthreatening commands, such as "Let me see your identification and registration."
  - Officers may increase their volume and shorten commands in an attempt to gain compliance. Short commands might include "Stop" or "Don't move."
- **Empty-hand control: Officers use bodily force to gain control of a situation.**
  - *Soft technique:* Officers use grabs, holds, and joint locks to restrain an individual.
  - *Hard technique:* Officers use punches and kicks to restrain an individual.
- **Less lethal methods: Officers use less lethal technologies to gain control of a situation.**
  - *Blunt impact:* Officers may use a baton or projectile to immobilize a combative person.
  - *Chemical:* Officers may use chemical sprays or projectiles embedded with chemicals to restrain an individual (e.g., pepper spray).
  - *Conducted energy devices (CED):* Officers may use CEDs to immobilize an individual. CEDs discharge a high-voltage, low-amperage jolt of electricity at a distance.
- **Lethal force: Officers use lethal weapons to gain control of a situation. These should be used only if a suspect poses a serious threat to the officer or another individual.**
  - Officers use deadly weapons such as firearms to stop an individual's actions.

An officer trying to correctly align the appropriate level of force in response to a perceived threat or to fulfill a law enforcement function, such as when officers lawfully arrest a violent felon, can seem mechanical in response to tense and evolving circumstances that officers face on the street. Those unfamiliar with police work must appreciate that an officer's decision to use some level of force must be made rapidly; there is no script, and rarely is there a prolonged opportunity for an officer to evaluate all choices and carefully weigh all alternatives. The "object"—a human being—against whom force is directed can be unpredictable, no matter how much an officer may know about the person and circumstances. In one of my criminal justice college classes, I cover legal issues involving the use of force. As a Federal Bureau of Investigation

(FBI) chief division counsel, I also examined these issues more closely with fellow agents. In the college classroom, I assume the role of a person against whom an arrest warrant has been issued. Student volunteers are then asked to arrest me (without a real weapon). The student "officer" might be told that I, a dangerous person wanted for resisting arrest and armed robbery, was walking along a street sidewalk. Without further guidance student "officers" would be instructed to arrest me using whatever words and actions they deem appropriate; they might also be provided with a bright red rubber gun and plastic handcuffs. Almost without exception, my brave student volunteers would be dumbfounded when I didn't follow their orders. Sometimes I would verbally provoke them; sometimes I would not or appear not to understand their directions; sometimes I would walk toward them showing no fear; and sometimes I would "resist" or act like I am reaching for an object in my jacket pocket. I inevitably observed fear, confusion, and even anger. Some student volunteers retreated, some didn't know what to say or do, and some were clearly frustrated. Some overreacted and "shot" me absent any apparent threat, even when I was compliant. These were all understandable responses given their lack of training. Students often found this both entertaining and intimidating, but more important, they better appreciated the rapid nature, difficulties, and ambiguities of these moments.

These lessons point to the importance of officer training in the application of force consistent with legal and policy standards that govern their choices. It serves the public to at least have some basic familiarity with them, too. One overlooked point is that the Fourth Amendment itself does not demand *perfect* choices, if such exist. An officer's choice does not have the benefit of 20/20 hindsight, but an officer must make *reasonable choices* and take *reasonable actions* considering the totality of circumstances at a particular moment. These decisions are a product of an officer's character, training, values, fears, and biases, as well as the multitude of rapidly evolving facts and circumstances before an officer. These decisions and actions have real and grave consequences, especially when they go wrong, such as in the tragic deaths of George Floyd and Breonna Taylor at the hands of police.

Deadly force, of course, is the final, most extreme, and most consequential use of force. It is no surprise that the decision to use deadly force is unmatched in the spectrum of police decisions. I have witnessed and sometimes participated in the unfolding process that follows the use of deadly force. No police action more significantly shapes public perception than the use of deadly force, as its use is fraught with consequences to the person against whom force is directed, the family, the officer, and the community. Other foreseeable consequences include intense media coverage and angry public debate, as well as multiple investigations conducted by a local police department through its internal affairs office, through a prosecutor's office, and by other agencies, such as a state police agency or the FBI. State and federal prosecutors may consider charges against an officer, and civilian review boards may weigh in. Unfortunately, in most instances, investigating and recreating facts and circumstances surrounding an officer's choice to use excessive or deadly force take time, precision, and effort. No two uses of force are identical, just as no two circumstances confronting an officer are exactly alike. A methodical, complete assessment of an officer's use of force frustrates the expectations of community and the press, who understandably want prompt answers. Compounding that may be issues over who or what agency conducts or leads the investigation.

No matter who conducts the investigation, the primary *legal* objective of any use-of-force investigation is to assess whether the officer's force meets objective legal standards, although there are other significant objectives as well, such as whether police department policies were followed. But primarily, an officer must meet or exceed what is legally required. Even if baseline Fourth Amendment legal standards are met, a police department may still choose to administratively discipline an officer who fails to meet department policies. There may also be relevant state law to consider. Moreover, there are other considerations at stake, including the rights and interests of the object of the force, and the officer's rights and interests. That said, each incident must be evaluated carefully even when officers, community, and press understandably want quick, clear answers.

Consistent with Fourth Amendment standards, when officers use force, including deadly force, they intentionally gain some control or termination of freedom over an individual. When an officer's use of force terminates an individual's freedom in some significant or meaningful way, the officer's action can be understood as a Fourth Amendment *seizure* of the person. An arrest, for example, is a use of force that represents a seizure; the arrest—a type of intentional seizure—terminates someone's freedom. Sometimes an officer may briefly detain someone, such as when stopping and frisking someone; this police action also terminates someone's freedom, however temporary that stop (or seizure) might be. And so does an officer's use of deadly force—in which an officer has asserted control and terminated someone's freedom, the consequences of which may be deadly.

So why is the word *seizure* so important? The Fourth Amendment speaks of the right of the people to be secure in their persons against unreasonable searches and *seizures*. U.S. Const., amend. IV, cl. 1 states, "The right of the people to be secure in their persons, houses, papers, and effects, against unreasonable searches and seizures, shall not be violated. ..." In other words, the government, through the police, must respect a person's inalienable right to be secure *against unreasonable* searches and *seizures* by the government. Any such seizure, by its very nature, must therefore be reasonable. The reasonableness standard extends to the underlying justification of whether to use force and how such force is applied. The Fourth Amendment's first clause, however, does not further define what a reasonable or unreasonable seizure is, but the Fourth Amendment's second clause, which establishes the warrant requirement, insists that "no Warrants shall issue, but upon *probable cause*, supported by Oath or affirmation, and particularly describing the place to be searched, and the persons or things to be *seized*" (emphasis added). Warrants, of course, include an arrest warrant, which clearly authorizes a seizure—one of a person by police. All such seizures must be reasonable. Admittedly, the Fourth Amendment does not elaborate on the meaning and full application of the reasonableness standard in the context of seizures and the use of force. That role has been left to the U.S. Supreme Court.

The Supreme Court addressed Fourth Amendment use-of-force standards in *Graham v. Connor* (1989). The court defined a constitutional standard in determining whether an officer has used excessive—and, hence, unreasonable—force. Under *Graham v. Connor*, police use of force is judged against an "objective reasonableness standard" required by the Fourth Amendment. The court stated that determining "whether the use of force to effect a particular seizure is 'reasonable' under the Fourth Amendment requires a careful balancing of the nature and quality of the intrusion on the individual's Fourth Amendment interests against the countervailing governmental interests at stake ..." (*Graham v. Connor*, 1989, pp. 396–397). Police departments' use-of-force policies must meet or exceed these standards. What follows are some key excerpts taken from the *Graham v. Connor* decision. These bullets help inform police and community how to evaluate an officer's use of force in a manner consistent with Fourth Amendment standards. I believe that all citizens, not just police, should have some familiarity with constitutional standards that govern police use of force, including that which is deadly:

- Our Fourth Amendment jurisprudence has long recognized that the right to make an arrest or investigatory stop necessarily carries with it the right to use some degree of physical coercion or threat thereof to effect it. ...
- Because "[t]he test of reasonableness under the Fourth Amendment is not capable of precise definition or mechanical application" ... its proper application requires careful attention to the facts and circumstances of each case, including the severity of the crime at issue, whether the suspect poses an immediate threat to the safety of the officers or others, and whether he is actively resisting arrest or attempting to evade arrest by flight. ...
- The "reasonableness" of a particular use of force must be judged from the perspective of a reasonable officer on the scene, rather than with the 20/20 vision of hindsight.
- With respect to a claim of excessive force, the same standard of reasonableness at the moment applies: "Not every push or shove, even if it may later seem unnecessary in the peace of a judge's chambers" ... violates the Fourth

Amendment. The calculus of reasonableness must embody allowance for the fact that police officers are often forced to make split-second judgments—in circumstances that are tense, uncertain, and rapidly evolving—about the amount of force that is necessary in a particular situation (*Graham v. Connor*, 1989, pp. 396–397).

As in other Fourth Amendment contexts, however, the "reasonableness" inquiry in an excessive force case is an objective one: The question is whether the officers' actions are "objectively reasonable" in light of the facts and circumstances confronting them, without regard to their underlying intent or motivation. An officer's bad or suspect intentions will not make a Fourth Amendment violation out of an objectively reasonable use of force, and an officer's good intentions will not make an objectively unreasonable use of force constitutional (*Graham v. Connor*, 1989, pp. 396–397).

In *Kingsley v. Hendrickson*, 576 U.S. 389 (2015), the U.S. Supreme Court cited some considerations that helped assess whether officers at a county jail had used objectively reasonable force when they removed a detainee from a cell after a detainee had refused to comply with their instructions. The detainee, Kingsley, had filed a civil lawsuit filed under 42 U.S.C. 1983, arguing that officers had used excessive force. In its decision, the Supreme Court cited an opinion by Judge Friendly for the Second Circuit Court of Appeals that involved a pretrial detainee's excessive force claim, which included these considerations:

- the officers' need for the use of force;
- the relationship between the extent of injury inflicted and the amount of force that was used;
- the extent of the injury; and
- whether force was applied in a good faith effort to maintain or restore discipline or maliciously and sadistically for the very purpose of causing harm *Kingsley v. Hendrickson*, 576 U.S. __2015 p. 12 found at https://www.justice.gov/sites/default/files/crt/legacy/2015/06/25/kingsleydecision.pdf.

While the cited cases involved jail settings, these considerations can help frame how to assess the reasonableness of an officer's actions in other circumstances involving the use of force—and whether the intentional use of force crossed "the constitutional line" (id). But to reiterate, whatever decision an officer makes involving the use of force, including deadly force, must be objectively reasonable.

Turning to the use of deadly force, what if an officer's otherwise reasonable assessment to use deadly force at the moment is wrong based on information learned *after* the incident—in 20/20 hindsight? What about a suspect who points a nonfunctioning Russian AK-47 assault rifle and threatens an officer? Would the officer's decision to fire their weapons under these circumstances, believing an assault weapon was about to be used against them, be deemed unreasonable or reasonable? The latter, of course. What this example illustrates is that some very reasonable decisions made in the heat of the moment may later be proven wrong *in fact*. What matters, however, is whether the officer's decision was reasonable "at the moment" the threat presented itself.

A more common circumstance, one filled with ambiguity and variations, occurs when officers see a suspect who appears to reach for a gun. This can happen after officers have ordered a suspect to stop, the suspect refuses and continues running, and, during the chase, the suspect appears to be reaching for an object—possibly a gun—in a waistband. Officers then fire their weapons and seriously wound or kill the suspect. Later investigation reveals that the object was a cell phone, a ubiquitous object of the modern world. Were the officer's actions and decision to use deadly force reasonable under the facts and circumstances at the time? Even more complex, if not legally but ethically or morally, is when *an officer's actions* themselves leading up to the decision to use force create an unstable and dangerous environment in which deadly force would more likely be used, even if it was deemed reasonable and necessary "at the moment." This is a developing area of study and debate, an area in which sound police policies may lessen the need to use deadly or other forms of force. Police should be mindful of being perceived as creating their own emergencies in which dangers are greatly—and perhaps unnecessarily—magnified by the tactics they elect to use.

For example, suppose officers execute a no-knock search warrant to search for drugs in a home implicated in a low-level drug investigation. No-knock warrants, authorized by a judge, allow police to ignore the typical requirement to announce their presence and purpose before making unconsented entry into a residence. And suppose that police, unaware of who may be inside, decide to execute the no-knock warrant at 2 a.m. Also unaware to police, occupants lawfully possess weapons. The use of deadly force and potential for danger to all involved rise exponentially compared to risks associated with the daytime execution of an ordinary search warrant involving police first knocking and announcing their presence and purpose and waiting for a reasonable time before making unconsented, forced entry. It should be noted that some states, such as Virginia, ban no-knock search warrants as a matter of state, not constitutional law (HB 5099, 2020).

To be clear, officers are not *required* to use deadly force when presented with a meaningful threat to themselves or others; they are not death squads meting out some perverse form of justice. The use of deadly force *is* a discretionary act to protect themselves and others as they perform lawfully authorized activities. But an officer's failure to use deadly force may also imperil the officer and result in death or serious bodily injury to themselves and others, including innocent lives. An officer may use deadly force only when necessary—that is, when the officer has probable cause or a reasonable belief that the suspect poses a significant threat of death or serious physical injury to the officer or others. This is easier to state than to apply.

That police have lawful authority to use force is not in dispute. But they must use it consistent with abstract legal standards, founded on a reasonableness standard that the Fourth Amendment imposes. Within this vacuum between police authority and its proper implementation lies officer discretion. Discretion implies that an officer makes choices that not every officer, faced with similar circumstances, will necessarily follow. Authority and power lie within this space, but this power can be abused (Vanagunas, 1974, p. 505). So while officers retain discretion in whether and what force to use, they must not abuse their discretion, as their choices will later be measured by a more objective although abstract standard of Fourth Amendment reasonableness. A central concern, then, is how to better ensure that officers make sound choices for all concerned, including officers themselves, the object of their use of force, and the community. In short, what options exist?

For example, a city police department could require its officers to always recite phrases, such as "Stop, or I'll shoot," before discharging a weapon even though no such specific Fourth Amendment standard requires such statement. But as noted above, any such deadly force policy cannot be *less* restrictive than baseline Fourth Amendment standards—it may be only more restrictive. An example of a deadly force policy found wanting—in this case, founded on state law—occurred when a Tennessee police officer followed state law and shot a fleeing felon who admittedly posed no threat to him. The case was *Tennessee v. Garner*, 471 U.S. 1 (1985), in which the Supreme Court examined a police officer's use of deadly force when the officer relied on a Tennessee law *that permitted officers to shoot fleeing felons*.

In the *Tennessee v. Garner* case, someone reported to police that a burglary was in progress. Two police officers responded to the scene, and one of them, Officer Elton Hymon, saw Edward Eugene Garner, the suspect. Officer Hymon described Garner as a 17- or 18-year-old male, about 5 feet 5 inches (in.) or 5 feet 7 in. tall. Garner was, in fact, age 15, but the officer's estimate of Garner's age was not central to the decision. Officer Hymon saw no sign that Garner was carrying a weapon, and based on these facts, he was "reasonably sure" that Garner was not armed. The Court described what happened next:

> While Garner was crouched at the base of the fence, Hymon called out "police, halt" and took a few steps toward him. Garner then began to

climb over the fence. Convinced that, if Garner made it over the fence, he would elude capture ... Hymon shot him. The bullet hit Garner in the back of the head. Garner was taken by ambulance to a hospital, where he died on the operating table. Ten dollars and a purse taken from the house were found on his body (p. 4).

Hymon justified his actions based on a Tennessee law that authorized a police officer to "use all the necessary means to effect the arrest," if "after notice of the intention to arrest the defendant, he either flee or forcibly resist" (Tenn. Code Ann. 40–7–108, 1982). As the Supreme Court noted, Tennessee courts construed this statute to allow the use of deadly force "only if a police officer has probable cause to believe that a person has committed a felony, the officer warns the person that he intends to arrest him, and the officer reasonably believes that no means less than such force will prevent the escape" (p.24).

Garner's father then filed a civil lawsuit in the Federal District Court for the Western District of Tennessee, in which he sought monetary damages under 42 U.S.C. 1983 for asserted violations of his son's constitutional rights. The federal district court found that the Tennessee law was constitutional and that the Officer Hymon "had employed the only reasonable and practicable means of preventing Garner's escape." As applied, the Tennessee law gave Officer Hymon the discretion to make such a fateful choice. The Supreme Court then examined the constitutionality of the Tennessee statute as applied here.

The Supreme Court found that within the meaning of the Fourth Amendment, Officer Hymon had "seized" Garner when he shot him. As this was deemed a Fourth Amendment seizure, the Court applied Fourth Amendment standards in examining the Tennessee law and the officer's reliance on this law to use deadly force. In delivering the majority opinion, Justice Byron White wrote:

> This case requires us to determine the constitutionality of the use of deadly force to prevent the escape of an apparently unarmed suspected felon. We conclude that such force may not be used unless it is necessary to prevent the escape and the officer has probable cause to believe that the suspect poses a significant threat of death or serious physical injury to the officer or others (p. 1).

The Court explained that the use of deadly force to prevent the escape of "an apparently unarmed felon" did not meet a constitutional standard even if it met the standard in the Tennessee law that then existed. As Justice White wrote, "It is not better that all felony suspects die than that they escape" (*Tennessee v. Garner*, 1985, p. 11). A portion of Justice White's opinion demands further mention:

> Where the suspect poses no immediate threat to the officer and no threat to others, the harm resulting from failing to apprehend him does not justify the use of deadly force to do so. It is no doubt unfortunate when a suspect who is in sight escapes, but the fact that the police arrive a little late or are a little slower afoot does not always justify killing the suspect. A police officer may not seize an unarmed, nondangerous suspect by shooting him dead. The Tennessee statute is unconstitutional insofar as it authorizes the use of deadly force against such fleeing suspects.
>
> It is not, however, unconstitutional on its face. Where the officer has probable cause to believe that the suspect poses a threat of serious physical harm, either to the officer or to others, it is not constitutionally unreasonable to prevent escape by using deadly force. Thus, if the suspect threatens the officer with a weapon or there is probable cause to believe that he has committed a crime involving the infliction or threatened infliction of serious physical harm, deadly force may be used if necessary to prevent escape, and if, where feasible, some warning has been given. As applied in such circumstances, the Tennessee statute would pass constitutional muster (*Tennessee v. Garner*, 1985, pp. 11–12).

Note the resemblance in the language of the U.S. Department of Justice's (1995) deadly force policy (1995) to language in the *Graham v. Connor* and *Tennessee v. Garner* decisions, which states in part:

> Law enforcement officers … of the Department of Justice may use deadly force only when necessary, that is, when the officer has a reasonable belief that the subject of such force poses an imminent danger of death or serious physical injury to the officer or to another person.

Nationally, police chiefs and police departments have wrestled with developing use-of-force (including deadly force) policies that build upon the Supreme Court's legal foundation. Many departments broaden use-of-force policies to more plainly incorporate practices and beliefs that embody core ethical standards and values. Admittedly, legal standards in the *Tennessee v. Graham* and *Garner v. Connor* decisions are not a "how-to" guide for the use of force, but they supply a framework upon which to develop training scenarios, standards, and considerations to guide an officer's decision-making.

Reimagining and Broadening Use-of-Force Standards

In March 2016, the Police Executive Research Forum (PERF), a research organization that focuses on critical policing issues, published *Guiding Principles on Use of Force*. Founded in 1976, PERF has identified best practices on such issues as reducing police use of force, developing community and problem-oriented policing, using technologies to deliver police services to the community, and developing and assessing crime reduction strategies. In its published guidance document, PERF set forth 30 principles, better known as the *PERF 30*; these 30 principles are *not laws* but guiding principles drawn from many sources, especially the United Kingdom (U.K.). The PERF 30 is complemented by a five-step Critical Decision-Making Model (CDM). The CDM is based on the National Decision Model, which has been used in the U.K. for several years. PERF's CDM is designed to meet the needs of U.S. police agencies and strengthen their critical thinking in a safe and effective manner (PERF 30, 2016, pp. 79–87). Some critics note that police in the U.S. face more readily available guns among the population and that they suffer far more deaths while in the line of duty than their U.K. counterparts. For example, in 2015 officers in the U.S. were six times more likely to be killed in the line of duty. Moreover, unlike the U.S., knives were the most common weapon wielded against police in the U.K. (HLSBuzz.org, 2016). See "Is PERF's 30 guiding principles the answer to excessive force?" for a fuller examination.

A circular diagram with connecting arrows depicts how the CDM works. Using CDM, officers begin by collecting information and assessing the situation, threats, and risks. In doing so, they must be mindful of authorized police powers and agency policy. After identifying options about whether and how to use force, officers select the best course of action, at which point they must act, review, and reassess as needed. Throughout the course of events, officers must be mindful of ethical standards, values, proportionality of response to a perceived threat, and the sanctity of human life. In a sense, the PERF 30, together with the CDM model, are both practical and aspirational. They are also ambitious, requiring considerable time, effort, expense, and long-term commitment to training and practice. Many would argue this is money well-spent. In a commentary about the PERF 30, former Hampton Police (Virginia) Police Chief Terry Sult shared these observations (Wexler, 2016):

> I think what the Supreme Court did in *Graham v. Connor* was give us
> an opportunity. What we have failed to realize is that they have given
> us the objective reasonable officer standard.

Who defines what the reasonable person standard is? We do, through policy, equipment, training and the teachings. ... If we don't refine and evolve what the reasonable person standard is through these initiatives ... the courts are going to do it for us. ... So I don't think there is a conflict between what the Court is doing and what we're doing here [in the PERF 30] (p. 17).

Critics aside, the PERF 30 deserves review and consideration, as many police departments have embraced all or parts of these values. A handful of notable PERF 30 (2016) principles follow (original emphases), along with my brief commentary. Policies 1–4 of the full report can be found at the link in the "References" section.

Policy 1: The *sanctity of human life* should be at the heart of everything an agency does (p. 34).

The first policy guides all others—it states a clear recognition of the sanctity of human life and, with it, the importance of treating all persons with dignity and respect.

Policy 2: Agencies should continue to develop best policies, practices, and training on use-of-force issues that go beyond the minimum requirements of *Graham v. Connor* (p. 35).

Use-of-force policies evolve over time and with experience. Change may be prompted by court decisions, scholarship, evidence-based findings, changing community standards, and even emerging technologies.

Policy 3: Police use of force must meet the test of *proportionality* (p. 38).

How an officer responds to a threat is at the heart of controversies surrounding the use of force. That's where the test of proportionality leans in. Policy 3's commentary poses these questions for an officer to consider:

- Am I using only the level of force necessary to mitigate the threat and safely achieve a lawful objective?
- Is there another, less injurious option available that will allow me to achieve the same objective as effectively and safely?
- Will my actions be viewed as appropriate—by my agency and by the general public—given the severity of the threat and totality of the circumstances (PERF, 2016, p. 38)?

Policy 3's discussion section insists this policy should *not* be understood that when officers decide what force "is necessary and appropriate to mitigate a threat ... *should stop and consider how their actions will be viewed by others*" (emphasis added; p. 38). What is deemed proportional should begin as officers approach an incident and continue throughout their decision-making. As always, police must consider the totality of the circumstances they face. How the public will view police actions "is not meant to be a 'check-the-box' step taken immediately before an officer uses force" (p. 39). If nothing else, the test of proportionality requires that officers consider and train on use of force from a broader perspective. However, proportionality should not be reduced to a mechanical, recipe-like approach to the use of force, where the "right" answer is self-evident in 20/20 hindsight. But it does encourage officers to ask hard questions. Regarding proportionality, Police Scotland Sergeant Jim Young poses the question, "Why use a sledgehammer to crack a nut?" And to him, the final question is "Was the force used the minimum amount or least injurious to achieve that lawful aim?" (PERF, 2016, p. 40). Some officers may balk at such an exacting requirement; the U.S. Supreme Court has not yet expressly imposed a "least injurious" option upon its Fourth Amendment calculation of reasonableness.

Policy 4: Adopt *de-escalation* as formal agency policy.

De-escalation policy and training figure prominently in efforts to minimize the likelihood of officers even needing to use force, let alone excessive force. But what is de-escalation? In the *National Consensus Policy and Discussion Paper on Use of Force* (2017), a collaborative effort among 11 of the most significant law enforcement and labor organizations in the U.S. and published by the International Chiefs of Police (IACP), defines *de-escalation* as:

> Taking action or communicating verbally or non-verbally during a potential force encounter in an attempt to stabilize the situation and reduce the immediacy of the threat so that more time, options, and resources can be called upon to resolve the situation without the use of force or with a reduction in the force necessary. De-escalation may include the use of such techniques as command presence, advisements, warning verbal persuasion, and tactical repositioning (p. 2).

Arnold Ventures, in partnership with the IACP, funded a study on de-escalation conducted by researchers from the University of Cincinnati and University of Nevada, Las Vegas. Although the evidence adduced in the research did not clearly reveal the effectiveness of de-escalation—more research is needed—the authors concluded that as it stands:

> De-escalation training is a promising practice; that is, a well-intended police reform whose consequences are largely unknown. While there are value-based and theoretical reasons to support de-escalation train-

ing, these are not solid empirical reasons. Based on accumulating anecdotes, professional expertise, and the limited, though generally positive trends identified in this systematic review across disciplines, we are confident that de-escalation training offers another valuable tool for individuals responding to incidents of crisis, aggression, or violence. However, recommendations that de-escalation must be used as a primary tool should await additional evidence regarding its effectiveness and any unintended consequences that may impact officer and public safety (pp. 33–34).

The authors acknowledged that police executives should not be expected to wait for further research to keep pace with mounting support and use of de-escalation training. The full report can be found at the link in the "References" section.

It takes little effort to find various use-of-force policies among law enforcement agencies, some of which adopt parts of the PERF 30. For a sample deadly force policy, see the Minneapolis Police Department's policy and procedures manual (the link is provided in the "References" section).

Policies such as these are designed to help officers make sound, reasonable decisions to protect themselves and others in a manner that promotes community trust in police. It is critical that all participants who debate or evaluate use-of-force policies or specific police actions recognize their complexity and ambiguity as they search for answers.

Collecting Data on Use of Force

There is widespread agreement that the use of force, especially deadly force, by police has momentous consequences to both community trust and the effectiveness of police. It is no surprise that there are efforts to systematically capture police use-of-force data at local, state, and national levels. For example, in partnership with law enforcement agencies, the FBI created a national use-of-force database in 2015 and began collecting data from law enforcement agencies on January 1, 2019. Participating police and investigative agencies are asked to supply incident, subject, and officer information in a series of questions and basic data requests. As noted in its website (the link is provided in the "References" section), the data collection includes:

- National-level statistics on law enforcement use-of-force incidents
- Basic information on the circumstances, subjects, and officers involved

The FBI website states that this collection effort "offers big-picture insights, rather than information on specific incidents" and, notably, "does not assess or report whether officers followed their department's policy or acted lawfully" (FBI, n.d.). Many in law enforcement believe such data could enhance transparency and improve police training. But some remain skeptical about its overall success given the challenges of systematically collecting such data from more than 18,000 state and local law enforcement agencies in the U.S. for a database in which participation is *voluntary*. Time will tell.

In the meantime, there are many questions and perspectives concerning the data that should be collected at local levels beyond those data sought in the FBI's national database. For example, Jim Cervera, a distinguished former Virginia Beach (VA) police chief, noted that departments might want to collect annual data about the number of times officers did *not* discharge a weapon when pointing one at a person. These numbers could be compared to the number of times officers discharged a weapon. There are many other sources of data that might capture how officers use force, especially in the context of arrests. For example, was a person charged with a serious crime arrested with or without incident? Or was a person who resisted arrest arrested with minimal force; if not, what level of force was used? Collecting and then sharing some or all such data—a form of transparency—is another opportunity for police to strengthen public trust and support. This is an area ripe for further study and collaboration.

Review Questions

1. If you were an officer planning to arrest someone wanted for attempted murder and bank robbery who is now believed to be sharing a residence with a violent ex-felon and is employed at Target, what might you consider in planning for and executing the arrest itself, including resources and how to respond to an accusee's actions when being confronted? Consider all options.
2. Review the use-of-force continuum above. Do you think officers should always abide by it? Why or why not?
3. Why is evaluating the proper use of force so difficult?
4. What is the Fourth Amendment legal standard for using force, including deadly force?
5. Do you believe the four-listed PERF policies should be adopted by all police departments? Why or why not?
6. Should a community have access to all police department use of force policies? Argue from both perspectives.
7. After reading this chapter, what do you believe are the most important skills and qualities for an officer to possess?

8. In addition to questions and data sought in the FBI's database, what other use-of-force questions or data might a local police department want to collect? And what data should be shared with a community?

References

Attorney general October 17, 1995 memorandum on resolution 14. (1995, October 1995). U.S. Department of Justice. https://www.justice.gov/archives/ag/attorney-general-october-17-1995-memorandum-resolution-14-attachment-0

BBC News. (2019, February 18). *North Korea's human rights: What's not being talked about.* https://www.bbc.com/news/world-asia-44234505

CHAPTER 31. An Act to amend and reenact § 19.2-56 of the Code of Virginia, relating to search warrants; provide notice of authority. HB 5099. (2020, October 28.) https://lis.virginia.gov/cgi-bin/legp604.exe?202+ful+CHAP0031

Ellis, J. J. (2000). *Founding brothers: The revolutionary generation.* Vintage Books.

Engel, R. S., McManus, H. D., and Herold, T. D. (2020). Does de-escalation training work? *Criminology & Public Policy, 19*(3), 721–759. https://doi.org/10.1111/1745-9133.12467

FBI. (n.d.). *National use-of-force data collection.* https://www.fbi.gov/services/cjis/ucr/use-of-force

Graham v. Connor, 490 U.S. 386 (1989). https://supreme.justia.com/cases/federal/us/490/386/

HLSBuzz.org. (2016, May 9). *Is PERF's 30 guiding principles the answer to excessive force?* Homeland Security, Medium. https://medium.com/homeland-security/is-perfs-30-guiding-principles-the-answer-to-excessive-force-eaff65049d3d

Human Rights Watch. (2019). *North Korea: Events of 2018.* https://www.hrw.org/world-report/2019/country-chapters/north-korea

International Chiefs of Police (IACP). (2017, October). *National consensus policy and discussion paper on use of force.* https://www.theiacp.org/sites/default/files/2020-07/National_Consensus_Policy_On_Use_Of_Force%2007102020%20v3.pdf

Kingsley v. Hendrickson, 576 U.S. 389 (2015). https://supreme.justia.com/cases/federal/us/576/14-6368/

Minneapolis Police Department. (2021, April 4). *The Minneapolis Police Department policy and procedure manual.* https://www.minneapolismn.gov/me-

dia/-www-content-assets/documents/MPD-Policy-and-Procedure-Manual.
pdf

National Institute of Justice, Office of Justice Programs. (2009, August 3). *The use-of-force continuum.* https://nij.ojp.gov/topics/articles/use-force-continuum

Orwell, G. (1983). *Nineteen eighty-four (1983 ed.).* Houghton Mifflin Harcourt.

Peel, R. (1829). *Nine principles of policing.*

Police Executive Research Forum (PERF). (2016 March). PERF's 30 Guiding Principles on Use of Force. *Guiding Principles on Use of Force,* 33–78.

Police Executive Research Forum (PERF). (2016, March). *Guiding principles on use of force.* Critical Issues in Policing series. https://www.policeforum.org/assets/30%20guiding%20principles.pdf

Smith, L. (2018, October 18). *I Was a Cop for 18 Years. I Witnessed and Participated in Abuses of Power.* Medium. https://gen.medium.com/i-was-a-cop-for-18-years-i-witnessed-and-participated-in-abuses-of-power-8d057c18f9ee.

Tennessee Code Title 40. Criminal Procedure § 40-7-108 (1982). https://codes.findlaw.com/tn/title-40-criminal-procedure/tn-code-sect-40-7-108.html

Tennessee v. Garner, 471 U.S. 1 (1985). https://supreme.justia.com/cases/federal/us/471/1/

U.S. Const., amend. IV, cl. 1.

Vanagunas, S. (1974). Toward checks and balances of police authority. *Marquette Law Review,* 57(3), 505–514. https://scholarship.law.marquette.edu/mulr/vol57/iss3/3

Wexler, C. (2016, March). Why we need to challenge conventional thinking on police use of force. *Guiding Principles on Use of Force,* 4–32. Police Executive Research Forum.

Image Credit

Facing the Legacy of Racism, Bias, and Inequality with Clarity, Purpose, and Action

Image 8

Peel Principle 5: The police seek and preserve public favor, not by pandering to public opinion, but by constantly demonstrating absolutely impartial service to law, in complete independence of policy, and without regard to the justice or injustice of the substance of individual laws, by ready offering of individual service and friendship to all members of the public without regard to their race or social standing, by ready exercise of courtesy and friendly good humor, and by ready offering of individual sacrifice in protecting and preserving life.

> *"We hold these truths to be self-evident, that all men are created equal, that they are endowed by their Creator with certain unalienable Rights, that among these are Life, Liberty and the pursuit of Happiness."* Declaration of Independence, 1776

"What, to the American slave, is your Fourth of July? I answer: a day that reveals to him, more than all other days in the year, the gross injustice and cruelty to which he is the constant victim. To him, your celebration is a sham; your boasted liberty, an unholy license; your national greatness, swelling vanity; your sounds of rejoicing are empty and heartless; your denunciation of tyrants, brass-fronted impudence; your shouts of liberty and equality, hollow mockery; your prayers and hymns, your sermons and thanksgivings, with all your religious parade and solemnity, mere bombast, fraud, deception, impiety, and hypocrisy—a thin veil to cover up crimes which would disgrace a nation of savages." Frederick Douglass, speech given at an event commemorating the signing of the Declaration of Independence held at Rochester's (New York) Corinthian Hall on July 5, 1852) in which he told his audience, "This Fourth of July is yours, not mine. You may rejoice, I must mourn"

Author's Introductory Note

As a white male born in the 1950s, I have not suffered the indignities and violence of racism; I have only witnessed them, too often from a comfortable distance. In the 1960s, I was not old enough to fully grasp the courage and struggles of civil rights leaders as they demanded change. I could only dimly sense their struggle to maintain self-control amidst their anger at the injustices. And I heard racist jokes and references among my parents' generation and knew that they were wrong, but I didn't directly challenge them. And I saw and continue to see the "casual" insensitivities, cruelties, and stark reminders of racism, from the names of Confederate figures (they are not "heroes" to all Americans) emblazoned on the public square to the casual, dehumanizing violence of too many police-citizen encounters captured on film and reported upon almost daily. I have long known that something very deep, very fundamental in society was flawed and wrong. The moral injustice is only too plain. But I now see younger, diverse generations who declaim the evils of racism that African Americans have decried for centuries, specifically in the context of police abuse and use of excessive force. My students are among them, and they give me fresh and intense perspectives on what is at stake and what cannot be ignored. That said, I do not write as a subject matter "expert" or scholar on racism. I can only do my best in sharing some observations and approaches to policing in the very real context of racism past and present and hope that others join the conversation and find ways to move beyond all-too-often entrenched attitudes and beliefs.

Slavery, Race, Inequality, and Law

Chapter 1 began by examining the legacy of slavery and racism in police work. Slavery, racism, and persistent inequalities also left enduring legacies in our nation's laws. First, read art. I, § 9, cl. 1 of the original U.S. Constitution of 1787, better known as the *Slave Trade Clause*:

> The Migration or Importation of such Persons as any of the States now existing shall think proper to admit, shall not be prohibited by the Congress prior to the Year one thousand eight hundred and eight, but a Tax or duty may be imposed on such Importation, not exceeding ten dollars for each Person.

Note that the word *slavery* does not appear in the Slave Trade Clause. Instead, the clause prohibited for 20 years any attempt by the *federal* government from limiting the importation of "persons" by existing state slave-holding governments. To be clear, "persons" were then understood primarily as enslaved African persons. To illustrate its effect, during this 20-year period the federal government could *not* pass a law that would prevent South Carolina or any other slave-holding state from importing slaves. The 20-year lifespan of the Slave Trade Clause, a political compromise between southern states and states that either abolished or contemplated abolishing slavery, remains a sad and shameful legacy.

Although the *importation* of slaves formally ended in 1808, slavery within and among states persisted as a "legal" institution five more decades, until the advent of the Civil War. The Declaration of Independence's avowed belief that "all men are created equal" could not be reconciled with the continued, sanctioned existence of slavery. In fact, in 1777 a "forgotten Black Founding Father," Prince Hall, made a similar point when he petitioned the Massachusetts legislature requesting emancipation and invoked "the resonant phrases and founding truths of the Declaration itself" (Hall, 2021).

During and after the Civil War (1861–1865), the U.S. government began to formally address the institution of slavery and its legacy. The Emancipation Proclamation, issued by President Abraham Lincoln on January 1, 1863, did not end slavery; it "freed only slaves held in the eleven Confederate states that had seceded, and only in the portion of those states not already under Union control" (Greene & McAward, 2021).

After the Civil War, three constitutional amendments, the Thirteenth, Fourteenth, and Fifteenth, addressed the abolition of slavery and the equal protection of the law in response to the historical oppression and brutality against Black people. The speed and efficacy of their impact, however, has been challenged. The first of these, the Thirteenth Amendment, was passed by Congress on January 31, 1865, and ratified by all states by December 6, 1865, nine months after the Civil War. The Thirteenth Amendment (1865) provides:

> **Section 1.** Neither slavery nor involuntary servitude, except as a punishment for crime whereof the party shall have been duly convicted, shall exist within the United States, or any place subject to their jurisdiction.

> **Section 2.** Congress shall have the power to enforce this article by appropriate legislation.

The Thirteenth Amendment abolished the most obvious and malevolent form of racism—slavery, something the Framers failed to address when the U.S. Constitution was ratified, an indelible stain in our nation's history. The amendment was a necessary and critical step forward. Congress in fact required former Confederate states to ratify the Thirteenth Amendment before they could regain federal representation. The Thirteenth Amendment also ensured that no state could reinstitute slavery through a revised state constitution.

Ratified three years later in 1868, U.S. Const., amend. 14, § 1 more broadly addressed discrimination. It provides:

> No State shall make or enforce any law which shall abridge the privileges or immunities of citizens of the United States; nor shall any State deprive any person of life, liberty, or property, without due process of law; nor deny to any person within its jurisdiction the equal protection of the laws.

The Fourteenth Amendment's specific purpose was to stop states from making or enforcing laws that would discriminate against Black people. The Fourteenth Amendment made clear that newly freed Black people were American citizens, something shamefully obvious in retrospect.

The Fourteenth Amendment's passage did not slow the enactment and enforcement of discriminatory laws among states. As state legislatures passed Jim Crow laws, segregation, a form of discrimination, flourished from the 1880s to the 1960s. Jim Crow laws institutionalized segregation and the unequal treatment of Black people in all facets of life, from busing to child custody to access to bathrooms to hair care to cohabitation to burial. The National Park Service (2018) provides an informative sampling of such laws. In this context it is important to remember that enforcement of Jim Crow laws often relied upon forcible *police* action directed toward Black people. Moreover, courts failed to intervene and too often, in the enforcement and punishment meted out through these unjust laws, were also complicit in the perpetuation of racism.

In 1896 this failure was especially clear when the U.S. Supreme Court examined a Louisiana law known as the *Separate Car Act*, which required separate railway cars for Black and White people. The case of course is *Plessy v. Ferguson* (1896). The basic facts are as follows: Homer Plessy (seven-eighths Caucasian) agreed to participate in a test to challenge the Separate Car Act. Plessy did so by sitting in a "Whites-only" car of a Louisiana train. When Plessy boarded the Whites-only car, he was told to vacate, but when he refused, he was arrested by police. Plessy was later convicted. He appealed the decision, claiming the act violated the Fourteenth Amendment's Equal Protection Clause. In a 7–1 majority decision, the Supreme Court stated that equal but separate accommodations for Black and White people did not violate the Equal Protection Clause. In short, the Court held that the Separate Car Act was constitutional, thus upholding Louisiana's state-imposed racial segregation. Justice Henry Brown, who wrote the majority opinion, conceded that the Fourteenth Amendment established equality for the races before the law but stated that separate treatment did not imply the inferiority of Black people. In his lone dissent, Justice John Marshall Harlan argued that the Constitution was color-blind, the United States had no class system, and, accordingly, all citizens should have equal access to civil rights. Justice Harlan was right.

In an *Atlantic* article entitled "The American Nightmare," Ibram X. Kendi pointed out that on May 19, 1896, "*The New York Times* allocated a single sentence on page 3 to reporting the U.S. Supreme Court's *Plessy v. Ferguson* decision." He further noted, "Constitutionalizing Jim Crow hardly made news in 1896. There was no there there. Americans already knew that equal rights had been lynched; *Plessy* was just the silently staged funeral." Think about the significance of this decision, whether as an adult, as a citizen, as a Black, or as a police officer. The highest court in the land gave its judicial imprimatur to racial segregation and, with it, the mechanisms behind it—the criminal justice system—a system that perpetuated racism and segregation. No one, especially police officers cloaked with state power and authority, should forget this history. At the same time, no one should ignore the modern Supreme Court's steady expansion of the Fourteenth Amendment's Equal Protection Clause since *Plessy*. Professor Brian T. Fitzpatrick of Vanderbilt Law School and Theodore M. Shaw, professor of law and director of the Center for Civil Rights at the University of North Carolina School of Law, wrote (2021):

> Although the original purpose was to protect [Black people] from discrimination, the broad wording has led the Supreme Court to hold

that all racial discrimination (including against whites, Hispanics, Asians, and Native Americans) is constitutionally suspect.

Since the 1960s, the Supreme Court had (not *has* as it is a steady, continuing expansion?) applied the Equal Protection Clause of the Fourteenth Amendment to prohibit states from passing laws that discriminate on bases besides race, particularly laws that discriminate against "suspect classifications," such as national origin, gender, immigration status, voting, access to courts, and wedlock status at birth. What this means is that laws that appear to discriminate against certain protected classifications are subject to heightened court scrutiny under the Equal Protection Clause. For a state to defend such laws, it must offer important, compelling reasons to justify their discriminatory nature. And now, following the Supreme Court decision *Obergefell v. Hodges* (2015), it appears that the court will apply the Equal Protection Clause to prohibit discrimination against gays and lesbians.

Moreover, on June 15, 2020, the Supreme Court held that *federal antidiscrimination laws* protect lesbian, bisexual, gay, transgender, and queer (LBGTQ) employees. The ruling clarified that Title VII of the Civil Rights Act of 1964, which prohibits discrimination "because of sex," includes LGBTQ employees. The majority opinion in *Bostock v. Clayton County* (2020), written by Justice Neil Gorsuch, stated in part:

> An employer who fires an individual for being homosexual or transgender fires that person for traits or actions it would not have questioned in members of a different sex. Sex plays a necessary and undisguisable role in the decision, exactly what Title VII forbids.

Laws that prohibit discrimination are not only just and moral, but they stand upon principles in the U.S. Constitution and federal law, such as Title VII of the Civil Rights Act of 1964, either of which are the supreme law of the land under Article VI of the Constitution. All of government must be mindful of the Equal Protection Clause's special importance and related federal and state laws that ban various forms of discrimination.

Then there is the Fifteenth Amendment (1869), enacted in 1870, which addresses race in the context of voting rights:

> **Section 1.** The right of citizens of the United States to vote shall not be denied or abridged by the United States or by any State on account of race, color, or previous condition of servitude.

Section 2. The Congress shall have power to enforce this article by appropriate legislation.

Much like the Fourteenth, Fifteenth Amendment rights and protections—here, voting—were largely "ignored and circumvented for nearly a century" (Pildes & Smith, n.d.). However, for about 20 years after the Fifteenth Amendment's adoption, Black men were permitted to vote, and they exercised their rights in large numbers. Many were elected to public office. In fact, there were 41 Black sheriffs during the post–Civil War Reconstruction Era (Facing History and Ourselves, 1996). But White people reacted swiftly and decisively—through what is known as the *Era of Disenfranchisement*—in which by 1890, states disemboweled Fifteenth Amendment rights and protections. Literacy tests, poll taxes, proof of good character, and other hurdles stood between Black men and their right to vote (and no women could even vote until the ratification of the Nineteenth Amendment in 1920). As a result, Black voting in the South dropped to extremely low levels from 1890 to 1965, despite the promise of the Fifteenth Amendment. So manifest racism lived on, and police and other government officials were part of the cultural fabric and institutions that made this possible. One can argue that a more contemporary version of efforts to deny or restrain voting still exists in various felony disenfranchisement laws and other laws. No matter, as the Voting Rights Act of 1965, directed at such abuses as Jim Crow laws, began to confront this injustice.

The Thirteenth Amendment, the Equal Protection Clause of the Fourteenth Amendment, the Fifteenth Amendment, and various civil rights laws speak to the unmistakable importance of laws that prohibit discrimination. They aim to serve and protect the individual, the community, and, ultimately, the common good. Those in government charged with upholding and enforcing the law should be particularly mindful. In that sense, police are charged with protecting and serving *all* citizens. There is no place for discrimination in policing. The pursuit of equality in human relations is a right and just thing to do, even if a particular citizen does not fall within a not-yet-protected constitutional or statutory classification. Each person, each citizen, deserves to be treated with dignity and respect and in accordance with the law. No exceptions. In exercising their lawful authority or in simple encounters with citizens, officers should act in response to what people do, not in response to who they are. This is what equal protection should look like in a broad sense in everyday policing.

These three amendments carry forward the promise and civic virtue of the Declaration of Independence, which begins:

> We hold these truths to be self-evident, that all men are created equal,
> that they are endowed by their Creator with certain unalienable

Rights, that among these are Life, Liberty and the pursuit of Happiness.—That to secure these rights, Governments are instituted among Men, deriving their just powers from the consent of the governed ... (Jefferson, 1776).

Taken together, they remind us that 1) governments—including police—derive their powers from the consent of the governed; 2) government was "instituted" to "secure these rights"; and 3) "all men are created equal" (Jefferson, 1776), meaning that equal protection of the laws is extended to all in similar cases and circumstances. In this compact, there is no place for policing practices deemed racist or discriminatory.

Racism, the unequal protection of laws, and other forms of discrimination undermine trust and cooperation among police, Black people, and other communities of color. Similarly, racial profiling and implicit or explicit racial bias do grave damage to community trust. On June 10, 2020, the *Washington Post* published a story by Radley Belko in which he compiled overwhelming evidence from various studies and research that indicated racial disparities in outcomes through profiling, higher arrest rates against Black people for misdemeanors and petty crimes, and higher rates for driver's license suspensions, ticket citations, traffic stops, and more. Add to this litany the documented consequences of the war on drugs, about which Belko noted, "Black people are consistently arrested, charged and convicted of drug crimes including possession, distribution and conspiracy at far higher rates than white people. This, despite research showing that both races use and sell drugs at about the same rate." The consequences serve as a gateway to the criminal justice system.

In a June 1996 *FBI Law Enforcement Bulletin* article titled "Combatting Bigotry in Law Enforcement," the authors noted, "Justice, including respect for human dignity and equal standing under the law, is simply antithetical to bigotry." This is more than sensitivity training. It is a "matter of teaching without equivocation the duties of speech and action that are incumbent on police, and of teaching what an oath to uphold the Constitution means" (DeLattre & Schofield, 1996). These are nonnegotiable responsibilities in the hard work of policing.

No matter whether any given police action is *legally* defensible on its face—and the vast majority are—there are practical consequences to anyone cited, arrested, or otherwise processed in the criminal justice system. Given the disparate outcomes described above, Black people find themselves enmeshed in the criminal justice system too often. By its very nature, the criminal justice system is an adversarial one. Look at criminal complaints or charges, which are captioned with phrases such as "State of Tennessee versus Citizen X." Anyone processed within the criminal justice system will incur real personal costs in time and expense due to missed work or job loss, disruptions in managing a household or caring for others, as well as costs, fines, legal fees, and other expenses stemming from citations or criminal charges. And then, of course, there is the physical and emotional toll among those who are incarcerated, one that extends to families and others who rely on them. Extensive research has documented the deleterious impact and almost incalculable toll of mass incarceration on individuals, their families, and their communities. There even appears to be a political consensus on the evils of overincarceration. Overincarceration or disproportionate incarceration does not serve the common good. Obviously, these observations do not minimize the real harm to victims and their families that results from violent or other serious crimes. The plight of crime victims matters in any calculation of the common good.

Dr. Martin Luther King, Jr.; the Law; and Racism

Dr. Martin Luther King, Jr., wrote powerfully about the role of law and racism in his August 1963 *Letter from Birmingham Jail*. In his response to the question of whether he would condone acts of civil disobedience that might violate the law, Dr. King distinguished between just and unjust laws. Just laws, he argued, must be obeyed. For example, Dr. King would never countenance murder or other clearly malevolent acts because such illegal acts are neither just nor moral. Dr. King explained the difference:

> I would agree with St. Augustine that "An unjust law is no law at all." Now, what is the difference between the two? How does one determine when a law is just or unjust? A just law is a man-made code that squares with the moral law, or the law of God. An unjust law is a code that is out of harmony with the moral law. To put it in the terms of St. Thomas Aquinas, an unjust law is a human law that is not rooted in eternal and natural law. Any law that uplifts human personality is just. Any law that degrades human personality is unjust.

Dr. King cited examples of unjust laws, such as segregation statutes, "because segregation distorts the soul and damages the personality. It gives the segregator a false sense of superiority and the segregated a false sense of inferiority" (1963). In the same sense, an unjust law is a "code that a majority inflicts on a minority that is not binding on itself" (King, 1963). This last statement speaks to both equality and the role of law. Laws that promote equality or prohibit discrimination are just laws.

In 1967, Dr. King told a group of White politicians attending the Hungry Club Forum at the Butler YMCA in Atlanta that "[in] 1863 the Negro was granted freedom from physical slavery through the Emancipation Proclamation. But he was not given land to make that freedom meaningful" (King, 2020). He next reminded his White audience that in 1875 the nation passed a civil rights bill, but its laws were not enforced. And finally, in referring to that watershed year of 1964 in the civil rights movement, Dr. King lamented that "the nation passed a weaker civil rights bill and even to this day has failed to enforce it in all of its dimensions" (id.). Add to this list of unrealized promises the glacial enforcement of the 1954 Supreme Court decision *Brown v. Board of Education* that outlawed segregation in public schools. The Court, remember, ordered that the states end such segregation with "all deliberate speed" (*Brown v. Board of Education*, 1954). The very vagueness of this standard gave segregationists the opportunity to either resist or slow the advance, and that is what they did. And why again is this significant? Because laws and rights, however aspirational, mean little unless they are understood, embraced, and enforced in letter and spirit. Their protections must be honored—and equally, too. Or, as Supreme Court Justice Robert H. Jackson wrote in a concurring opinion in *Railway Express Agency, Inc. et al. v. New York* (1949), "Courts can take no better measure to assure that laws will be just than to require that laws be equal in operation." So can police.

Our nation's past reminds us that laws and proclamations, including those that *establish and protect civil rights and the equality of* all *citizens*—which Dr. King would describe as just—did not unilaterally abolish the remnants of slavery, let alone racism and its legacy. Just laws aimed at addressing inequality or preserving, protecting, and promoting rights were and are *not self-enforcing*; they require state support and enforcement. When U.S. Supreme Court Justice Neil Gorsuch spoke before the American Bar Association in 2020, he noted that a bill of rights without meaningful enforcement is useless, pointing to his belief that North Korea's bill of rights are more extensive than ours (Boykin & Onyejekwe, 2020). So without engagement and enforcement, their protections are aspirational, if not meaningless. When institutions of government—and that includes police—neglect to honor just laws, citizens and communities who might derive protection and a sense of equality grow skeptical, cynical, and even contemptuous. This compromises individual and community support for the machinery of justice and the rule of law. History has shown that this is not a formula for a free and secure civil society for all people. When there is civil strife or manifest evidence of inequality, institutions of government must honor and enforce such just laws. Lip service is not enough.

Contemporary Examples of Policing and Discrimination

Consider today the consequences of unequal police *enforcement* in the context of race, in particular the practice of stop-and-frisk, which, as I have explained to students, is itself clearly constitutional. As noted in this book, there *is* a legal standard that must be met to justify a lawful *Terry* stop: Police must have "specific and articulable facts" that indicate that the person to be **stopped** is currently or is about to be engaged in criminal activity. There is likewise a legal standard that must be met to justify a lawful frisk for weapons: whether an officer has a reasonable suspicion that the suspect (the person lawfully stopped) is armed and dangerous. Officers, however, sometimes fail to meet legal standards, such as when they stop and frisk a young Black male for no apparent reason other than perhaps the color of his skin—where reasonable suspicion of criminal activity is absent. In these circumstances, police actions appear racist and unlawful. The other constitutional shortcoming occurs when police departments direct their officers to stop and frisk, by custom or policy, communities or individuals where race or ethnicity is a component (or another protected classification group). That, too, is racist and unlawful. These twin concerns were revealed in a successful class-action lawsuit based on allegations of widespread New York City Police Department (NYPD) stop-and-frisk practices against Black and Hispanic people in violation of the Fourth Amendment's prohibition against unreasonable search and seizures and the Fourteenth Amendment's Equal Protection Clause, *Floyd v. City of New York* (2013). The court found that the NYPD made 4.4 million stops over an eight-and-a-half-year period. More than 80% of these 4.4 million stops were of Black or Hispanic people. More than half of the time, the police also frisked those they stopped. Lives were disrupted, too often unnecessarily and unlawfully.

The judge, Federal District Court Judge Shira A. Scheindlin, wrote powerfully about her concerns. In her introduction, she wrote (2013; case citations are omitted):

> New Yorkers are rightly proud of their city and seek to make it as safe as the largest city in America can be. New Yorkers also treasure their liberty. Countless individuals have come to New York in pursuit of that liberty. The goals of liberty and safety may be in tension, but they can coexist—indeed the Constitution mandates it.
>
> Plaintiffs—blacks and Hispanics who were stopped—argue that the NYPD's use of stop and frisk violated their constitutional rights in two ways: (1) they were stopped without a legal basis in violation of the Fourth Amendment, and (2) they were targeted for stops because of their race in violation of the Fourteenth Amendment. ...
>
> ... This case is not about the effectiveness of stop and frisk in deterring or combating crime. This Court's mandate is solely to judge the constitutionality of police behavior, not its effectiveness as a law enforcement tool. Many police practices may be useful for fighting crime—preventive detention or coerced confessions, for example—but because they are unconstitutional, they cannot be used, no matter how effective ...

... This case is about whether the City has a policy or custom of violating the Constitution by making unlawful stops and conducting unlawful frisks.

... While it is true that any one stop is a limited intrusion in duration and deprivation of liberty, each stop is also a demeaning and humiliating experience. No one should live in fear of being stopped whenever he leaves his home to go about the activities of daily life. Those who are routinely subjected to stops are overwhelmingly people of color, and they are justifiably troubled to be singled out when many of them have done nothing to attract the unwanted attention. Some plaintiffs testified that stops make them feel unwelcome in some parts of the City, and distrustful of the police. This alienation cannot be good for the police, the community, or its leaders.

Later in her opinion, Judge Scheindlin wrote (2013):

The idea of universal suspicion without individual evidence is what Americans find abhorrent and what black men in America must constantly fight. It is pervasive in policing policies—like stop-and-frisk, and ... neighborhood watch—regardless of the collateral damage done to the majority of innocents. It's like burning down a house to rid it of mice.

Judge Scheindlin rightly points to the importance of individualized suspicion in any police-citizen encounter before police assert some level of force or authority, particularly physical force. When police actions imply or reveal racial or other forms of discrimination, communities, and individuals suffer, and so does trust.

Racism is not confined to overt physical or verbal abuse by law enforcement officers. It can be subtle and unaccountable. Consider the Federal Bureau of Investigation's (FBI) zealous investigations of Dr. Martin Luther King, Jr., and other Black activists in the 1960s and 1970s. What was often lacking was unmistakable evidence that these groups or individuals were either committing federal crimes or threatening national security, evidence that might otherwise justify an investigation. That left the specter of race as an alternative explanation. Compounding the wrong were illegal or overly aggressive investigative activities, including the use of illegal wiretaps. These and similar investigations by other federal agencies were the subjects of a U.S. Senate committee report documenting the many wrongs directed against Black leaders and others. This Senate committee, later referred to as the Church Committee, was established in 1975 to investigate federal intelligence operations "and determine the extent, if any, to which illegal, improper, or unethical activities were engaged in by any agency of the Federal Government." ("Senate Select Committee to Study Governmental Operations with Respect to Intelligence Activities," 1976). Among other outcomes, the almost immediate aftermath of the Church Committee report was the promulgation of the first version of the attorney general guidelines that limited various FBI activities and operations—representing checks and balances on the abuse of power.

A more recent example of overzealous and illegal police activities was documented in a 2020 article published by ProPublica titled "The Police Have Been Spying on Black Reporters and Activists for Years. I Know Because I'm One of Them." The article was written by Wendi C. Thomas, a Black journalist who has covered police in Memphis. In open federal court, a Memphis Police Department officer admitted that he was spying on Thomas without providing any lawfully sufficient reason why. Thomas's article reveals that she was on a long list of "prominent black journalists and activists who have been subjected to police surveillance over decades." What led to the courtroom drama was a successful lawsuit filed by the American Civil Liberties Union against the Memphis Police Department alleging that the department violated a 1978 consent decree barring surveillance of residents for political purposes. The officer testified that he had used a fake Facebook account to monitor protest activity and follow current events connected to Black Lives Matter (2020). Thomas was unable to obtain clear answers about why she was targeted for surveillance. This type of police activity does no justice to the First Amendment.

I cannot overstate the importance of officers being able to articulate and justify law enforcement actions as they exercise their investigative and coercive powers. Any police action deemed capricious or arbitrary invites scrutiny; this is only compounded when race or other forms of discrimination exist.

Earning Trust and Difficult Conversations

Research and studies reveal a significant racial confidence gap in police performance. For example, the Pew Research Center amply demonstrated these differences in a 2016 report. Similarly, there are demonstrable disparities in legal outcomes involving race and policing. In a paper entitled *Racial Disparities in Legal Outcomes: On Policing, Charging Decisions, and Criminal Trial Proceedings* (Sommers & Marotta, 2014), the authors noted that "behavioral science research and actual policing data identify a statistically significant relationship showing that [Black and Latino people] are perceived and treated differently than [White people], by ordinary citizens and police" (p. 105). They suggested strategies and policy interventions that include identifying "when such racial disparities are most likely" and then modifying "police procedures accordingly. ..." (p. 105). Some disparities, such as shooter bias, are most evident when police are tired, rushed, or cannot see well, "though some of these circumstances are unavoidable during actual policing" (p. 105). Obviously a more diverse police force would reduce bias, too. The authors conclude that to "effectively reduce bias ... training must allow officers that there is no actual relationship between target race and threat" (p. 105). There are ongoing and developing efforts to address these issues, but a multidisciplinary approach through legislation, policy, and guidelines supported by research and realized by training are essential.

Police may gain trust by how they enforce the law through such practices as procedural justice (see Chapter 10 for a fuller examination). Moreover, police may earn trust by their faithful adherence to the letter and spirit of the Constitution and rule of law and by their respect for the dignity and equality of every human being. They must make each encounter matter. These choices are stronger and more effective when coupled with appropriate police transparency, accountability, and oversight. Again, there is no place for discrimination in policing. Within this space, there is ample opportunity for finding common ground among community and police. Many police departments are moving in that direction.

At the federal level, the U.S. Department of Justice issued guidance for federal law enforcement agencies regarding the use of race, ethnicity, gender, national origin, religion, sexual orientation, or gender identity, most recently modified in 2014. That guidance reflected "the Federal Government's ongoing commitment to keeping the Nation safe while upholding our dedication to the ideal of equal justice under the law" (p. 2). As Norfolk (Virginia) FBI's Chief division counsel, I used that guidance to instruct, counsel, and emphasize the central message of these guidelines, namely: "The Constitution protects individuals against the invidious use of irrelevant characteristics" as the sole basis of law enforcement actions (U.S. Department of Justice, 2014, p. 3). Race, for example, should be considered by law enforcement officers only when there is an unmistakably legitimate law enforcement purpose. For example, it is one thing for officers to identify someone racing from the scene of a bank robbery as Black, White, or green for purposes of identification; it is another for law enforcement officers to target Black people because of the color of their skin through such tactics as stop-and-frisk.

There remains another concern—a lack of open, honest, and productive dialogue about the challenges that communities and police face in their necessary but complex relationship, especially in the context of racism both past and present. Some might call these "difficult conversations." Difficult conversations are designed to "achieve effective communication across the gulf of real differences in experiences, beliefs, and feelings," to which Roger Fisher referred in his foreword in the widely acclaimed book *Difficult Conversations: How to Discuss What Matters Most* (Stone, Patton, & Heen,

2010). The concepts outlined in this book have been applied successfully in personal, business, and government settings. It is impossible to condense the depth and fullness of *Difficult Conversations* in the space of a few pages; however, I will share or modify some of the book's points that resonate in the context of police-citizen conversations both in general and more specifically in the context of overt and implicit bias and racism.

Like all difficult conversations, one about racism and policing requires the engagement of "mind and heart," which is not exactly how most officers view their work in which control plays such a key part (Fisher, p. xvii). These conversations need not be limited to formal meetings between the community and police; they might occur in more spontaneous encounters. Through training and self-awareness, police are better equipped to discuss such issues in any context, planned or not.

Learning how to have difficult conversations supplemented by training in procedural justice, community policing, implicit bias, and other matters is a good beginning, but will this move a status quo marked by anger, hostility, and distrust? If not, why not? Perhaps we do not skillfully manage difficult conversations needed to implement meaningful change. We too often avoid conflict and differing perspectives, which are "an engine for rapid learning and innovation" (Stone, Patton, & Heen, 2010, p. xvii). Instead, we retreat to our familiar places of distrust and misunderstanding. Second, the death knell to many meaningful but difficult conversations is that we presume our view is right and that anyone who opposes our belief is simply wrong, self-interested, or uninformed. When this happens, one or both sides may give up or grow ever more apart and resentful—and nothing is fixed. And nothing is learned.

What does a difficult conversation look like? The authors explain that each difficult conversation is really three conversations:

- The "What Happened?" Conversation: Who said or did what? Who is right? Who meant what? Who is to blame?
- The Feelings Conversation: Are my feelings valid? Should I acknowledge them or not? What about the other person's feelings, and what do I do about it?
- The Identity Conversation: This is an internal debate over whether we are competent or not, a good or bad person, worthy of love or not, and "what impact might it have on our self-image and self-esteem, our future and our well-being?" Will our answers to these questions leave us balanced, or off-center and anxious? (Stone, Patton, & Heen, 2010, p. 8)

These questions can help frame any difficult conversation, including questions raised at police-community forums, not those triggered by a flashpoint event such as a disputed police shooting. These conversations can promote honesty, clarity, and even curiosity, but more important, they may alter or soften preconceived notions, and dignity and respect might supplant fear and distrust. Perhaps this approach can help establish safer, freer, stronger, and more trusting communities. For example, a difficult conversation might address differing views and concerns about the role of law and lead to common ground about the law's important role in shaping a safer, more secure, more just, and freer society and the police's role in equally enforcing the law. It may seem like a civics lesson, but it is an important one in which many voices must be present and respected.

In Episode 9 of *Uncomfortable Conversations with a Black Man*, former National Football League linebacker Emmanuel Acho posed this question to a group of four White Petaluma, CA, Police Department officers: "[Do] you think we'll ever get to the point where Black children look to cops as helpers as opposed to the enemy?" This is a challenge police must face in many communities of color. That said, police cannot unilaterally make quick and easy fixes, but they can move the needle despite a history begetting understandable hostility. Over time police may earn trust through listening, learning, and acknowledging past and present wrongs of racism and other forms of discrimination. Police and community together may also consider what Acho (n.d.) observed: "I would say that proximity breeds care and distance breeds fear. ... There is not enough proximity. ..." Greater proximity between officers—especially White officers—and Black people, beyond coercive law enforcement actions, is always a step forward.

Police (and others, of course) cannot ignore the skepticism, deep-seated anger, and loss of trust among Black people. Meaningful conversations on policing, race, and discrimination, discussions that move the needle away from hardened or comfortable positions, are not easy. It is easier to take umbrage at the slightest offense in words and opinions and then retreat to the relative "safety" of like minds. That safety is illusory. It is also wildly optimistic to think that a few difficult conversations will yield immediate change. In the introduction of *Difficult Conversations* (2010), the authors warned:

> So it is best to keep your goals realistic. Eliminating fear and anxiety is an unrealistic goal. Reducing fear and anxiety and learning to manage that which remains are more obtainable. Achieving perfect results with no risk will not happen. Getting better results in the face of tolerable odds might (p. xxxii).

Dissolving barriers to reconciliation and finding common ground are short-term and long-term investments in the common good—not easy but immeasurably important to our nation.

Conclusion

There is no one-size-fits-all solution that informs how to address racism, bias, and inequality in the work of policing. However, practices that help dispel the threat or reality of discrimination and bias are worth the effort. In the meantime, police departments can take the initiative, however imperfect, to address these problems. This is an opportunity that engages and demands the better natures of all who want something better, something that equally secures the rights of *all* citizens, recognizes historical wrongs, and supports safe communities. Significant improvements to police-community relations will not be the product of a few difficult conversations or any single strategy. But these conversations may at least open some minds. Individual and corporate actions by police officers, supported by strong leadership, also matter, especially when they are borne of a culture that values, among other things, foundational American principles, justice, and the inherent dignity of every human being.

Review Questions

1. Read the opening quote from a speech by Frederick Douglas. Share your reaction. Is it "patriotic" to review our nation's history in a manner that acknowledges both its achievements and its shortcomings? Why or why not?
2. Describe the costs associated with being charged with a crime. Do you know someone who was charged with a serious crime? If so, what did you learn?
3. Give examples of how race might be properly and improperly used in police work.
4. Working with others, script a "necessary conversation" between police and community. What topics might you raise, and how would you present them, considering more than one perspective?
5. If you were a police chief, what measures would you implement to reduce bias and racism? Would you work jointly with the community? If so, how would you identify community participants?

References

Acho, E. (n.d.). *A conversation with the police—Uncomfortable conversations with a Black man, Ep. 9.* YouTube. https://www.youtube.com/watch?v=pM-HpZQWKT4

Belko, R. (2020, June 10). There's overwhelming evidence that the criminal justice system is racist. Here's the proof. *Washington Post.* https://www.washingtonpost.com/graphics/2020/opinions/systemic-racism-police-evidence-criminal-justice-system/

Bostock v. Clayton County. (n.d.). Oyez. Retrieved June 28, 2021, from https://www.oyez.org/cases/2019/17-1618.

Boykin, N., & Onyejekwe, K. C. (2020, February 18). *Republic or Bust: Keynote, A Conversation Between Justice Neil Gorsuch and Judge John Sparks, Jr.* American Bar Association. https://www.americanbar.org/groups/judicial/publications/appellate_issues/2020/winter/republic-or-bust/

Brown v. Board of Education, 347 U.S. 483 (1954). https://www.oyez.org/cases/1940-1955/347us483

DeLattre, E.J., & Schofield, D. L. (1996, June). Combatting bigotry in law enforcement. *FBI Law Enforcement Bulletin*, 65(6).

Fitzpatrick, B. T., & Shaw, T. M. (2021). *The Equal Protection Clause.* https://constitutioncenter.org/interactive-constitution/interpretation/amendment-xiv/clauses/702

Facing History and Ourselves. (1996). *Black officeholders in the South.* https://www.facinghistory.org/reconstruction-era/black-officeholders-south

Floyd v. City of New York, 959 F. Supp. 2d 540 (S.D.N.Y. 2013).

Greene, J., & McAward, J. M. (2021). *The Thirteenth Amendment.* Interactive Constitution. https://constitutioncenter.org/interactive-constitution/interpretation/amendment-xiii/interps/137

Hall, D. (2021, February 10). A forgotten Black founding father: Why I've made it my mission to teach others about Prince Hall. *The Atlantic.* https://www.theatlantic.com/magazine/archive/2021/03/prince-hall-forgotten-founder/617791/

Jefferson, T. (1776). *The Declaration of Independence.*

Kendi, I. X. (2020, June 1). *The American nightmare.* The Atlantic. https://www.theatlantic.com/ideas/archive/2020/06/american-nightmare/612457/

King, M. L., Jr. (1994). *Letter from the Birmingham jail.* Harper San Francisco.

King, M. L. (2020, March 7). *Martin Luther King Jr. Saw Three Evils in the World.* The Atlantic. https://www.theatlantic.com/magazine/archive/2018/02/martin-luther-king-hungry-club-forum/552533/

National Park Service. (2018, April 17). *Jim Crow laws.* https://www.nps.gov/malu/learn/education/jim_crow_laws.htm

Obergefell v. Hodges, 576 U.S. 644 (2015). https://www.supremecourt.gov/opinions/14pdf/14-556_3204.pdf

Peel, R. (1829). *Nine principles of policing.*

Pew Research Center. (2016, September 29). *The racial confidence gap in police performance.* https://www.pewsocialtrends.org/wp-content/uploads/sites/3/2016/09/ST_2016.09.29_Police-Final.pdf

Pildes, R. H., & Smith, B. A. (n.d.). *The Fifteenth Amendment.* https://constitutioncenter.org/interactive-constitution/interpretation/amendment-xv/interps/141

Plessy v. Ferguson, 163 U.S. 537 (1896). https://supreme.justia.com/cases/federal/us/163/537/

Railway Express Agency, Inc. et al. v. New York, 336 U.S. 106 (1949). https://casetext.com/case/railway-express-agency-v-people-of-state-of-new-york#p112

Senate Select Committee to Study Governmental Operations with Respect to Intelligence Activities. U.S. Senate. (1976, April 29). https://www.senate.gov/about/powers-procedures/investigations/church-committee.htm

Sommers, S. R., & Marotta, S. A. (2014). Racial disparities in legal outcomes: On policing, charging decisions, and criminal trial proceedings. *Policy Insights from the Behavioral and Brain Sciences, 1*(1), 103–111. https://doi.org/10.1177%2F2372732214548431

Stone, D., Patton, B., & Heen, S. (2010). *Difficult conversations: How to discuss what matters most.* Penguin Books.

Thomas, W. C. (2020, June 9). *The police have been spying on Black reporters and activists for years. I know because I'm one of them.* ProPublica. https://www.propublica.org/article/the-police-have-been-spying-on-black-reporters-and-activists-for-years-i-know-because-im-one-of-them?utm_source=pardot&utm_medium=email&utm_campaign=major investigations&utm_content=feature

U.S. Const., amend. 13.

U.S. Const., amend. 15.

U.S. Const. art. I, § 9, cl. 1.

U.S. Department of Justice. (2014, December). *Guidance for federal law enforcement agencies regarding the use of race, ethnicity, gender, national origin, religion, sexual orientation, or gender identity.* https://www.dhs.gov/sites/default/files/publications/use-of-race-policy_0.pdf

Image Credit

Chapter 9

Evaluating Police Strategies, Tactics, and Militarization

The importance of caution

Image 9

Peel Principle 1: The basic mission for which police exist is to prevent crime and disorder as an alternative to the repression of crime and disorder by military force and severity of legal punishment.

> *"Whoever, except in cases and under circumstances expressly authorized by the Constitution or Act of Congress, willfully uses any part of the Army or the Air Force as a posse comitatus or otherwise to execute the laws shall be fined under this title or imprisoned not more than two years, or both."* Posse Comitatus Act, June 18, 1878

Concerns About Military's Influence in Domestic Policing

No one can dispute the primary role of the U.S. Armed Forces in protecting and preserving the security, rights, and freedoms that "We the People" enjoy from attack or interference by foreign adversaries. What is less clear is the proper role of the U.S Armed Forces in domestic affairs. Our nation's founders, mindful of the presence and activities of British soldiers before independence was gained, had grave concerns about the presence and influence of a professional military in the nation's domestic affairs. Note what James Madison said when addressing the Constitutional Convention in Philadelphia on June 29, 1787 (Preble, 2019):

> A standing military force, with an overgrown Executive will not long be safe companions to liberty. The means of defence against foreign danger, have been always the instruments of tyranny at home.

Although Madison favored a strong central government, he, like others at the convention, feared the dangers of a permanent army. A tangible American expression that reflects the deep concern about a military presence in domestic affairs is the Third Amendment of the Bill of Rights (1787), which states: "No Soldier shall, in time of peace be quartered in any house, without the consent of the Owner, nor in time of war, but in a manner to be prescribed by law." As Gordon S. Wood, university professor and professor of history emeritus at Brown University, wrote, the Third Amendment (n.d.):

> [Suggests] the individual's right of domestic privacy—that people are protected from governmental intrusion into their homes; and it is the only part of the Constitution that deals directly with the relationship between the rights of individuals and the military in both peace and war—rights that emphasize the importance of civilian control over the armed forces.

As Radley Balko noted in his book *The Rise of the Warrior Cop: The Militarization of America's Police Forces* (2013), the Third Amendment embodies a broad sentiment about militarism in a free society (p. 16). As Balko observed, "Ultimately, the Founders decided that a standing army was a necessary evil, but the role of soldiers would be only to dispel foreign threats, not to enforce laws against American citizens" (p. 16).

In 1776, well before the Third Amendment was ratified, Samuel Adams expressed concern about the dangers of a professional army, describing it as "always dangerous to the Liberties of the People" (Adams, 1776). Why? Because soldiers, he believed, were conditioned to obey their officers' orders unthinkingly and were more likely to consider themselves separate from the people. Adams cautioned that the power of a standing army "should be watchd [sic] with a jealous Eye" (1776).

The concern about unthinking obedience to authority, however, is not limited to those who serve in the military. The concern is more universal. Consider Yale psychologist Stanley Milgram's groundbreaking although controversial experiments in the 1960s revealing the willing, deferential obedience by people to ostensibly legitimate authorities, no matter how brutal the consequences to other human beings. Study participants were instructed by an authority figure to deliver increasingly high-voltage shocks to someone—an actor—in another room. The actors would scream, eventually going silent as the shocks became stronger (Milgram, 1963). Although many participants expressed deep reservations while following instructions to administer purportedly higher, life-threatening voltage to another human being, they overwhelmingly did so. Later studies by Milgram, however, revealed that rebellious peers reduced obedience levels—food for thought perhaps for those who dislike nonconformists. A predisposition to unthinkingly obey ostensibly legitimate authority creates one set of dangers. Organizations or individuals having legitimate authority but lacking sufficient oversight or accountability create another, one more fully examined in the next chapter. These general observations and findings about human nature should play a role in the execution of existing or proposed police tactics, strategies, and equipment in their role to protect and serve.

Law enforcement strategies, tactics, and equipment have changed over the past 50 years. As a rookie Federal Bureau of Investigation (FBI) agent in 1985, I was issued a Smith and Wesson Model 13 six-shot .357 Magnum revolver, a well-made, reliable handgun first manufactured in 1974 for use by police and military. To many agents, it seemed like a logical choice for civilian law enforcement, at least until April 11, 1986, when a shootout occurred in Dade County, Florida. During the firefight, FBI Special Agents Jerry L. Dove and Benjamin P. Grogan were killed, and five other agents were wounded. The carnage ended only after Special Agent Ed Mireles heroically fired his Model 13 revolver, killing William Russell Matix and Michael Lee Platt. Both Matix and Platt were military veterans turned serial bank robbers. Platt, who was shot 12 times and wounded, fired at least 42 rounds from a Ruger Mini-14 .223 Remington semi-automatic rifle before he died. The event received nationwide attention and sent shockwaves through the FBI and other law enforcement agencies. The events were dramatized in an NBC made-for-television movie, *In the Line of Duty: The F.B.I. Murders* (1988). The immediate impact was attention called to the fact that FBI agents were outgunned and outmaneuvered, so the FBI and other law enforcement agencies began to reevaluate existing tactics and weapons needed to ensure that law enforcement officers would not be at a clear disadvantage in dangerous circumstances. These efforts led to sweeping changes in FBI policy and practices. By the late 1980s through the 1990s, all street agents transitioned from using revolvers to semiautomatic pistols; there were many other changes that go beyond the scope of this book, but suffice it to say, weaponry, protective gear, and tactical training changed. These changes were in addition to the continued development and deployment of FBI field office Special Weapons and Tactics (SWAT) teams and the famed Hostage Rescue Team. Police departments nationwide also instituted broad changes before and during this time.

Observers might note that FBI and many other law enforcement agency use-of-force practices adopted a more intimidating model in tactics and weaponry to meet evolving, dangerous threats. That said, communities should not minimize the very legitimate concerns among all law enforcement officers. The world has changed. Machine guns, assault rifles, other high-powered weapons, and guns in general have become increasingly commonplace. A 2017 NBC News report revealed that, "one out of every five firearms purchased in this country is an AR-style rifle, according to a NSSF [National Shooting Sports Foundation] estimate. Americans now own an estimated 15 million AR-15s, gun groups say" (Schuppe, 2017). A 2019 BBC News statistical analysis, citing a 2018 Small Arms Survey stated, "While it is difficult to know exactly how many guns civilians own around the world, by every estimate the U.S. with more than 390 million, is far out in front." Using a measure of the number of firearms per 100 residents, the U.S. led the world with 120.5 firearms per 100 residents, followed by Yemen at 52.8—a country that has compulsory military service. Standing at number six in the world, neighbor Canada had 34.7 per 100 residents. When widely available guns find their way into the wrong hands, police are at greater risk. Although no one doubts that weapons are overwhelmingly owned by law-abiding citizens, they are also possessed by people who should not have access to them. This is not about Second Amendment politics or advocacy; it is about the reality faced by law enforcement officers.

Given these circumstances, law enforcement agencies understandably looked to the U.S. military for tactical insight and equipment, especially since the mid-1980s, and likewise recruited and welcomed military personnel for their undeniable skills, training, and experience. The move toward practices and equipment used by our world-class U.S. military is hardly surprising. Moreover, veterans already populate the ranks of police and law enforcement agencies; statistics reveal that veterans who served their country honorably have long favored policing as a civilian career. According to an analysis of U.S. Census data by Gregory B. Lewis and Rahul Pathak of Georgia State University for the Marshall Project, "today just 6 percent of the population at large has served in the military, but 19 percent of police officers are veterans" (Weichselbaum & Schwartzapfel, 2017). This is no small statistical difference. It is also understandable because both the U.S. military and civilian police agencies commonly draw people who seek purpose and opportunity in these callings, although there are also other draws.

But where have these developments taken contemporary policing? In a 2017 *FBI Law Enforcement Bulletin* article, Dr. Scott W. Phillips examined issues relating to police departments that have chosen "to follow the principles of the military model." A total of 370 police leaders from diverse departments large and small attending the FBI National Academy during a two-month period in 2015 responded to a survey that contained various questions about SWAT policies and procedures. One interesting takeaway was that police leaders are sharply divided over whether police departments become more militarized when they:

- possess an armored vehicle;
- deploy SWAT for routine patrol or no-knock warrants (where police do not knock and announce their presence before executing a warrant);
- conduct military training for SWAT teams; or
- adopt military-style uniforms or weapons for patrol officers (Phillips, 2017).

Americans are also divided. This point was driven home in a 2017 study by Emily Ekins sponsored by the CATO Institute, whose data revealed the following:

> 54% say police using military equipment is going too far, while 46% say it's necessary for law enforcement purposes. Majorities across racial groups oppose police using military weapons and armored vehicles (58% of blacks, 53% of whites and 51% of Latinos). Most Republicans (65%) believe police need to use military weapons, while 60% of both Democrats and independents believe police using such equipment goes too far (p. 6).

Among citizens, and certainly among police, there *are* broadly competing beliefs about what constitutes good policing—or at least what defines the proper role of police. For example, there is a divide between those who favor the "warrior" mindset and those who favor the "servant" mindset. The servant mindset is many things. It is Sir Robert Peel's *Nine Principles of Policing*, referred to throughout this book. It is, more recently, the principles articulated in the Police Executive Research Forum 30 principles in Chapter 7. It is community policing. It is procedural justice. Even the police motto "to serve and protect" connotes an image of this mindset. In its various iterations, the servant mindset dissolves the "us-versus-them" divide between police and community. It is aspirational and, many argue, effective; others disagree. It is a topic worthy of open and honest dialogue and continuing research.

More provocative is the continued currency of the warrior mindset among many officers. In a significant and informative *Harvard Law Review Forum* article, Seth Stoughton, assistant professor of law at the University of South Carolina School of Law (2015), defined the warrior mindset:

> What is the warrior mindset? In its most restrictive sense, it refers to the mental tenacity and attitude that officers, like soldiers, are taught to adopt in the face of a life-threatening struggle. In this context, the warrior mindset refers to a bone-deep commitment to survive a bad situation no matter the odds or difficulty, to not give up even when it is mentally and physically easier to do so. So narrowly defined, the concept is difficult for anyone to criticize. Unfortunately, the homage paid to the Warrior has expanded that uncontroversial definition beyond all recognition (p. 226).

Fear—and with it, the instinct to survive—can and must play a role in any law enforcement officer's mind. Fear is not always irrational. There is a place for it as officers face daily and unpredictable dangers in their efforts to serve and protect their community. Like anyone, officers want to return safely to their homes and families when their workday ends. There is no doubt, too, that situational awareness *must* play an important part of safe and effective policing. But does that mean a warrior mindset *must* be the *primary* response to the communities that police inhabit? Perhaps not.

Dr. Stoughton did not minimize the importance of officer vigilance or the will to survive. Officers need to be mentally tough and physically prepared for the worst *when* appropriate. Communities should respect the powerful interest in self-preservation. But is *hyper*vigilance the best strategy in all police-citizen encounters? As Dr. Stoughton (2015) argued, the answer is no:

> The warrior mindset has mutated into the warrior mentality. ... From their earliest days in the academy, would-be officers are told that their prime objective, the proverbial "first rule of law enforcement," is to go home at the end of every shift. But they are taught that they live in an intensely hostile world. A world that is, quite literally, gunning for them. As early as the first day of the police academy, the dangers officers face are depicted in graphic and heart-wrenching recordings

Seth Stoughton, "Law Enforcement's 'Warrior' Problem," *Harvard Law Review*, vol. 128, no. 6. Copyright © 2015 by Harvard Law Review Association.

that capture a fallen officer's last moments. Death, they are told, is constantly a single, small misstep away. A recent article written by an officer for *Police Magazine* opens with this description: "The dangers we expose ourselves to every time we go [on duty] are almost immeasurable. We know this the day we sign up and the academy certainly does a good job of hammering the point home." For example, training materials at the New Mexico Police Academy hammer that point quite explicitly, informing recruits that the suspects they will be dealing with "are mentally prepared to react violently." Each recruit is told, in these words, "[Y]ou could die today, tomorrow, or next Friday." Under this warrior worldview, officers are locked in intermittent and unpredictable combat with unknown but highly lethal enemies. As a result, officers learn to be afraid. That isn't the word used in law enforcement circles, of course. Vigilant, attentive, cautious, alert, or observant are the terms that appear most often in police publications. But make no mistake, officers don't learn to be vigilant, attentive, cautious, alert, and observant just because it's fun. They do so because they are afraid. Fear is ubiquitous in law enforcement (pp. 226–227).

Dr. Stoughton (2015) explained that the warrior mentality "creates a substantial, if invisible, barrier to true community policing" (p. 228). Although he acknowledged that "community policing" is a nebulous phrase in its understanding and application, nearly all can agree that its primary goal is to build meaningful, trusting, and collaborative relationships between police and community. A hypervigilant safety-at-all-cost focus on officer safety makes this difficult, if not impossible. To demonstrate, Dr. Stoughton proposed a thought experiment:

Imagine that you are a rookie police officer driving down the street, windows down, and looking for people in the community with whom you can begin building positive relationships. But you have been told (repeatedly) that your survival depends on believing that everyone you see—literally everyone—is capable of, and may very well be interested in, killing you. Put in that position, would you actually get out of your car and approach someone? And if you did, would you stroll up to start a casual conversation or would you advance cautiously, ask for identification, run a criminal background check, and request consent to search ... and then, maybe, try to start that casual conversation? The latter, of course, is what many officers are taught to do. It is what I was taught to do as a rookie officer. My first ever "consensual encounter," only hours into my first day of field training, followed exactly that pattern. It takes no great imagination to recognize how badly that approach, repeated over hundreds or thousands of police/civilian interactions in any given jurisdiction, hinders the creation of meaningful, collaborative relationships (pp. 228–229).

He then questioned whether the warrior mentality makes policing safer or less safe for police and community (2015, p. 229). It is true that officers *must be* trained to manage and control—by their words and actions—the space in which they work. This *is* a critical component when officers face potentially dangerous situations. But, as Dr. Stoughton noted, if officers believe that an "unquestioned command" tone and presence is the safest approach in most police-citizen encounters, anything less than full compliance will more likely cause officers to view a noncompliant citizen as "the enemy" (Stoughton, 2015, pp. 229–230). Any law enforcement officer knows that citizen noncompliance, *especially in response to and in the context of emerging dangers*, triggers powerful survival emotions and trained responses. But not all police-citizen encounters are like that. When all interactions are viewed through the prism of compliance or noncompliance, tensions are likely to flare, raising the potential for otherwise avoidable violence, especially among communities where police are already distrusted. Even among communities more favorably disposed to police, there is little gained and something lost in community support when an officer assumes a command presence gratuitously. Dr. Stoughton (2015) quoted Sue Rahr, a former sheriff, director of the Washington State Criminal Justice Training Commission, and member of President Obama's Task Force on Twenty-First Century Policing, who said, "We do our recruits no favor if we train them to approach every situation as a war. To do so sets them up to create unnecessary resistance and risk of injury" (p. 230).

Most telling is a finding that of the 10 most destructive and violent riots in United States history, half were in response to perceived police abuses (Stoughton, 2015, p. 230). Although we can argue about details, hypervigilance and overly aggressive tactics can "needlessly create use of force situations" that can fan the flames of social tensions (Stoughton, 2015, p. 230). Recent history repeatedly attests to widespread social tensions and civil unrest in response to police abuse or overly aggressive tactics. Witness what happened in Ferguson, MO, beginning on August, 10, 2014, when police shot 18-year-old Michael Brown, followed by violent encounters between protestors and police, who adopted a militaristic response as the crowds gathered.

In a study published in the *Washington Post* on June 30, 2017, reporters Ryan Welch and Jack Mewhirter posed another salient question: Does military equipment lead police officers to be more violent? The reporters, together with Casey Delhanty and Jason Wilks, published their research findings. This is how they proceeded:

> We used anthropologist Peter Kraska's definition of militarization: the embrace and implementation of an ideology that stresses the use of force as a good way to solve problems. In this definition, militarization occurs along four dimensions—material, cultural, organizational and operational. We posit that when law enforcement receives more military materials—weapons, vehicles and tools—it becomes more militarized along the other three axes as well. They use more military language, create elite units like SWAT teams, and become more likely to jump into high-risk situations. Militarization makes every problem—even a car of teenagers driving away from a party—look like a nail that should be hit with an AR15 hammer.

Their collected data about transfers of military equipment from the Department of Defense (DOD) revealed an interesting trend about the course of events since 1996. Passed that year, the National Defense Authorization Act authorized the defense secretary to give to local law enforcement DOD's excess military equipment free of charge under what is commonly known as the *1033 Program*. During the following two decades, military transfers skyrocketed. Their analysis included a chart that shows this dramatic expansion, one that accelerated after the September 11, 2001, terrorist attacks. For example, in 1998, the DOD transferred about $9.4 million in excess military equipment to 290 law enforcement agencies. By 2014, the DOD had transferred nearly $800 million in equipment to 3,029 law enforcement agencies. Between 2006 and 2014, law enforcement agencies received "an array of military equipment worth over $1.5 billion: more than 6,000 mine-resistant, ambush-protected vehicles (MRAPs), 79,288 assault rifles, 205 grenade launchers, 11,959 bayonets, 50 airplanes, 422 helicopters, and $3.6 million in camouflage and other 'deception equipment'" (Welch & Mewhirter, 2017). Analyzing the data and controlling for other factors, the authors concluded that counties that asked for and received military equipment for law enforcement agencies were associated with more civilians killed each year by police. That is a sobering thought, one calling for further inquiry and review.

In a June 2014 study entitled *War Comes Home: The Excessive Militarization of American Policing*, the American Civil Liberties Union (ACLU) collected data from local law enforcement agencies about the deployment of SWAT teams in 2011 and 2012. Among other trends, their data revealed that SWAT teams were commonly used to "to execute search warrants in low-level drug investigations ..." (ACLU, 2015,

p. 5). More specifically, 79 percent of SWAT deployments "were for the purpose of executing a search warrant, most commonly in drug investigations. Only a small handful of deployments (7 percent) were for hostage, barricade, or active shooter scenarios" (ACLU, 2015, p. 5). By contrast, the International Association of Chiefs of Police (IACP) and the National Tactical Officers Association (NTOA) sponsored a study entitled *National Special Weapons and Tactics (SWAT) Study: A National Assessment of Critical Trends and Issues from 2009 to 2013* (2014) that found that the "most common incident involving activation of a SWAT team from 2009 through 2013 was a high-risk warrant service incident" (p. vi). There are considerable differences in methodology, approach, goals, and results between the two studies. Each deserves scrutiny. In particular, the ACLU study found a lack of clear or consistent standards establishing when SWAT teams should be deployed, and it decried the lack of restraints or internal policies, let alone the lack of public oversight that might limit the deployment of SWAT teams. Of note were the following two findings, the first about the force and violence associated with SWAT deployments and the second about the impact on communities of color (ACLU, 2014):

> SWAT deployments often and unnecessarily entailed the use of violent tactics and equipment, including armored personnel carriers; use of violent tactics and equipment was shown to increase the risk of bodily harm and property damage. Of the incidents studied in which SWAT was deployed to search for drugs in a person's home, the SWAT teams either forced or probably forced entry into a person's home using a battering ram or other breaching device 65 percent of the time. For drug investigations, the SWAT teams studied were almost twice as likely to force entry into a person's home than not, and they were more than twice as likely to use forced entry in drug investigations than in other cases. In some instances, the use of violent tactics and equipment caused property damage, injury, and/or death (p. 6).

> The use of paramilitary weapons and tactics primarily impacted people of color; when paramilitary tactics were used in drug searches, the primary targets were people of color, whereas when paramilitary tactics were used in hostage or barricade scenarios, the primary targets were white. Overall, 42 percent of people impacted by a SWAT deployment to execute a search warrant were Black and 12 percent were Latino. This means that of the people impacted by deployments for warrants, at least 54 percent were minorities. Of the deployments in which all the people impacted were minorities, 68 percent were in drug cases, and 61 percent of all the people impacted by SWAT raids

in drug cases were minorities. In addition, the incidents we studied revealed stark, often extreme, racial disparities in the use of SWAT locally, especially in cases involving search warrants (p. 5).

The IACP/NTOA study (2014), in contrast, focused more on what happened after SWAT teams were deployed; there were no recommendations for improvement. The study's conclusion was as follows:

> The results clearly reveal the composition of agency SWAT teams, protocols, practices, training procedures, and community relations and demonstrate police leaders have a powerful resource in SWAT teams. Throughout the survey, law enforcement agencies articulated clear protocols and practices that promote public safety. Overall, this survey reveals SWAT operations are in demand based on incidents within communities, and the teams are professional with extensive training, policies, and procedures in place; additionally, the teams are more likely to utilize less-lethal solutions and are necessary to keep communities safer (p. 20).

Make no mistake—the execution of search or arrest warrants can be a very dangerous business. Sometimes the dangers posed by wanted suspects to police are known; sometimes the dangers that a residence about to be searched presents to police are known. These known dangers, let alone what is unknown, may place officers at grave risk. That said, there *is* a place for SWAT operations where SWAT skill sets, training, and resources make safe and successful outcomes for police more likely. And to be clear, SWAT deployment is not limited to the execution of warrants. But the *decision* to deploy SWAT, just like the decision to use force, should be subject to standards resulting in a rational, intelligent choice, not a choice by default. But to be clear, the Fourth Amendment itself does not govern *whether* police have the inherent legal authority to deploy SWAT *as a tactic* per se. No matter what tactics are chosen or how they are deployed, the Fourth Amendment always protects the right of the people "against unreasonable searches and seizures." And even if a Fourth Amendment reasonableness standard does not directly apply to the decision to deploy SWAT, that decision *should* be informed and reasonable. It need not be a "perfect" decision with the benefit of 20/20 hindsight, but it should never be routine or presumed to cover an overly expansive list of designated crimes or circumstances. There are also advantages in providing some level of public transparency in policies justifying SWAT deployment. Why? It promotes greater accountability, and with it, public trust. The precise nature of what greater transparency and oversight might look like are subjects that deserve attention by police, elected officials, academic researchers, and the public, as a great deal is at stake.

Legal Limits Imposed on Use of Military in Domestic Policing

Embedded in U.S. law are restraints placed on the role and activities of the U.S. armed forces in domestic affairs. Collectively, these laws ensure that civilian, not military, authorities are the primary enforcers of civil and criminal law in the U.S. Absent extraordinary circumstances, U.S. military personnel must not act as civilian law *enforcers*—in general, soldiers must not assert their power and authority against civilians, especially those involving the exercise of coercive powers such as arrests. Although U.S. military personnel take an oath to support and defend the U.S. Constitution against all enemies, *foreign and domestic*, Americans have long resisted military involvement in civilian affairs, as noted earlier in this chapter.

But how did this come about? American resistance dates to traditions born in England, first acknowledged in *Magna Carta: The Great Charter of Liberties of King John* (1215) and later in U.S. laws limiting the use of posse comitatus. As a general concept, *posse comitatus* refers to the ability of a sheriff to seek assistance to enforce the law in the event of a civil disorder. Its most tangible expression in the U.S. is found in the Posse Comitatus Act (PCA), first enacted in 1878 but later codified as 18 U.S.C. § 1385. The PCA states:

> Whoever, except in cases and under circumstances expressly authorized by the Constitution or Act of Congress, willfully uses any part of the Army or the Air Force as a posse comitatus or otherwise to execute the laws shall be fined under this title or imprisoned not more than two years, or both.

Note that a violation of the PCA is not merely a civil matter—it is a *crime* to willfully use any part of the Army or Air Force as a posse comitatus to execute the laws.

In 2017, Congress reaffirmed the PCA's continued importance in 6 U.S.C. § 466, which provides:

> (a) Findings

> Congress finds the following:

> (1) Section 1385 of title 18 (commonly known as the "Posse Comitatus Act") prohibits the use of the Armed Forces as a posse comitatus to ex-

ecute the laws except in cases and under circumstances expressly authorized by the Constitution or Act of Congress.

(2) Enacted in 1878, the Posse Comitatus Act was expressly intended to prevent United States Marshals, on their own initiative, from calling on the Army for assistance in enforcing Federal law.

(3) The Posse Comitatus Act has served the Nation well in limiting the use of the Armed Forces to enforce the law.

(4) Nevertheless, by its express terms, the Posse Comitatus Act is not a complete barrier to the use of the Armed Forces for a range of domestic purposes, including law enforcement functions, when the use of the Armed Forces is authorized by Act of Congress or the President determines that the use of the Armed Forces is required to fulfill the President's obligations under the Constitution to respond promptly in time of war, insurrection, or other serious emergency.

(5) Existing laws, including chapter 13 of title 10 (commonly known as the "Insurrection Act"), and the Robert T. Stafford Disaster Relief and Emergency Assistance Act (42 U.S.C. 5121 et seq.), grant the President broad powers that may be invoked in the event of domestic emergencies, including an attack against the Nation using weapons of mass destruction, and these laws specifically authorize the President to use the Armed Forces to help restore public order.

(b) Sense of Congress

Congress reaffirms the continued importance of section 1385 of title 18, and it is the sense of Congress that nothing in this chapter should be construed to alter the applicability of such section to any use of the Armed Forces as a posse comitatus to execute the laws.

Those interested in a more complete background should read the Congressional Research Service (CRS) report by legislative attorney Jennifer K. Elsea titled *The Posse Comitatus Act and Related Matters: The Use of the Military to Execute Civilian Law*.

As noted above, the PCA as amended criminalizes "the willful use of any part of the Army or Air Force to execute the law unless expressly authorized by the Constitution or an act of Congress." There *are* statutory exceptions, such as federal laws that allow the president to use military force to suppress insurrection or to enforce federal authority, in 10 U.S.C. §§ 251–255, and laws that authorize the DOD to provide federal, state, and local police with *information, equipment, and personnel*, in 10 U.S.C. §§ 271–284. The CRS report (Elsea, 2018) cites court decisions that reveal PCA violations: "(a) when the Armed Forces perform tasks assigned to an organ of civil government, or (b) the Armed Forces perform tasks assigned to them solely for purposes of civilian government" (p. 2).

Congress, courts, and the U.S. military alike have long believed that the domestic use of the U.S. Armed Forces to enforce the law is limited to special circumstances. Why? Gene Healy of the CATO Institute (2005) quoted a federal court judge who summarized the danger that the PCA was designed to meet: "Military personnel must be trained to operate under circumstances where the protection of constitutional freedoms cannot receive the consideration needed in order to assure their preservation." This statement captures a key concern and reality.

In short, there is a legal and cultural tradition of resistance to call upon the military in domestic policing unless there is clearly defined authority to address extraordinary events that overwhelm the capacity of domestic civilian capacities to address them. As noted, constitutional freedoms *are* at stake. This is not some hypothetical musing. This is a real concern even among those who have actively served in the U.S. Armed Forces. Healy also quoted Army Lt. Gen. Russell Honore, commander of the federal troops who supported domestic authorities in New Orleans during Hurricane Katrina, during which time Lt. General Honore ordered his soldiers to keep their guns pointed down. Lt. General Honore said, "[t]his isn't Iraq. Soldiers are trained to be warriors, not peace officers—which is as it should be. But putting full-time warriors into a civilian policing situation can result in serious collateral damage to American life and liberty" (Healy, 2005). The general's plainspoken advice might extend to civilian police who favor the warrior mentality. (Another excellent reference may be found in Peter B. Kraska's "Militarization and Policing—Its Relevance to 21st Century Police" [2007].)

Conclusion

Must officers choose to be *either* a servant of the people or a militaristic warrior? Or is this a false choice? Some have suggested that a more aspirational model might be that of guardian or hero. In an era of community policing, police are called upon to perform many competing roles, perhaps too many. Some are coercive; others are supportive. In *Citizens, Cops and Power: Recognizing the Limits of Community* (2006), Steve Herbert wrote, "The police's coercive role means that they are not good community builders, and thus we fool ourselves—and harm communities—by holding onto the more elaborate rhetoric of community policing" (p. 139). Police and communities must assess these choices.

When police exercise coercive powers in a manner that too closely resemble military action or powers that gratuitously involve force, people take notice. Christopher David, a graduate of the U.S. Naval Academy and former member of the Navy's Civil Engineer Corps, took notice on July 18, 2020, when he was confronted in Portland, OR, by unidentified federal officers who broke his hand and unleashed a chemical irritant on him after he wanted to know what the officers involved thought of the oath to which they had sworn—to protect and defend the Constitution. The way in which the law enforcement officers responded to David's question did not elevate their standing in the minds of most Americans. Police must question the message their actions convey when they are called upon to protect and serve the people. This requires self-awareness and self-discipline, not blind obedience. What matters more is obedience to the Constitution in support of the common good and respect for the dignity of every human being.

Review Questions

1. Do you think it is difficult for police officers to transition from foreign battlefields to civilian streets? Why or why not? If possible, find such an officer and ask.
2. What beneficial qualities gained by serving in the military are also beneficial qualities for serving as civilian police? What qualities are not?
3. Should the community know more about police tactics or weaponry? Consider both perspectives.
4. Suppose again that you are a police chief. What choices in training, tactics, strategy, equipment, or clothing, if any, might you consider in adopting a less militaristic approach without unnecessarily endangering the work that officers perform?
5. Find and describe a recent newsworthy event in which police were accused of being too militaristic. Do you agree with the criticism? Why or why not?

References

Adams, S. (1776, January 7). *Letter to James Warren*. Manuscripts and Archives Division, The New York Public Library. https://digitalcollections.nypl.org/items/01a38720-1954-0134-2e91-00505686a51c

American Civil Liberties Union (ACLU). (2014, June). *War comes home: The excessive militarizatoin of American policing.* https://www.aclu.org/sites/default/files/field_document/jus14-warcomeshome-text-rel1.pdf

Balko, R. (2013). *Rise of the warrior cop: The militarization of America's police forces.* PublicAffairs.

BBC News. (2019, April 8). *America's gun culture in charts.* https://www.bbc.com/news/world-us-canada-41488081

Ekins, E. (2017). *Policing in America: Understanding public attitudes toward police. Results from a national survey.* https://www.cato.org/sites/cato.org/files/survey-reports/pdf/policing-in-america-august-1-2017.pdf

Elsea, J. K. (2018, November 6). *The Posse Comitatus Act and related matters: The use of the military to execute civilian law.* Congressional Research Service. https://fas.org/sgp/crs/natsec/R42659.pdf

Healy, G. (2005, October 7). What of 'Posse Comitatus'? CATO Institute. https://www.cato.org/commentary/what-posse-comitatus

Herbert, S. (2006). *Citizens, cops and power: Recognizing the limits of community.* University of Chicago Press.

Holt, J. C. (1992). *Magna Carta.* Cambridge University Press.

International Association of Chiefs of Police (IACP) & National Tactical Officers Association (NTOA). (2014). *National* Special Weapons *and* Tactics *(SWAT) study: A national assessment of critical trends and issues from 2009 to 2013.* https://ntoa.org/pdf/swatstudy.pdf

Kraska, P. B. (2007, December 13). Militarization and policing—Its relevance to 21st century police. *Policing: A Journal of Policy and Practice, 1*(4), 501–513. https://doi.org/10.1093/police/pam065

Lewis, G. B., & Pathak, R. (2014). The employment of veterans in state and local government. *PMAP Publications, 11.* https://scholarworks.gsu.edu/cgi/viewcontent.cgi?article=1009&context=pmap_facpubs

Milgram, S. (1963). Behavioral study of obedience. *Journal of Abnormal Psychology, 67,* 371–378. https://doi.org/10.1037/h0040525

Peel, R. (1829). *Nine principles of policing.*

Phillips, S. W. (2017, August 14). Police militarization. *FBI Law Enforcement Bulletin.* https://leb.fbi.gov/articles/featured-articles/police-militarization

Posse Comitatus Act, 18 U.S.C. § 1385 (1878).

Preble, C. A. (2019, March 4). *The Founders' foreign policy.* CATO Institute. https://www.cato.org/blog/founders-foreign-policy

Schuppe, J. (2017, December 27). *America's rifle: Why so many people love the AR-15.* NBC News. https://www.nbcnews.com/news/us-news/america-s-rifle-why-so-many-people-love-ar-15-n831171

Stoughton, S. (2015, April 10). Law enforcement's 'warrior' problem. *Harvard Law Review Forum, 128*(6), 225–234. https://harvardlawreview.org/2015/04/law-enforcements-warrior-problem/

U.S. Const., amend 3.

U.S. Const., amend 4.

Weichselbaum, S., & Schwartzapfel, B. (2017, March 30). *When warriors put on the badge*. The Marshall Project. https://www.themarshallproject.org/2017/03/30/when-warriors-put-on-the-badge

Welch, R., & Mewhirter, J. (2017, June 30). Does military equipment lead police officers to be more violent? We did the research. *Washington Post.* https://www.washingtonpost.com/news/monkey-cage/wp/2017/06/30/does-military-equipment-lead-police-officers-to-be-more-violent-we-did-the-research/

Wood, G. S. (n.d.). *The Third Amendment.* https://constitutioncenter.org/interactive-constitution/interpretation/amendment-iii/interps/123

Image Credit

Chapter 10

Procedural Justice, Character, Professionalism, and Accountability Contribute to Community Trust

Image 10

Peel Principle 5: To seek and preserve public favor, not by pandering to public opinion, but by constantly demonstrating absolute impartial service to law, in complete independence of policy, and without regard to the justice or injustice of the substance of individual laws, by ready offering of individual service and friendship to all members of the public without regard to their wealth or social standing, by ready exercise of courtesy and friendly good humor, and by ready offering of individual sacrifice in protecting and preserving life.

"The accountability of individual police officers is a fundamental issue for police executives. ... The enduring concern of police executives to ensure accountability in American policing is a reflection of their professional commitment." Kelling, Wasserman, & Williams, 1988, p. 1

Procedural Justice, Community Policing, and Other Practices

Gaining community trust is not easy. Success relies on police revealing a culture of values, traits, and commitment to law in their everyday work. Success also relies on police taking actions and forming partnerships within a community that inspire confidence. Those familiar with modern policing practices know that gaining trust is a central goal of the widely discussed strategy of community policing. More specifically, "[community] policing is a philosophy that promotes organizational strategies that support the systematic use of partnerships and problem-solving techniques to proactively address the immediate conditions that give rise to public safety issues such as crime, social disorder, and fear of crime" (U.S. Department of Justice, 2014, p. 3). Partnerships are built on trust.

First, some words of caution. Neither police nor community should rely on police reform or specific police practices to unilaterally create safe and healthy communities. Governmental or third-party interventions *alone* at any level, no matter how creative or just or aspirational they are, are not likely to establish free, secure, just, or thriving communities. But unilateral and repeated unwise, discriminatory, or unlawful police actions can do grave damage to communities, reminding us of the Hippocratic oath's injunction "First, do not harm." Sustainable change founded on partnerships and problem-solving techniques also relies on continuity of effort. Continuity is critical to the efforts of police and community, as it is true for nearly any meaningful human endeavor that seeks good and lasting change.

Turn to procedural justice, "which deals with the process of policing, not the outcomes of policing. It's not about what an officer does, but rather *how* he or she does it" (emphasis added; Kenyon, 2019). Process matters. But what is procedural justice? Procedural Justice for Law Enforcement: An Overview (Kunard & Moe, 2014) explained that procedural justice refers to the idea that the *fairness* in the processes used to resolve disputes matters greatly. The following excerpt emphasizes the part of procedural justice that focuses on the quality of communication between officers and community members in a variety of situations (Kunard & Moe, 2014):

> The ways in which community members develop opinions about a specific interaction with an officer (their assessment) is based primarily

upon two things: the outcome of the encounter (whether they received a ticket, for example) and the process of the encounter (how the officer came to the decision about whether to give a ticket and whether the officer explained their decision-making process). In short, procedural justice is concerned not exactly with what officers do, but also with the way they do it. Research has shown that often the process is more important than the outcome of the encounter in shaping a community member's assessment of the interaction (Sunshine and Tyler, 2003; Tyler and Huo, 2002). In fact, in a study conducted in 2008, researchers interviewed New Yorkers both prior to and following a personal experience with the police. The people who received a traffic citation from an officer who treated them fairly tended to view the police more favorably and were significantly more willing to cooperate with the police than they had been before that encounter (Tyler and Fagan, 2008). ... Psychologists, sociologists, and criminologists alike have studied the pillars of procedural justice in police-community interactions. The main finding from this body of research is that "police can achieve positive changes in citizen attitudes to police through adopting procedural justice dialogue as a component part of any type of police intervention," (Masserole et al., 2012) (p. 3).

The publication credits research in this area led by Tom Tyler at New York University in which Dr. Tyler (National Initiative for Building Community Trust and Justice, n.d.) identified four main components, or "pillars," of procedural justice, namely fairness, voice, transparency, and impartiality. His contributions demand attention. Any community that values freedom and rights, including those central to our nation's founding and proclaimed by Dr. Martin Luther King, Jr., and others, should expect fairness, a voice, transparency and impartiality in policing. It is hard to imagine anything less as a precondition to creating a culture of trust and responsibility.

As Dr. Matthew Kenyon explained in *Rethinking Procedural Justice: Perceptions, Attitudes, and Framing* (2019), procedural justice does not prescribe particular outcomes, but instead establishes four basic rules (voice, transparency, impartiality, and fairness) that police should consider in the process of interacting with community members:

1. Allow the person to explain his or her side of the story.
2. Be transparent about the decisions you make.
3. Show care and concern for the person's safety.

4. Be respectful and avoid name calling or offensive terms.

These processes build trust. Whether they are understood as police *tactics* or not, they are also the right thing to do. Dr. Kenyon (2019) lists these five promising benefits based on supporting research:

1. Procedural justice can help the public to see the police as more effective crime fighters. ...
2. Procedural justice can encourage victims to report their victimization to police. ...
3. Procedural justice can encourage the public to participate in crime prevention programs. ...
4. Procedural justice can lead to increased cooperation from the public. ...
5. Procedural justice can lead to increased compliance with officer directives, especially when dealing with offenders.

While words, tactics, and actions by police influence individual and community perceptions and behaviors, attention must also be directed to evidence showing *what really works in reducing crime*. All crime reduction tactics are not equal, whether they are effective in reducing crime or not. Draconian measures aimed at promoting security alone—and perhaps the reduction of crime—may incite abiding distrust, resentment, and violence. And anything resembling a police state belies the rights and freedoms promised in the Constitution. Security and freedom need not be incompatible goals. That said, what are some common proactive policing practices that can still honor constitutional values, and do they work?

In 2017, the National Academy of Science, Engineering, and Medicine issued a news release regarding proactive policing practices and the role of racial bias. Researchers evaluated the efficacy of various police tactics designed to reduce crime. Dina Fine Maron (2017) reviewed the research findings and published an article in *Scientific American* in which she explained that the research findings did not conclusively show that proactive police policies such as stop-and-frisk are effective unless they are highly focused "on areas with high concentrations of crime or robberies." But when police resources are deliberately focused in areas with higher crime rates ("hot-spotting") or directed toward high-rate offenders, the results are more promising (Maron, 2017). Fortunately, the evidence does not indicate that crime was simply displaced to another neighborhood. Moreover, when businesses or building owners work with police, results are also promising. In short, tailored plans designed to understand and address specific problems seem to be more effective in reducing crime (Maron, 2017). Expansive, unfocused tactics, such as "broken windows" policing, "in which officers crack down on even small instances of disorder before they overwhelm a neighborhood" (Maron, 2017), are not typically effective unless efforts are focused on a small number of high-crime streets. However, some police chiefs attest to the effectiveness of broken windows policing when it is carefully targeted and monitored. Let us be clear, however—continuing research will help more confidently predict what works in reducing crime.

Some focused practices, such as stop-and-frisk, are risky, especially if they are 1) not performed within the letter and spirit of the law (see Chapter 8 regarding stop-and-frisks), 2) loosely monitored, 3) done in a manner that raises the specter of racism, or 4) conducted without some transparency and community support. There can be no compromise in police professionalism, and there must be a strict, documented accounting of such practices, subject to prompt and ongoing internal and even external review.

What about the general effectiveness of community policing and procedural justice? Research on community policing did not clearly point to its effectiveness, but much research remains, and it may take more time to measure the long-term results. It is not a leap of faith to believe that procedural justice practices, once fully implemented, will strengthen trust and ultimately reduce crime. But concrete, measurable benefits may not be quickly realized, as perceptions and behaviors change slowly and less predictably over time. There is reason for optimism provided efforts do not abate. Professor Tyler's four pillars of procedural justice—fairness, a voice, transparency, and impartiality in policing—are compelling and they make sense. They honor the inalienable rights and expectations of "We the People" articulated in the Constitution and underscore the importance of treating each person with dignity and respect.

Police power in the context of police-citizen encounters has dominated the analysis so far, but this is only part of the story. Beyond training and experience, behind every police officer's choice of words and actions, is individual character. Character drives every exercise of police power and authority, from split-second to less volatile police-citizen encounters. If, in fact, character matters, consider a few traits and values that encourage—or, when absent, undermine—trust among police, citizens, and community. They are, I believe, key to developing lasting trust when communities perceive an imbalance of *power*, which exists in most police-citizen encounters.

Character Traits

Anyone who has taken the oath of office and carried the badge and gun knows—and feels—not only the authority and power that these experiences confer on the holder, but pride in their profession, too. However, unfettered pride can stonewall and even blind self-awareness and induce arrogance. To counteract any such tendency, police departments, police, and those who aspire to serve in law enforcement might remember the old saw "With great power comes great responsibility." There are far too many reminders, both historical and fictional, of the dangers of abuse of power. George Orwell's familiar 1949 classic, *Nineteen Eighty-Four*, is a potent example. In one passage, Big Brother, the leader of Oceania, a dystopian, totalitarian state in which the ruling party wields total power "for its own sake" over the people, counselled George Winston, the novel's protagonist who had fought to resist such control:

> There will be no curiosity, no enjoyment of the process of life. All competing pleasures will be destroyed. But always—do not forget this, Winston—always there will be the intoxication of power, constantly increasing and constantly growing subtler. Always, at every moment, there will be the thrill of victory, the sensation of trampling on an enemy who is helpless. If you want a picture of the future, imagine a boot stamping on a human face—forever (Part Three, Chapter 3).

A boot stamping on a human face is an unacceptable vision. An officer placing a knee on the neck of a suspect for a prolonged time with no visible concern about the risk of injury or death is an unacceptable vision. A better vision is officers who use their power and authority for legitimate law enforcement purposes reasonably and responsibly—without exceptions. In this sense, police truly support a free society and safe communities.

While external checks and balances are essential to minimize abuse, a more powerful check may be internal—an officer's character. Law enforcement agencies know this and must seek police candidates who not only demonstrate certain skills and aptitudes suitable for policing but also possess good character and values. It is fatuous to believe that police academies manufacture good character, but they can reinforce and promote it. Mentors and colleagues can do the same, as can communities. That said, here are some key character traits and values that check power and authority inherent in policing. Be mindful that these traits often overlap and support other traits.

Dedication to Honesty, Facts, and Truth

The importance of a deep-seated commitment to honesty, facts, and integrity is self-evident and expressed throughout the book. A principal component of policing is observation and the investigation of facts—the pursuit of truth, unmoved by bias, unswayed by heuristics, and unwilling to alter or withhold evidence of either guilt or innocence. If law enforcement systematically fails in this task, the criminal justice system is compromised. When facts no longer matter, in a sense all freedoms are at risk. As Professor Timothy Snyder wrote in *On Tyranny: Twenty Lessons from the Twentieth Century* (2017):

> To abandon facts is to abandon freedom. If nothing is true, then no
> one can criticize power, because there is no basis upon which to do so.
> If nothing is true, then all is spectacle (p. 65).

This represents the abandonment of reason, the absence of critical thinking. Evidence becomes irrelevant or something to manipulate or perhaps ignore. It is a seedbed of fascism. Police must dedicate themselves to honesty, facts, and truth in their vital work in service to justice and public safety.

Humility

Individual and corporate (as in agencies themselves) humility can deepen and strengthen trust and relationships with a community. Why? And what is humility, or what is it not? Humility dampens excessive pride and blindness. Dr. Karl Albrecht (2017) provides a sense of the meaning of humility and its power:

> It's a subtle concept, and I find myself having to frame it mostly in
> terms of what it is not. My conception of humility is what you have
> when you give up certain self-aggrandizing thought patterns, reflexes,
> and behaviors. I offer the proposition—and the value judgment—that
> humility is a kind of liberation, a paradoxical state of freedom from
> the culturally imposed norms of narcissistic "me-first" thinking.

By contrast, individuals or institutions so often trumpet their every achievement, status, power, or personal influence, no matter their significance. The ready access to social media allows us to inflate our pride by normalizing and encouraging every opportunity to proclaim our qualities and achievements, perhaps to remind us that we are "better" than others. At an individual level, excessive pride feeds personal insecurity, not character, and it's a hollow pursuit, one that can shackle rather than expand our basic humanity. At an institutional level it can blind an organization to its faults and the need for change. Humility is not like that. In his book *Wishful Thinking: A Seeker's ABC* (1993), Frederic Buechner wrote, "True humility doesn't consist of thinking ill of yourself but of not thinking of yourself much differently from the way you'd be apt to think of anybody else." His description reminds us of the Peelian principle that "police at all times should maintain a relationship with the public that gives reality to the historic tradition that *the police are the public and the public are the police*" (Peel, 1829). Officers must remember that they remain public *servants*, not overseers. Humility crosses divides and fosters trust.

There are *practical advantages* to humility. Some business publications extol humility as a positive trait in the business world, such as what *Forbes* contributor Jeff

Boss wrote in a March 1, 2015 article, when he cited 13 habits of humble people, among them situational awareness, curiosity, an ability to listen, and a willingness to accept responsibility—all relevant qualities in good policing. Humility grounds us in our relations with others. It is not passive or weak—it strengthens the holder, and that includes police.

If this is true, how can police and police departments cultivate and practice humility? By reinforcing and practicing the venerable police motto "to serve and protect," with the emphasis on "serve." By demonstrating in training and practice that humility *works* in the real world, for example:

- A humble officer, recognizing human fallibility, presumes less and investigates all relevant facts in a criminal investigation, wherever the facts lead.
- A humble officer knows that the person against whom coercive force is directed is also a human being and that a sense of proportionality in whether and how to use force against that human being matters—that the blind, indiscriminate use of force is wrong.
- A humble officer knows that sometimes it is better to walk away from an angry verbal confrontation provided no one is endangered.
- A humble officer in riot gear facing a group of angry protesters might acknowledge that these protesters may have a legitimate beef, that the protesters are exercising their rights, and that they are human beings, fellow citizens, and not the enemy. And should an officer's personal approval of the source of the protest matter? This is not easy—it takes strength and self-control. Protesters might also recognize that officers have a difficult job in maintaining the peace when the potential for violence or the destruction of property exists.
- In a noncoercive setting, humble officers know that they are not judge and jury and that there is a constitutional responsibility to disclose evidence favorable to the accused—evidence that might reasonably negate a defendant's guilt, reduce a defendant's potential sentence, or undermine the credibility of a government witness. It is an issue of fundamental fairness and a cornerstone of justice. "We the People" deserve nothing less.

In their hiring and training practices, police departments must also be wary of those who relish the exercise of raw power, those too wrapped in the "grandeur" of the power of the badge and gun. It is unwise, even perilous, to issue a gun and badge to those who view the proper role of police as first a wielder of power, a warrior if you will, rather than as a servant. I have known a few such aspiring law enforcement officers; I could not envision them holding the authority to use force, including deadly force, against fellow citizens without becoming real dangers to the public. And history has repeatedly shown that one act of police brutality can spark profound anger and distrust, especially among African Americans and communities of color. George Floyd's death is but one notable reminder.

The unwise exercise of police power does little to promote a positive, lasting influence within a community. Rather, real, positive influence is derived from an officer's commitment to law, service, and the common good, in which both humility and empathy are key attributes. In a 2013 Scholars Strategy Network article, Chad Posick, assistant professor and graduate coordinator in the Department of Criminal Justice and Criminology at Georgia Southern University, explained:

> Research on citizen interactions with the police has consistently indicated that the way officers behave determines how they are evaluated by people with whom they interact. When we probe in detail, it turns out community members have more positive evaluations of the police when officers communicate that they understand the issues that matter to community members. Studies specifically show that the police are more likely to be trusted and considered effective at their jobs when they display empathy with the community's concerns.

Officers have daily cause to exercise lawful power and authority in their many and diverse citizen encounters, but when done so from a position of humility and self-discipline, they are more grounded and immune from the allure of power and its corrupting influence. While police departments cannot manufacture humility through training alone, they can promote it. Words and actions among colleagues can demonstrate and even model it. The reverse is true. For example, an officer may need to arrest a resistant suspect lawfully yet forcefully, but an officer's taunting and boastful words and heavy-handed conduct after the suspect is in custody do not advance the dignity of the officer or the interests of justice. By contrast, an officer who firmly but professionally arrests someone *accused* of a crime, avoiding any gratuitous displays of anger, has informed all those around him about his character and the impartial nature of justice. That, too, takes self-control. Derek Chauvin, the officer who forcefully placed his knee on the neck of George Floyd for about nine minutes, failed to demonstrate humility or strength, but instead demonstrated brute and dehumanizing force. Just one such event, captured on video, can trigger a national response. Less volatile police-citizen encounters also offer such a window of opportunity, where *humility and strength* are revealed in the self-control and respect an officer shows to others. Or those qualities may be absent. Either way, people notice.

Consider the power dynamic between police and citizens in other contexts. So often it is the officer who is necessarily "in charge" in a police-citizen encounter. But there are occasions (and police can be more mindful of such opportunities) when an officer might simply be *present*. Some examples? Attend a formal or informal gathering without an agenda, listen to a citizen, and show interest and curiosity in people and their culture. Sometimes nothing more is needed. Obviously policing demands far more than that, but police are *always* ambassadors whether they like it or not, and an officer can reveal a basic humanity and humility in any encounter. Undoubtedly, most officers already recognize the value of these encounters, but more efforts are needed, especially in communities where distrust is commonplace.

Police need support from other sources of influence within a community. For example, various agents of informal social control described in Chapter 4, such as families, schools, and community institutions, are often better positioned to reinforce the positive value of humility. Police, parents, schools, and secular and religious community leaders may choose to respond constructively to the dehumanizing influence of false pride and lack of humility by offering better examples of real humility and the respect and dignity that it implies in human interactions.

Curiosity and Open-Mindedness

A July 29, 2019, article by David Epstein adapted from his book *Range: Why Generalists Triumph in a Specialized World* appeared in the *Washington Post Weekly*. In it, Epstein referred to open-mindedness as a "superpower." People who possess this quality, he wrote, routinely do something that rarely occurs in most of us: "They imagine their own views as hypotheses in need of testing." What a fresh, powerful approach to understanding ourselves, our work, our conduct, and our relationship with others. These people aim not to impose their perspective on others "but to encourage others to help them disprove what they already believe" (Epstein, 2019). Those who hold this "superpower" don't run from contrary evidence or views or counterarguments—they examine them in the spirit of a trait called *science curiosity* (a term used by Epstein, 2019). Research revealed that "science-curious people always chose to look at new evidence, whether it aligned with their beliefs or not" (Epstein, 2019). Not every police-citizen encounter permits the time and reflection for open-mindedness, but many do.

The importance of this trait in police work, investigative or otherwise, cannot be overstated. How often have documentaries or research initiatives revealed mistakes by federal, state, and local agencies—including decisions made in good faith—where the absence of open-mindedness, of "science curiosity," contributed to unjust actions or outcomes (even those made in good faith), such as those exonerated by the efforts of others who take a fresh look at all available evidence? In investigative work, open-mindedness is lacking when investigators cherry-pick details to fit preconceived notions or rely overly on questionable investigative techniques and results. Witness the continued findings and overturned convictions realized through the work of the Innocence Project (https://www.innocenceproject.org/), where investigators were found to have relied too greatly on questionable eyewitness testimony or confessions. Members of the Innocence Project, I note, include former law enforcement officials. Also recall what was recounted in Chapter 5 about the investigation of Centennial Olympic Park bombing during the 1996 Summer Olympics in Atlanta, when two people died and more than 100 people were injured after a 40-pound bomb filled with nails and screws exploded. Circumstantial evidence, including a Federal Bureau of Investigation profile, pointed to security guard Richard Jewell. Tunnel vision and a lack of curiosity plagued the investigation until the real culprit, Eric Rudolph, was identified. This is not a political issue; it is a commitment to constitutional principles and character upon which justice might be better realized.

That same curiosity and open-mindedness may also strengthen police-community relations in other contexts. When feasible, police are encouraged to be curious about those whom they serve, including their culture and customs or anything that matters to them. It is an opportunity to develop trust and strengthen relationships among community members, which is at the heart of community policing.

Accountability

An effective means to reduce police abuses of power involves establishing and enforcing legal, regulatory, and ethical standards and making police accountable in meeting those standards. Real accountability requires elements of internal and external supervision, oversight, and transparency. There must also be standards imposed on police to report clear instances of abuse. Collectively, this approach checks the worst of human impulses, impulses that thrive without some transparency, oversight, and ultimately accountability. A clear example where accountability was absent involved the gross acts of torture of Iraqi prisoners by a handful of military police at Abu Ghraib Prison in Iraq (see a 2014 *New Yorker* article by Seymour M. Hersh). Hersh (2014) cited a 53-page report that was not meant for public release by Major General Antonio M. Taguba, which listed some of the wrongdoing perpetrated by soldiers of the 372nd Military Police Company and also by members of the American intelligence community:

> Breaking chemical lights and pouring the phosphoric liquid on detainees; pouring cold water on naked detainees; beating detainees with a broom handle and a chair; threatening male detainees with rape; allowing a military police guard to stitch the wound of a detainee who was injured after being slammed against the wall in his cell;

sodomizing a detainee with a chemical light and perhaps a broom stick, and using military working dogs to frighten and intimidate detainees with threats of attack, and in one instance actually biting a detainee.

It is easier and perhaps more comforting to dismiss actions of those involved as the product of "a few bad apples." It is harder for an organization and those in positions of leadership to assess what systemic and situational conditions created an absence of oversight and accountability and then to do something about it. For more insight, watch Dr. Philip Zimbardo during a 2008 TED Talk examine the psychology of evil as seen at Abu Ghraib (the link is provided in the "References" section).

What happened at Abu Ghraib graphically illustrates the collective and human capacity for evil where power exists, one that feeds upon systems and circumstances that allow its growth. What happened within Baltimore Police Department's Gun Trace Task Force, described by former Officer Larry Smith in his personal account earlier in the book, is but another example. Within this context, power and the human capacity for evil are linked. That is why police departments and individual acts of policing, with their inherent power, must be accountable to the people.

Departments can begin by empowering and protecting officers who question, intervene and report when their colleagues commit serious misconduct that does not meet legal, ethical, or policy standards governing police. The International Association of Chiefs of Police (IACP) published a paper titled *Peer Bystander Intervention in Law Enforcement Agencies* (2020) that supports the establishment of such policies and practices. There are also practical reasons. Once ingrained within a department's culture, tangible benefits may follow, such as "fewer citizen complaints, fewer incidents of misconduct, a decrease in the use of excessive force, an increase in officer safety and wellness, fewer disciplinary issues, increased retention of employees, and increased trust from the community" (IACP, 2020, p. 1). Such an approach can better bridge the divide between community and police. The IACP recommends implementing a standalone "Duty to Intervene" separate from an agency's use-of-force policy, one that may also include a clause prohibiting retaliation. The IACP (2020) position paper lays out specific suggestions to officers to determine how to intervene when a colleague is engaging in misconduct.

Some states have either enacted or considered *laws* that require officers to report misconduct. For example, New Hampshire requires New Hampshire police officers who witness misconduct by fellow officers to report it to a superior officer (Citizens Count, 2020). By contrast, Virginia's efforts to impose mandatory reporting requirements were ultimately rejected by a state senate committee (Elson, 2021). There are many perspectives and concerns, sometimes competing, that frame any proposed legislative response, including the precise nature of what misconduct triggers mandatory reporting, to whom or what body should a report be filed, what internal or external processes should be followed, privacy and due process concerns of the affected officers, the public's right to know, and many more. The wisdom and efficacy of any legislative approach is fertile ground for further research, debate and analysis. In the meantime, police departments can more forcefully address such concerns and consider IACP or other recommendations. In addition to internal and external standards imposed on police by law, policy, or other directives, many states and localities grapple with the most effective use of civilian oversight boards (COB). COBs represent an opportunity for communities to monitor and perhaps discipline police malfeasance. The precise composition and power of such boards are subjects of much debate as communities typically vie for more oversight, and police departments seek limits on the power and span of work of COBs. Each has understandable needs and concerns in ensuring police most effectively serve and protect communities. Here are some questions to consider, some of which might lead to difficult conversations:

1. What should be the essential functions of a COB?
2. What powers would be entrusted to a COB? Subpoena or broad disciplinary powers or something else?
3. How would COB members be selected? What qualifications, if any, would be required?
4. Should COB members be compensated? Why or why not?
5. Should members serve for a designated term? Could they be removed for cause, and if so, by whom and how?
6. Who or what might oversee a COB, and what might such oversight look like?

Consider these and other questions from the perspectives of lawmakers, external administrative bodies, police, and community members. In short, together they must search for common ground and ultimately find answers that promote community and officer safety, individual rights, equality, law, and justice.

General Observations

The IACP provides resources that benefit both law enforcement and the community. For example, IACP.org has an online resource entitled "Steps to Building Trust" (2018). The guide offers steps for executive and command-level officers, steps for front-line officers, and steps for community stakeholders, with the latter two more relevant to the general audience. Common themes are the importance of engaging the community in many forms, role-modelling, using discretion, being transparent, training, and so forth.

Efforts to explain and otherwise demystify police work are also encouraged. Much is expected. Consider two messages directed to front-line officers:

- Work with law enforcement leaders to develop consistent and strategic messaging about expectations for building relationships with the community, particularly regarding how officers should interact with citizens in a difficult or emotionally charged situation.
- Encourage community stakeholders to participate in programs that increase community trust, such as citizen police academies, Neighborhood Watch, and National Night Out initiatives.

The IACP guide (2018) encourages officers to get out of their patrol vehicles; "build relationships" by way of "serving as a community coach for youth sports" and participating in pick-up games of basketball; and more. Humanizing the face of police authority and finding the humanity in others are powerful antidotes to misunderstanding and distrust. The community is not the enemy. Learning about how about people relate and the challenges they face also promotes trust. Trusted partnerships founded on mutual dignity and respect between police and community may in some small measure bend, in Dr. King's words, the "arc of the moral universe … toward justice" (King, 1968).

Review Questions

1. Why do you trust certain individuals or institutions?
2. Identify strengths and weaknesses of procedural justice. Create a scenario or script in which an officer incorporates procedural justice while exercising power and authority.
3. Do you agree that humility is important in policing? Why or why not?
4. What other qualities are central to just and effective policing? Rank the top five and justify.
5. How might the community support police who demonstrate the most important qualities in policing?
6. Can communities expect police to be such model citizens? Do they have a choice?
7. How might communities attract the most capable and deserving police candidates? Or what might undermine such efforts?
8. What other measures might enhance police accountability?

References

Albrecht, K. (2015, January 8). *The paradoxical power of humility.* Psychology Today. https://www.psychologytoday.com/us/blog/brainsnacks/201501/the-paradoxical-power-humility

Buechner, F. (1993). *Wishful thinking: A seeker's ABC.* HarperOne.

Citizens Count. (2020, June 3). *How New Hampshire investigates police misconduct.* Concord Monitor. https://www.concordmonitor.com/In-NH-internal-affairs-investigations-come-before-police-misconduct-is-reported-to-the-state-34596737

Elson, S. (2021, February 17). *Virginia lawmakers kill bill requiring law enforcement to report misconduct by fellow officers.* The Virginian-Pilot. https://www.pilotonline.com/government/virginia/vp-nw-virginia-officer-accountability-bill-20210217-2piearryvvatflz7gemzaypda4-story.html

Epstein, D. (2019, July 29). Opinion: Chances are, you're not as open-minded as you think. *Washington Post.* https://www.washingtonpost.com/opinions/chances-are-youre-not-as-open-minded-as-you-think/2019/07/20/0319d308-aa4f-11e9-9214-246e594de5d5_story.html

Hersh, S. M. (2004, May 10). Torture at Abu Ghraib. *New Yorker.* https://www.newyorker.com/magazine/2004/05/10/torture-at-abu-ghraib

International Association of Chiefs of Police (IACP). (2020). *Peer bystander intervention in law enforcement agencies.* https://www.theiacp.org/sites/default/files/2020-08/243806_IACP_CPE_Bystander_Intervention_p2.pdf

IACP. (2018, August 15). *Steps to building trust.* https://www.theiacp.org/resources/steps-to-building-trust

Kelling, G. L., Wasserman, R., & Williams, H. (1988, November). Police accountability and community policing. *Perspectives on Policing, 7,* 1–7. https://www.ojp.gov/pdffiles1/nij/114211.pdf

Kenyon, M. D. (2019, October 16). Rethinking procedural justice: Perceptions, attitudes, and framing. *Police Chief Online.* https://www.policechiefmagazine.org/rethinking-procedural-justice/

King, M. L. K., Jr. (1968, March 31). *Remaining awake through a great revolution.* Washington National Cathedral. https://cathedral.org/MLK50/

Kunard, L., & Moe, C. (2014). *Procedural justice for law enforcement: An overview.* U.S. Department of Justice Office of Community Oriented Policing Services. https://cops.usdoj.gov/RIC/Publications/cops-p333-pub.pdf

Maron, D. F. (2017, November 9). Science says these police tactics reduce crime. *Scientific American.* https://www.scientificamerican.com/article/science-says-these-police-tactics-reduce-crime/

National Academy of Science, Engineering, and Medicine. (2017, November 9). *A number of proactive policing practices are successful at reducing crime; insufficient evidence on role of racial bias.* https://www.nationalacademies.org/news/2017/11/a-number-of-proactive-policing-practices-are-successful-at-reducing-crime-insufficient-evidence-on-role-of-racial-bias

Orwell, G. (1983). *Nineteen eighty-four (1983 ed.).* Houghton Mifflin Harcourt.

Peel, R. (1829). *Nine principles of policing.*

Posick, C. (2013, March 2013). *The role of empathy in crime, policing, and justice.* Scholars Strategy Network. https://scholars.org/brief/role-empathy-crime-policing-and-justice

Procedural Justice. National Initiative for Building Community Trust and Justice. (n.d.). https://trustandjustice.org/resources/intervention/procedural-justice

Snyder, T. (2017). *On tyranny: Twenty lessons from the twentieth century.* Tim Duggan Books.

U.S. Department of Justice. (2014a). *Community policing defined.* Office of Community Oriented Policing Services. https://cops.usdoj.gov/RIC/Publications/cops-p157-pub.pdf

Zimbardo, P. (2008). *The psychology of evil.* TED Talks, TED2008. https://www.ted.com/talks/philip_zimbardo_the_psychology_of_evil/transcript?language=en

"How New Hampshire investigates police misconduct," by Citizens Count, 6/3/2020, retrieved on 6/10/2021 at https://www.concordmonitor.com/In-NH-internal-affairs-investigations-come-before-police-misconduct-is-reported-to-the-state-34596737.

"Virginia Lawmakers kill bill requiring law enforcement to report misconduct by fellow officers," by Sarah Elson, Capital News Service, 2/17/2021 retrieved 6/10/2021 at https://www.pilotonline.com/government/virginia/vp-nw-virginia-officer-accountability-bill-20210217-2piearryvvatflz7gemzaypda4-story.html.

Image Credit

CPSIA information can be obtained
at www.ICGtesting.com
Printed in the USA
LVHW022351090822
725456LV00002B/27

9 781793 506504